REFLEC

FO

DAILY PRAYER

REFLECTIONS
FOR
DAILY PRAYER

ADVENT **2013** TO
EVE OF ADVENT **2014**

IAN ADAMS
CHRISTOPHER COCKSWORTH
STEPHEN CONWAY
STEPHEN COTTRELL
STEVEN CROFT
PAUL KENNEDY
BARBARA MOSSE
NADIM NASSAR
MARK OAKLEY
HELEN ORCHARD
SUE PICKERING
JOHN PRITCHARD
ANGELA TILBY
CATHERINE WILLIAMS

Church House Publishing
Church House
Great Smith Street
London SW1P 3AZ

ISBN 978 0 7151 4362 9

Published 2013 by Church House Publishing
Copyright © The Archbishops' Council 2013

The opinions expressed in this book are those of the
authors and do not necessarily reflect the official policy of
the General Synod or The Archbishops' Council of the
Church of England.

Designed and typeset by Hugh Hillyard-Parker
Printed and bound by CPI Group (UK) Ltd, Croydon, CR0 4YY

What do you think of *Reflections for Daily Prayer*?

We'd love to hear from you – simply email us at

publishing@churchofengland.org

or write to us at

Church House Publishing, Church House,
Great Smith Street, London SW1P 3AZ.

Visit **www.dailyprayer.org.uk** for more
information on the *Reflections* series, ordering
and subscriptions.

Contents

About the authors

Ian Adams is a poet, writer and artist. He is the creator of the daily Morning Bell, author of *Cave Refectory Road: monastic rhythms for contemporary living* and *Running Over Rocks: spiritual practices to transform tough times*. Ian is an Anglican priest, director of StillPoint, and co-founder of Beloved Life. For more information visit: www.about.me/ianadams

Christopher Cocksworth is the Bishop of Coventry. He read Theology at the University of Manchester. After teaching in secondary education, he trained for ordination and pursued doctoral studies, serving in parochial and chaplaincy ministry and in theological education, latterly as Principal of Ridley Hall, Cambridge. Christopher is married to Charlotte and they have five children.

Stephen Conway became Bishop of Ely in late 2010. He grew up in multicultural South London, read Modern History at Oxford and taught in Scotland. He trained for the priesthood in Cambridge. He served for twenty years in Durham and then as Area Bishop of Ramsbury in Salisbury.

Stephen Cottrell is the Bishop of Chelmsford. Before this he was Bishop of Reading and has worked in parishes in London, Chichester, and Huddersfield and as Pastor of Peterborough Cathedral. He is a well-known writer and speaker on evangelism, spirituality and catechesis. His best-selling *How to Pray* (CHP) and *How to Live* (CHP) have recently been reissued.

Steven Croft is the Bishop of Sheffield. He was previously Warden of Cranmer Hall, and team leader of Fresh Expressions. He is the author of a number of books including *Jesus People: what next for the church?* and *The Advent Calendar*, a novel for children and adults.

Paul Kennedy is Rector of East Winchester, a socially diverse multi-parish benefice. He is also a Benedictine oblate at the Anglican Alton Abbey and blogs at http://earofyourheart.com/wp/. Paul is married to Paula, a teacher, and they have three sons. When not in the parishes, Paul enjoys cycling and surfing.

Barbara Mosse is an Anglican priest and writer, and is a Scholar in Residence at Sarum College, Salisbury. Alongside parish work, she has varied chaplaincy experience in prison, university, community mental health and hospital. She is the author of *The Treasures of Darkness* (Canterbury Press 2003), and *Encircling the Christian Year* (BRF 2012).

Nadim Nassar is an Anglican priest, and is the Director and Co-Founder of the Awareness Foundation and co-author of the Awareness Course. Born and raised in Lattakia, Syria, he studied theology at the Near East School of Theology in Beirut during the Lebanese Civil War. He has lectured at different universities in London and has appeared on TV and radio around the world.

Mark Oakley is Canon Chancellor of St Paul's Cathedral. A former Chaplain to the Bishop of London and Rector of St Paul's, Covent Garden, he is also the author of *The Collage of God* (2001) and various anthologies, articles and reviews, usually in the areas of faith, poetry and literature.

Helen Orchard is Team Vicar of St Matthew's Church in the Wimbledon Team. She was previously Chaplain-Fellow at Exeter College, Oxford and before ordination worked for the National Health Service. Her publications include works on John's Gospel and on spirituality and healthcare.

Sue Pickering is a New Zealand Anglican priest and has been involved nationally in the formation of spiritual directors. A Canon at Taranaki Cathedral, Sue is currently chaplain to a retirement village. Her publications include retreat resources, an introduction to spiritual direction, and articles on contemplative spirituality in everyday life.

John Pritchard is the Bishop of Oxford. Prior to that he has been Bishop of Jarrow, Archdeacon of Canterbury and Warden of Cranmer Hall, Durham. His only ambition was to be a vicar, which he was in Taunton for eight happy years. He enjoys armchair sport, walking, reading, music, theatre and recovering.

Angela Tilby is a Canon of Christ Church, Oxford and is Continuing Ministerial Development Adviser for the Diocese of Oxford. Prior to that she has been Vice-Principal of Westcott House, Cambridge and a senior producer at the BBC, where she made several acclaimed television programmes and series.

Catherine Williams works as a Selection Secretary for the Ministry Division of the Archbishops' Council and is National Adviser for Vocations. She has worked in both parish ministry and at diocesan level, most recently as Vocations Officer and Assistant Diocesan Director of Ordinands for the Diocese of Gloucester. She continues to be involved in vocational discernment, ministerial consultancy and spiritual direction.

About *Reflections for Daily Prayer*

Based on the *Common Worship Lectionary* readings for Morning Prayer, these daily reflections are designed to refresh and inspire times of personal prayer. The aim is to provide rich, contemporary and engaging insights into Scripture.

Each page lists the Lectionary readings for the day, with the main psalms for that day highlighted in **bold**. The Collect of the day – either the *Common Worship* collect or the shorter additional Collect – is also included.

For those using this book in conjunction with a service of Morning Prayer, the following conventions apply: a psalm printed in parentheses is omitted if it has been used as the opening canticle at that office; a psalm marked with an asterisk may be shortened if desired.

A short reflection is provided on either the Old or New Testament reading. Popular writers, experienced ministers, biblical scholars and theologians will be contributing to this series. They all bring their own emphases, enthusiasms and approaches to biblical interpretation to bear.

Regular users of Morning Prayer and *Time to Pray* (from *Common Worship: Daily Prayer*) and anyone who follows the Lectionary for their regular Bible reading will benefit from the rich variety of traditions represented in these stimulating and accessible pieces.

Finally, for the first time, this year's volume includes both a simple form of Common Worship: Morning Prayer (see inside front and back covers) and a short form of Night Prayer – also known as Compline – (see pp. 324–7), particularly for the benefit of those readers who are new to the habit of the Daily Office or for any reader while travelling.

The importance of daily prayer

Daily prayer is a way of sustaining that most special of all relationships. It helps if we want to pray, but it can be sufficient to want to want to pray, or even to want to want to want to pray! The direction of the heart is what matters, not its achievements. Gradually we are shaped and changed by the practice of daily prayer. Apprentices in prayer never graduate, but we become a little bit more the people God wants us to be.

Prayer isn't a technique; it's a relationship, and it starts in the most ordinary, instinctive reactions to everyday life:

- **Gratitude**: good things are always happening to us, however small.
- **Wonder**: we often see amazing things in nature and in people but pass them by.
- **Need**: we bump into scores of needs every day.
- **Sorrow**: we mess up.

Prayer is taking those instincts and stretching them out before God. The rules then are: start small, stay natural, be honest.

Here are four ways of putting some structure around daily prayer.

1 **The Quiet Time**. This is the classic way of reading a passage of the Bible, using Bible reading reflections like those in this book, and then praying naturally about the way the passage has struck you, taking to God the questions, resolutions, hopes, fears and other responses that have arisen within you.

2 **The Daily Office**. This is a structured way of reading Scripture and psalms, and praying for individuals, the world, the day ahead, etc. It keeps us anchored in the Lectionary, the basic reading of the Church, and so ensures that we engage with the breadth of Scripture, rather than just with our favourite passages. It also puts us in living touch with countless others around the world who are doing something similar. There is a simple form of Morning Prayer on the inside front and back covers of this book, and a form of Night Prayer (Compline) on pp. 324–7. Fuller forms can be found in *Common Worship: Daily Prayer.*

3 **Holy Reading**. Also known as *Lectio Divina*, this is a tried and trusted way of feeding and meditating on the Bible, described more fully on pages 6–7 of this book. In essence, here is how it is done:

- *Read:* Read the passage slowly until a phrase catches your attention.
- *Reflect:* Chew the phrase carefully, drawing the goodness out of it.
- *Respond:* Pray about the thoughts and feelings that have surfaced in you.
- *Rest:* You may want to rest in silence for a while.
- *Repeat:* Carry on with the passage …

4 **Silence**. In our distracted culture some people are drawn more to silence than to words. This will involve *centring* (hunkering down), *focusing* on a short biblical phrase (e.g. 'Come, Holy Spirit'), *waiting* (repeating the phrase as necessary), and *ending* (perhaps with the Lord's Prayer). The length of time is irrelevant.

There are, of course, as many ways of praying as there are people to pray. There are no right or wrong ways to pray. 'Pray as you can, not as you can't', is wise advice. The most important thing is to make sure there is sufficient structure to keep prayer going when it's a struggle as well as when it's a joy. Prayer is too important to leave to chance.

+John Pritchard

Lectio Divina – a way of reading the Bible

Lectio Divina is a contemplative way of reading the Bible. It dates back to the early centuries of the Christian Church and was established as a monastic practice by Benedict in the 6th century. It is a way of praying the Scriptures that leads us deeper into God's word. We slow down. We read a short passage more than once. We chew it over slowly and carefully. We savour it. Scripture begins to speak to us in a new way. It speaks to us personally, and aids that union we have with God through Christ who is himself the Living Word.

Make sure you are sitting comfortably. Breathe slowly and deeply. Ask God to speak to you through the passage that you are about to read.

This way of praying starts with our silence. We often make the mistake of thinking prayer is about what we say to God. It is actually the other way round. God wants to speak to us. He will do this through the Scriptures. So don't worry about what to say. Don't worry if nothing jumps out at you at first. God is patient. He will wait for the opportunity to get in. He will give you a word and lead you to understand its meaning for you today.

First reading: Listen

As you read the passage listen for a word or phrase that attracts you. Allow it to arise from the passage as if it is God's word for you today. Sit in silence repeating the word or phrase in your head.

Then say the word or phrase aloud.

Second reading: Ponder

As you read the passage again, ask how this word or phrase speaks to your life and why it has connected with you. Ponder it carefully. Don't worry if you get distracted – it may be part of your response to offer to God. Sit in silence and then frame a single sentence that begins to say aloud what this word or phrase says to you.

Third reading: Pray

As you read the passage for the last time, ask what Christ is calling from you. What is it that you need to do or consider or relinquish or take on as a result of what God is saying to you in this word or phrase? In the silence that follows the reading, pray for the grace of the Spirit to plant this word in your heart.

If you are in a group, talk for a few minutes and pray with each other.

If you are on your own, speak your prayer to God either aloud or in the silence of your heart.

If there is time, you may even want to read the passage a fourth time, and then end with the same silence before God with which you began.

+Stephen Cottrell

Monday 2 December

Psalms **50**, 54 or **1**, 2, 3
Isaiah 25.1-9
Matthew 12.1-21

Matthew 12.1-21

'He will not break a bruised reed' (v.20)

Matthew's Gospel is a portrait of Jesus. The writer's whole purpose is to paint a picture of 'the Messiah, the Son of David, the Son of Abraham' (Matthew 1.1). The three episodes in today's passage are linked by the palette of gentleness and compassion (Matthew 11.29).

First, Jesus is gentle with his own disciples and defends them when they are hungry, even on the sabbath. Rules are important but, left to themselves, they can crush people. The interpretation of rules through the lens of compassion is essential.

Second, Jesus is gentle with the man with the withered hand, presented to him as a trap and a test case on the Sabbath. The man's hand is healed. The immense worth and value of every person is affirmed. The Pharisees' rage intensifies only to build to a confrontation in the rest of the chapter.

Finally, Jesus is gentle with the crowds who come to him for healing. All are made well. The quotation from Isaiah's servant song (vv.18–21) draws out what it means to be filled with God's Spirit. Even the hidden nature of Jesus' ministry was foretold by the prophets. The power of God finds paths of gentleness.

In the Christian community, all power must be tempered by restraint, humility and compassion. Let this same gentleness be evident to all you meet today (Philippians 4.5).

COLLECT

Almighty God,
give us grace to cast away the works of darkness
and to put on the armour of light,
now in the time of this mortal life,
in which your Son Jesus Christ came to us in great humility;
that on the last day,
when he shall come again in his glorious majesty
    to judge the living and the dead,
we may rise to the life immortal;
through him who is alive and reigns with you,
in the unity of the Holy Spirit,
one God, now and for ever.

Tuesday 3 December

Matthew 12.22-37

'... the kingdom of God has come to you' (v.28)

Yesterday's picture of gentleness and compassion contrasts with today's portrait of strength. Meekness is not the same as weakness. Steel and determination are part of the character of Christ and the Christian.

The person healed in this episode suffers threefold: a demoniac who is both blind and mute. We are meant to savour the wonder of the healing before we move on to the controversy. Only when we have seen the miracle does the debate fall into perspective.

It is clear to all who witness the miracle that Jesus has great power. But what is its source? The Pharisees advance a theory that the power over evil comes from the prince of evil. Jesus demolishes their argument first with devastating logic: how can Satan be divided against himself? He follows through then with a confident affirmation and explanation of his own power. In the terms of the question, the healing is possible only because the strong man has been tied up and now his property is plundered.

But, in making their case, the Pharisees have made the mistake of acknowledging that a great deed of power has indeed been done. Jesus shows the crowd that this is indeed a miracle and that a great good cannot flow from evil. The only alternative is that the kingdom of God is breaking in.

Almighty God,
as your kingdom dawns,
turn us from the darkness of sin to the
light of holiness,
that we may be ready to meet you
in our Lord and Saviour, Jesus Christ.

COLLECT

Wednesday 4 December

Matthew 12.38-end

'... something greater than Solomon is here!' (v.42)

In this one chapter we have seen two public miracles and many private ones, yet still the scribes and Pharisees ask for a sign! Jesus points them both backwards and forwards: backwards to the sign of the prophet Jonah and forwards to his own death and resurrection.

At every point the reader is invited to look more deeply into the question about who Jesus is against the great canvas of salvation history. Jonah is the most effective of the great missionary prophets. He was saved from the belly of the fish and called even the great city of Nineveh to repentance – a great sign and a fruitful ministry. Yet something even greater than Jonah is here. Solomon is the wisest of the scribes of old. Even the Queen of the South came to seek his wisdom. There are bold hints in both stories of the nations coming to know God in Christ. Yet something greater even than Solomon is here in this meek, steely, wonder-working ... carpenter from Nazareth?

For suddenly we are taken back (via another paragraph of judgement) from the sweep of history to the immediate and the domestic. Jesus' mother and brothers are outside. Can this man who stands out against the sweep of history be the same one who grew up in Nazareth? Earth and heaven combine. God is indeed in what otherwise seemed ordinary. And because God is present, every relationship is transformed.

COLLECT

Almighty God,
give us grace to cast away the works of darkness
and to put on the armour of light,
now in the time of this mortal life,
in which your Son Jesus Christ came to us in great humility;
that on the last day,
when he shall come again in his glorious majesty
    to judge the living and the dead,
we may rise to the life immortal;
through him who is alive and reigns with you,
in the unity of the Holy Spirit,
one God, now and for ever.

Psalms **42**, 43 *or* 14, **15**, 16
Isaiah 28.14-end
Matthew 13.1-23

Matthew 13.1-23

'A sower went out to sow' (v.3)

The parable of the sower is in part a challenge to the crowds to provoke them to thought and help them ponder what it means to follow Christ. There are clues here about the commitment and perseverance required to be a disciple and about the fruit that is evidence of a transformed life.

But the parable is also instruction to the disciples. For every disciple will share in sowing the seed of the word of God. For that reason, every disciple needs some understanding of what happens when the word is sown.

Not every seed bears fruit. Some is snatched away. Note another walk-on part for the evil one. Some takes root, but never matures. New believers must be prepared for the times of trial that will come. Some seed begins to grow, but riches and the lure of wealth choke the new life. New believers must be well taught and pastored as the seed grows. And some bears fruit in abundance.

The one who sows the seed must be prepared for all of this. It is foolish to sow the seed and not be alert to the care of the crop as that seed begins to grow. There is life and creativity in the word, the message that is sown.

Where are you sowing the word of life today, this month and this year? Are you sowing in abundance?

Almighty God,
as your kingdom dawns,
turn us from the darkness of sin to the
light of holiness,
that we may be ready to meet you
in our Lord and Saviour, Jesus Christ.

COLLECT

Friday 6 December

Psalms **25**, 26 *or* 17, **19**
Isaiah 29.1-14
Matthew 13.24-43

Matthew 13.24-43

'... an enemy came and sowed weeds among the wheat' (v.25)

The two parables of the sower and the weeds are vital for understanding in detail the life of the local church. The first gives us our way of understanding why some flourish in the Christian life and others do not. The second gives us a vital insight into the imperfection of the Christian Church.

Many of us can idealize the Church in our thinking and teaching. After all, the Church in Scripture is described by many powerful images: the very body of Christ, the bride of Christ, the people of God and so on.

It helps to remember that Jesus describes the kingdom as a mixed field of wheat and weeds. In tomorrow's reading it will be a great dragnet full of all kinds of fish, some good and some bad. The kingdom is not, of course, identical with the Church. But what applies to the kingdom here applies also to the Church.

We believe, this side of the last judgement, that the Church on earth is imperfect, mixed up, messy and often difficult. Every local church – even yours – is a field of wheat with weeds sown in the midst. The two are intermingled and cannot be separated.

We need to be realistic about the state of the Church in every generation. Only in that way will we develop wise pastoral responses, realistic vision and humility as a Church before the wider world.

COLLECT

Almighty God,
give us grace to cast away the works of darkness
and to put on the armour of light,
now in the time of this mortal life,
in which your Son Jesus Christ came to us in great humility;
that on the last day,
when he shall come again in his glorious majesty
    to judge the living and the dead,
we may rise to the life immortal;
through him who is alive and reigns with you,
in the unity of the Holy Spirit,
one God, now and for ever.

Psalms **9**, 10 *or* 20, 21, **23**
Isaiah 29.15-end
Matthew 13.44-end

Matthew 13.44-end

'... one pearl of great value' (v.46)

The parables of the hidden treasure and the pearl of great price are a matching set. Together they describe the mystery that some people stumble on the kingdom almost by accident when they are looking for something else. Others search diligently all their lives and in the end find what they are looking for.

But when you find the kingdom – the reign of God on earth of justice, peace and presence – whether by accident or design, the response is exactly the same. You know this is what you have been searching for all your life. You know this is worth everything. And so you go and sell everything you have and buy the field or the pearl.

Sometimes people read these parables as if they are about sacrifice. The emphasis is placed on the words 'sells all that he has' (v.44). We focus on what we might be called to give up to discover the kingdom and follow God's call.

But that's not the point at all. The parables are about value not sacrifice. Is the man digging the field richer at the beginning or at the end of the story? Is the merchant better off after he sells everything or before?

When Paul writes of the surpassing value of knowing Christ Jesus my Lord, he is not exaggerating (Philippians 3.8). Knowing God in Jesus Christ and discovering the kingdom is the greatest treasure this world affords and lasts into the next. How does the value of the kingdom affect our values in this world?

Almighty God,
as your kingdom dawns,
turn us from the darkness of sin to the
light of holiness,
that we may be ready to meet you
in our Lord and Saviour, Jesus Christ.

COLLECT

Monday 9 December

Matthew 14.1-12

'Herod the ruler' (v. 1)

For a moment the story moves away from Jesus, though references to him frame the story about the death of John the Baptist at the beginning and end of the passage. John is a major historical figure and a major figure in Matthew's story: in Chapter 3, we have the story of his preaching and Jesus' baptism; in Chapter 11, we read of the messengers he sent from prison and Jesus' assessment of his ministry.

Now the story of John is brought to an end. We learn again of John's passion for truth through his public condemnation of the king's adultery. We see some of the conflict in Herod's own mind between his desires and his fears. We see some of the conflict and manipulation in his own family. The picture is not an attractive one.

There are a number of contrasts here, not least between John (who has not risen from the dead) and Jesus (who will indeed rise). But the greatest is between the kingdom of heaven, the constant theme of the chapter of parables, and the kingdom of this world, focused in Herod. God's kingdom is one of truth not falsehood, holiness not sin, justice not capriciousness, peace not violence, protection of children not manipulation and sexualization.

The story calls us to value the kingdom of heaven in contrast to the rulers we see around us and to pray with greater passion to our Father in heaven: your kingdom come.

COLLECT

O Lord, raise up, we pray, your power
and come among us,
and with great might succour us;
that whereas, through our sins and wickedness
we are grievously hindered
in running the race that is set before us,
your bountiful grace and mercy
may speedily help and deliver us;
through Jesus Christ your Son our Lord,
to whom with you and the Holy Spirit,
be honour and glory, now and for ever.

Psalms **56**, 57 *or* 32, **36**
Isaiah 30.19-end
Matthew 14.13-end

Matthew 14.13-end

'... by himself to pray' (v.23)

The crowds seem bigger, the ministry more public, the miracles even greater. The feeding of the 5000 recalls the ministry of Moses and manna in the wilderness. The walking on water recalls the great nature miracles of the Old Testament. The healing of the sick in Gennesaret is greater than anything seen among the prophets.

How does Jesus respond to this larger, more public canvas? It is no accident that as the crowds grow, on two occasions in this passage Matthew tells us deliberately that Jesus takes time to be by himself. In the opening verse, the withdrawal is in response to the news of the death of John the Baptist. We might speculate that Jesus is taking time to grieve and to take stock about what John's death means for his own ministry. In verse 23 we are specifically told that Jesus went up the mountain by himself to pray.

The lesson is a valuable one. The more public the ministry, the more this needs to be balanced by times of withdrawal and solitude. The more on display we are, the more we need to tend our private world. This is in part about paying attention to our emotions, our inner self. It is in part about paying attention to God's direction and call and values in the midst of tumultuous events around us and within us.

Almighty God,
purify our hearts and minds,
that when your Son Jesus Christ comes again as
judge and saviour
we may be ready to receive him,
who is our Lord and our God.

COLLECT

Psalms **62**, 63 *or* **34**
Isaiah 31
Matthew 15.1-20

Matthew 15.1-20

'For out of the heart come evil intentions ...' (v.19)

For Jesus, it seems that every conversation is a controversy and every step on his journey is fenced about with arguments. The focus swings back to the Pharisees and scribes again, leaving for a moment the needs of the crowds and the disciples. In Chapter 13, Matthew shows us teaching through parables; in Chapter 15, we see him teaching through debate.

What is the heart of that teaching? Integrity and character. The scribes and Pharisees believe you can do all that is needed through the keeping of rules. According to Jesus, this approach is nowhere near enough. The heart is corrupt and so will corrupt even the keeping of rules and traditions – even laws given by God. Jesus is reaching back to a different teaching in the prophets about the transformation and renewal of the heart: the inner person, the mind and the will.

The Bible teaches about human depravity and sin in many different ways, but this is one of the starkest passages in the teaching of Jesus himself. The evil that people do and the desire to break the commandments come from within. It is because of this great capacity for evil within us that women and men need a saviour. It is because the human heart is so utterly corrupt that Jesus makes this journey to the cross: 'Christ died for our sins in accordance with the scriptures' (1 Corinthians 15.3).

COLLECT

O Lord, raise up, we pray, your power
and come among us,
and with great might succour us;
that whereas, through our sins and wickedness
we are grievously hindered
in running the race that is set before us,
your bountiful grace and mercy
may speedily help and deliver us;
through Jesus Christ your Son our Lord,
to whom with you and the Holy Spirit,
be honour and glory, now and for ever.

Psalms 53, **54**, 60 *or* **37***
Isaiah 32
Matthew 15.21-28

Matthew 15.21-28

'And her daughter was healed instantly' (v.28)

Another attempt to withdraw from the crowds and an encounter that disturbs us. Our sympathies are all with the woman, of course. She is a foreigner and a gentile. Her daughter is tormented and in her need she sees Jesus as the only grounds for hope, and so she shouts and keeps shouting and kneels and begs for mercy. We are impatient with the disciples who want to protect Jesus' retreat and their own privacy. We recoil even from the words of Jesus who seems to insult the woman and all her race.

The term 'dogs' (v.26) is softened a little, to be sure, when we know that the original refers to household pets – and young ones at that. 'Puppies' might be a better translation. There are strands of affection and respect in Jesus' first response. In the woman's reply there is boldness and wit as well as respect and faith.

The passage echoes in Jesus' life the stories of Elijah and Elisha, both of whom raise up the children of widows (1 Kings 17 and 2 Kings 4). In Elijah's case, the widow was also in the territory of Sidon. Both of the healing stories in Kings are elaborate and difficult. Jesus heals instantly, with just a word. Something greater than the greatest of the prophets is here.

Almighty God,
purify our hearts and minds,
that when your Son Jesus Christ comes again as
judge and saviour
we may be ready to receive him,
who is our Lord and our God.

COLLECT

Friday 13 December

Psalms 85, **86** *or* **31**
Isaiah 33.1-22
Matthew 15.29-end

Matthew 15.29-end

'... seven baskets full' (v.37)

The themes of the symphony are interwoven and still building. After the interlude in Sidon, we return to Galilee again, to the public ministry and the vast crowds. This is an extraordinary season of grace.

Like Mark, Matthew records two miracles of Jesus feeding the crowds in the wilderness. The whole passage has rich Old Testament allusions once again. In telling us that Jesus went up the mountain, Matthew points us back to Sinai and the giving of the law and echoes the prophecies of Isaiah and the great feast on Mount Zion (Isaiah 25.6). 'Bread in the desert' (v.33) echoes, of course, the stories of Moses and manna in the wilderness during the Exodus. The story looks forward as well to the life of the Church and the Eucharist: the same actions of taking, giving thanks, breaking and giving are present.

But the main contrast is between the need and the resources, and this is the reason the whole Church loves this story. There are 4000 men in the crowd plus women and children. The disciples have just seven loaves and two fish. Yet when offered to Jesus, these sparse resources are enough and more than enough. The leftovers would feed another hundred or so.

COLLECT

O Lord, raise up, we pray, your power
and come among us,
and with great might succour us;
that whereas, through our sins and wickedness
we are grievously hindered
in running the race that is set before us,
your bountiful grace and mercy
may speedily help and deliver us;
through Jesus Christ your Son our Lord,
to whom with you and the Holy Spirit,
be honour and glory, now and for ever.

Psalms **145** *or* 41, **42**, 43
Isaiah 35
Matthew 16.1-12

Matthew 16.1-12

'Yeast' (v.6)

We are about to leave the Pharisees and Sadducees for a season, but they will be back in Chapter 19. However, we cannot forget their teaching. Jesus uses the powerful image of yeast. In Matthew 13.33, yeast is an image of the kingdom. But in today's passage, yeast is the image for the kingdom's opposite: false teaching that can spread through and corrupt individuals and communities.

Wrong ideas are immensely powerful in shaping lives, in shaping culture and in shaping nations. We live in a time when people have become casual about truth and where the instincts of the Church are to avoid controversy in the interests of fellowship and unity.

It is timely, then, to remember that yeast is an image of the power of false teaching as well as of the kingdom. It's timely to remember the care Jesus takes to refute his opponents by his words as well as his actions. It's timely to remember that controversy, difficult debate and seasons of mission often go hand in hand in Christian history. What is taught in our churches week by week affects the lives of families and communities and society for a generation.

James writes, 'Not many of you should become teachers' (James 3.1). If you are called to a teaching ministry, realize afresh its importance and value. If you are not, then pray for those who are. Yeast effects change.

Almighty God,
purify our hearts and minds,
that when your Son Jesus Christ comes again as
judge and saviour
we may be ready to receive him,
who is our Lord and our God.

COLLECT

19

Matthew 16.13-end

'Get behind me, Satan! You are a stumbling-block to me' (v.23)

A vicar colleague admitted how uncomfortable he has become going out to dinner. There is a widening gap between how his family live their life and how the other guests live theirs. Discussion focuses upon the latest gadgets and property values, and his reaction is a mixture of alienation and jealousy. He aims to set 'his mind on divine things', but the 'human things' remain ever present. Sadly, he will be avoiding pre-Christmas dinner parties.

Peter, by divine inspiration, recognizes Jesus as the Messiah and Son of God. In return he is blessed by God and, like Abraham, his name is changed to reflect a new relationship with God, but this is no guarantee of getting things right in the future. Immediately, he misunderstands and is called Satan and a stumbling-block as his mind returns from the divine to human concerns. He recognizes the divine Messiah but places human expectations upon him. Surely, he would presume, a Messiah should lead an army and expel Roman occupiers, not suffer and die.

Peter is fearful. He has just recognized the Messiah, but his human understanding is crushed by predictions of suffering and death. Perhaps in confusion, and hurt by the dire predictions, he does not hear that Jesus will rise again. Do human concerns about presents, menus and guests prevent us from hearing, once again, our seasonal good news of Emmanuel, God with us?

COLLECT

O Lord Jesus Christ,
who at your first coming sent your messenger
to prepare your way before you:
grant that the ministers and stewards of your mysteries
may likewise so prepare and make ready your way
by turning the hearts of the disobedient to the wisdom of the just,
that at your second coming to judge the world
we may be found an acceptable people in your sight;
for you are alive and reign with the Father
in the unity of the Holy Spirit,
one God, now and for ever.

Matthew 17.1-13

*'his face shone like the sun,
and his clothes became dazzling white' (v.2)*

'Tell me and I'll forget; show me and I may remember; involve me and I'll understand' runs a Chinese proverb. The transfiguration follows on from Jesus *telling* his disciples about his forthcoming suffering, death and resurrection. However, from the example of Peter, it seems that they struggled to understand and grasp what was predicted. The experience of the transfiguration is needed to unpack and make memorable Jesus' mission. The disciples are involved by climbing the mountain together, being enveloped by cloud and then hearing the voice.

They experience what Matthew calls, in biblical Greek, the *metamorpho,* from which we get 'metamorphosis': that process by which caterpillars become butterflies, or a nymph becomes a dragonfly. It is a radical change that comes from within. The seed of, and drive to, change is part of the nature of the creature.

Gregory of Palamas, the 14th-century Orthodox monk and bishop, refers to the *energies* of God that come forth from Jesus on the mountain, enacting this metamorphosis. It should be the goal of all Christians to glow with the *energies* of God as we metaphorically climb our mountain to become 'partakers of the divine nature' (2 Peter 1.4, *AV*). The Orthodox tradition refers to this as *theosis* or 'divinization'. The divine nature resides within each of us from our creation in God's image. Our task of evangelism is not to put Jesus into people but to draw him out.

God for whom we watch and wait,
you sent John the Baptist to prepare the way of your Son:
give us courage to speak the truth,
to hunger for justice,
and to suffer for the cause of right,
with Jesus Christ our Lord.

COLLECT

21

Matthew 17.14-21

'[Jesus] said to them, "Because of your little faith"' (v.20)

The disciples come down from a high. They experience the mountain-top transfiguration, but then are brought crashing to earth by their inability to heal. Jesus accuses them of having 'little faith'. It's a rebuke that stopped a family member coming to church after hearing that those who had tragically lost a son were questioned on their littleness of faith. How do *we* understand this encounter?

Perhaps we focus on the father's cry 'Lord, have mercy'. *Mercy* is rich in meaning, much of which is lost in English. It's the cry of several gospel figures, e.g. blind Bartimaeus, and it's used in the Jesus Prayer: Lord Jesus Christ, Son of God, have mercy on me. The Greek word is *eleos*, which has the same root as the word for olive oil – oil that is used both in celebration and in healing, bringing soothing comfort to physical and psychological wounds. The Hebrew word is *hesed* or 'steadfast love', recalling the steadfast love of God for his people – a love that never diminishes.

The father's cry for mercy is a cry for love and soothing care. A cry that asks others to feel for his epileptic son the way that he feels. Perhaps the response of Jesus that faith the size of a mustard seed can move a mountain is about moving those mountainous barriers to compassion within our own heart. Faith, if it's a relationship of steadfast love, breaks down barriers.

O Lord Jesus Christ,
who at your first coming sent your messenger
to prepare your way before you:
grant that the ministers and stewards of your mysteries
may likewise so prepare and make ready your way
by turning the hearts of the disobedient to the wisdom of the just,
that at your second coming to judge the world
we may be found an acceptable people in your sight;
for you are alive and reign with the Father
in the unity of the Holy Spirit,
one God, now and for ever.

Matthew 17.22-end

'... when you open [the fish's] mouth, you will find a coin' (v.27)

Despite my previous career in finance, it's the fish rather than the attitude to taxes that catches my attention. From where does this strange passage come? It is only in Matthew's Gospel and there is nothing like it elsewhere in the New Testament. It shows both that Matthew has a source of information that eludes Mark, Luke and John, and also that this is a unique symbolic tradition. Why the fish? The coin could have been left on the pavement or miraculously dropped into Peter's hand.

To attempt an explanation, it's necessary to explore the Jewish tradition of *midrash*, which refers to the way in which stories and symbols inherited by a religious tradition give a deeper level of meaning to that tradition's scriptures and practices. To what inherited symbols could the coin in the fish's mouth be alluding? The Hebrew Scriptures refer to Jonah – the reluctant prophet bringing salvation to the city of Ninevah – who was vomited from the fish's belly. Local tradition also referred to fish carrying their young in their mouths. For the Palestinian Jews, who first heard Matthew's Gospel, these images would be invoked and could be linked to a new prophet bringing salvation or a new age being nurtured in their midst.

Alternatively, if you find these conjectures fanciful, you can reflect upon the teaching on taxes. This may be summed up as: let's go along with payment, even if we disagree – at least it avoids scandal.

God for whom we watch and wait,
you sent John the Baptist to prepare the way of your Son:
give us courage to speak the truth,
to hunger for justice,
and to suffer for the cause of right,
with Jesus Christ our Lord.

COLLECT

Psalms **46**, 95
Zephaniah 3.1-13
Matthew 18.1-20

Matthew 18.1-20

'... point out the fault when the two of you are alone' (v.15)

Christmas can be a time of tension but, fortunately, we are given guidance on resolving conflict: first, go to the person alone; only if there is no resolution, do we get a few others involved; only then should the conflict become widely known; and finally the broken relationship is acknowledged.

In this approach we hear the view of the other person and perhaps realize that the fault lies not with them but with us – or, more often, with a combination of people and misunderstandings. The process starts in private, and it's far easier to acknowledge fault when it's done before only one or two people, thus avoiding public humiliation. Wisdom comes in honouring the position of the other person and avoiding gossiping and point scoring.

In the 6th century, Benedict wrote a rule for monks that incorporated Jesus' approach to conflict resolution. He was also at pains to avoid *murmuratio*, or grumbling, which could undermine any community as surely as it undermined the Israelites, with their hardened hearts, wandering in the wilderness. Grumbling goes *viral* like a flashmob as people can gossip and plot over coffee and in cliques. The response for Jesus and Benedict is attentiveness. If someone upsets you, don't gossip about them but instead make time and space for them. Listen, understand and respond with love. If, finally, you have to acknowledge a broken relationship, you can do so knowing you worked for peace and reconciliation.

COLLECT

O Lord Jesus Christ,
who at your first coming sent your messenger
to prepare your way before you:
grant that the ministers and stewards of your mysteries
may likewise so prepare and make ready your way
by turning the hearts of the disobedient to the wisdom of the just,
that at your second coming to judge the world
we may be found an acceptable people in your sight;
for you are alive and reign with the Father
in the unity of the Holy Spirit,
one God, now and for ever.

Psalms **121**, 122, 123
Zephaniah 3.14-end
Matthew 18.21-end

Matthew 18.21-end

'... one who owed him ten thousand talents' (v.24)

Peter thinks he's generous in forgiving seven times, but it's mean according to Jesus' scale of 77 times – or, in other words, so many times that it is impossible to keep track. Jesus tells a parable to demonstrate forgiveness where one who owed 10,000 talents is forgiven his debts – personal debts that, today, may not bail out a country's banking system, but do amount to perhaps £5bn!

This is written during an extended eurozone crisis. Germany's leaders are clear that they cannot continually bail out countries that fail to get their finances in order. Greece is considering electing a government that may not even try. Can Germany forgive Greece's different financial principles? Can Greece listen to Germany's concerns without recalling the Nazi occupation of World War Two? Is it possible to forgive without counting the cost and feeling the weight of history?

Jesus says that forgiveness needs to be both experienced and lived out. The one forgiven the equivalent of multi-billion pound debts fails to forgive the one owing 100 denarii or 100 day's wages – a debt that, given time, could have been paid off. It's striking that as soon as there's a failure in living out forgiveness, there's also a failure in being forgiven. The first servant is dragged before the king to be thrown into debtors' prison. So there does appear to be a limit to forgiveness. Not a numerical limit but a limit imposed in failing to live it out – forgive us our sins, as we forgive those who sin against us.

God for whom we watch and wait,
you sent John the Baptist to prepare the way of your Son:
give us courage to speak the truth,
to hunger for justice,
and to suffer for the cause of right,
with Jesus Christ our Lord.

COLLECT

Monday 23 December

Matthew 19.1-12

'Is it lawful for a man to divorce his wife for any cause?' (v.3)

Marriage questions were dangerous: John the baptist was executed because he criticized Herod Antipas and Herodias for marrying. This isn't just a debate on marriage law; it's an opportunity to catch Jesus out once and for all. Jesus responds by affirming Jewish tradition, not an expedient measure introduced by Moses but the understanding that we are created male and female, and that we become one flesh in marriage. However, in Matthew's account, Jesus then introduces an exception, allowing divorce on the grounds of *pornia*, an unclear word here translated as 'unchastity' (v.9). In Mark's and Luke's account there are no exceptions, so how do we approach issues of divorce and remarriage?

Most parishes now remarry divorced people. Reaching out with compassion, and allowing repentance and a new beginning, has tended to override the traditional understanding barring remarriage. This is broadly welcomed but leads to the questioning of other inherited traditions: can only a man be a bishop; or can marriage only be between a man and a woman?

It's a question about how we understand God's will for us personally and as a Church in our society. The Church will always be built upon the witness of the Bible, and this witness is enriched by other traditional and contemporary insights. Slavery, once allowed by the Church because it was accepted in the Bible, is now recognized as abhorrent. How might the Church's attitude to contemporary issues evolve over time?

COLLECT

God our redeemer,
who prepared the Blessed Virgin Mary
to be the mother of your Son:
grant that, as she looked for his coming as our saviour,
so we may be ready to greet him
when he comes again as our judge;
who is alive and reigns with you,
in the unity of the Holy Spirit,
one God, now and for ever.

Tuesday 24 December

Christmas Eve

Matthew 19.13-15

'... it is to such as these that the kingdom of heaven belongs' (v.14)

Christmas is often called a time for children. With wonder, a child gazes upon the decorations and the stocking awaiting Santa. However, I don't think Jesus is calling for a childlike innocence, more the realization that the kingdom of heaven is a gift not a reward. These children are brought to Jesus – they don't come through their own effort – and later Judaism recognized that religious duties come aged 12 or 13 with the *Bar Mitzvah*. The kingdom belongs to children because it's a gift freely given, not a reward for effort.

The emphasis on free gift, or grace, instead of works is *the* theme in the teaching of Martin Luther, the reformer of the 1500s. Justification, by which a person is righteous before God, is by faith and not by works: 'All have sinned and are justified freely, without their own works and merits, by His grace.'

The gift Christians celebrate at Christmas is the life, death and resurrection of Jesus Christ – a gift that is freely given and that we receive through faith regardless of our worth. Thus the kingdom, the presence of Jesus, belongs to those who can receive it as a child would. On receiving this gift we are, according to the Lutheran tradition, a 'saint and a sinner at the same time'. A saint in receipt of the wonderful gift of justification; a sinner as we inevitably fall short in the trials and temptations of life.

Almighty God,
you make us glad with the yearly remembrance
of the birth of your Son Jesus Christ:
grant that, as we joyfully receive him as our redeemer,
so we may with sure confidence behold him
when he shall come to be our judge;
who is alive and reigns with you,
in the unity of the Holy Spirit,
one God, now and for ever.

COLLECT

Wednesday 25 December

Christmas Day

Psalms **110**, 117
Isaiah 62.1-5
Matthew 1.18-end

Matthew 1.18-end

'... he will save his people from their sins' (v.21)

On Christmas morning, we recall the angel announcing to Joseph the birth, name and identity of this new child. It's the identity 'saviour' that casts a shadow over this new life.

American singer-songwriter Lana Del Rey sang, 'We were born to die'. This is a truism for all mortal beings, but for Jesus, the Saviour, this is poignantly true. Jesus, in obedience, chooses to embrace all that it means to be human by – as St Paul tells the Philippians – emptying himself of the divine nature (Philippians 2.7) and following the call to crucifixion. He becomes frail humanity, and then embraces all the joys and sorrows of human experience.

The church father, Athanasius of Alexandria, explained the incarnation with the phrase, 'He was made man that we might be made God'. This child was divine, but he is born into the mess of a stable, enjoyed family life with Mary and Joseph, but died in pain and humiliation. He even embraced that most human of conditions, doubt, with the cry, 'My God, my God, why have you forsaken me?' (Matthew 27.46). To be fully human, Jesus had to experience the fullness of a mortal life: love and fear; joy and pain; friendship and death. It's only in this total embrace of human nature that human nature can become divine.

This season's Evening Prayer recalls God's almighty Word leaping from a heavenly throne. The incarnation is God inviting us to make the return leap with his Word.

COLLECT

Almighty God,
you have given us your only-begotten Son
to take our nature upon him
and as at this time to be born of a pure virgin:
grant that we, who have been born again
and made your children by adoption and grace,
may daily be renewed by your Holy Spirit;
through Jesus Christ your Son our Lord,
who is alive and reigns with you,
in the unity of the Holy Spirit,
one God, now and for ever.

Psalms **13**, 31.1-8, 150
Jeremiah 26.12-15
Acts 6

Thursday 26 December

Stephen, deacon, first martyr

Acts 6

'... like the face of an angel' (v.15)

I liked training for ordination at St Stephen's House. Stephen was one of the first seven servants, *diakonia*, from which we get the word deacon. 'The diaconate is the ministry... of distributing the Church's aid to the poor' wrote Luther, but in Stephen we see this expanding to include the unpacking of the Scriptures and preaching. However, one thing disturbed me: the exaltation of his martyrdom.

In death Stephen becomes a sort of second Christ: he is 'transfigured' when his face becomes like that of an angel; like Jesus he forgives his executioners; and he commends his spirit to God. Before his death he is granted a vision of Christ. Fulgentius, bishop of Ruspe, says, Christ's 'soldier leaves the tabernacle of his body and goes triumphantly to heaven.' In popular devotion Stephen is called the 'Proto-Martyr' – the first person to die for Christian faith.

However, I would like to recall his life rather than his death. Christianity has too often reflected upon death, as shown in the way our creeds jump from Jesus' birth, by Mary, to his death, by Pontius Pilate. There is no credal reflection upon his earthly life and ministry, upon healings or parables. The reality of the incarnation – of the Word made flesh – is the life of Jesus and the fullness of life experienced by his followers. Christianity is an 'en-fleshed' faith with primary concern for justice and righteousness, in this life; otherwise it is rightly called the opiate of the masses.

COLLECT

Gracious Father,
who gave the first martyr Stephen
grace to pray for those who took up stones against him:
grant that in all our sufferings for the truth
we may learn to love even our enemies
and to seek forgiveness for those who desire our hurt,
looking up to heaven to him who was crucified for us,
Jesus Christ, our mediator and advocate,
who is alive and reigns with you,
in the unity of the Holy Spirit,
one God, now and for ever.

Friday 27 December

John, Apostle and Evangelist

Psalms **21**, 147.13-end
Exodus 33.12-end
1 John 2.1-11

1 John 2.1-11

'For the sins of the whole world' (v.2)

'Jesus is Lord', proclaimed the early Church. However, what does it mean for a life of faith? Creeds emerged, but our passage from John is a good pre-credal summary. Jesus is: an advocate with the Father; the atoning sacrifice for sins; and the true light.

The word translated 'advocate' (v.1) is the Greek *paraclete* – literally the one 'called alongside'. This image evokes the courtroom where the paraclete is our advocate or defence lawyer pleading our cause before the Father. John's writing is pragmatic and recognizes that sin remains a problem for those who are in Christ Jesus.

The atoning sacrifice comes from the Jerusalem temple, where animal sacrifices were offered to help people accept God's forgiveness symbolically. God is not appeased by animal sacrifices but the sacrifice enables the sinner to offer something that enables them to accept forgiveness. In the same way, Jesus – the atoning sacrifice for sin – is not sacrificed to offer anything to the Father; he is sacrificed so that we may accept the free gift of forgiveness. The price for sin is paid *for* us rather than *to* the Father. Jesus could be seen as the perfect scapegoat bearing the price of sins away from us.

Jesus, the true light, is the example of a God-orientated life. A Christian cannot walk in the dark, nor can they walk out of love. The model of Jesus called sacrificially alongside us reorientates our life towards others.

COLLECT

Merciful Lord,
cast your bright beams of light upon the Church:
that, being enlightened by the teaching
of your blessed apostle and evangelist Saint John,
we may so walk in the light of your truth
that we may at last attain to the light of everlasting life;
through Jesus Christ your incarnate Son our Lord,
who is alive and reigns with you,
in the unity of the Holy Spirit,
one God, now and for ever.

Psalms **36**, 146
Baruch 4.21-27
or Genesis 37.13-20
Matthew 18.1-10

Saturday 28 December

The Holy Innocents

Matthew 18.1-10

'... their angels continually see the face of my Father in heaven' (v.10)

Following Christmas, Matthew's Gospel commemorates a horrific event: the killing of young boys around Bethlehem.

The historic account may be questioned, especially as it's not recalled in the other Gospels or histories. However, the profound tragedy is that the killing of a few tens of boys by Herod the Great was not an exceptional event. Just another outrage by a corrupt regime whose king murdered his own sons to consolidate power. Still, the event is not recalled elsewhere, so why does Matthew include it?

In our eucharistic reading for today (Matthew 2.13-18), Matthew's account uses inherited symbols from the Hebrew Scriptures to demonstrate that Jesus fulfils Israel's longing. Rachel weeping for her children recalls the Exile, when Israel was expelled to Babylon and later experienced liberation through God's intervention. Pharaoh of the Exodus, who killed all the Hebrew boys, is replaced by the infanticide of Herod again killing young Hebrew boys. Moses the prophet of God who escaped the slaughter, is replaced by Jesus who is called to a similar vocation of leadership. In Matthew's retelling of the massacre, he points to God's intervention just as the Exodus was a time of divine intervention. However, while the experience of the first followers of Jesus is grounded in the Hebrew Scriptures, it's not contained by them. The Jesus experience is witnessed to by those first followers of *The Way* who grew in faith reflecting upon inherited Scripture while being inspired by the Holy Spirit.

COLLECT

Heavenly Father,
whose children suffered at the hands of Herod,
though they had done no wrong:
by the suffering of your Son
and by the innocence of our lives
frustrate all evil designs
and establish your reign of justice and peace;
through Jesus Christ your Son our Lord,
who is alive and reigns with you,
in the unity of the Holy Spirit,
one God, now and for ever.

31

Monday 30 December

Psalms 111, 112, **113**
Jonah 2
Colossians 1.15-23

Jonah 2

'I remembered the Lord' (v.7)

We encounter Jonah as disaster befalls him on his reluctant adventure. He has already made a determined effort to scupper the preaching tour to Nineveh by heading off in the opposite direction (Jonah 1.3), ending up in the unlikely habitat of a whale's belly (Jonah 1.17). Now he's in real trouble.

However unusual his physical predicament, Jonah's spiritual and psychological state may well feel familiar. Jonah is 'everyman', or at least every Christian. Most of us have, at some point, travelled at speed in the opposite direction to our intended destination. Most have experienced the descent into the pit of despair, where the waters close in and the weeds wrap round our head. What brings us back up is that, at the last gasp – 'as my life was ebbing away' – we remember the Lord. Not that we remember God exists, or can be petitioned, or blamed or cursed for our predicament. But that we remember God is essentially good and to be praised. Jonah responds with the voice of thanksgiving because he remembers, despite his circumstances, that the Lord is God and, with this, moves from self-pity to worship. This, as much as his undignified arrival on the beach, is his deliverance.

COLLECT

Almighty God,
who wonderfully created us in your own image
and yet more wonderfully restored us
through your Son Jesus Christ:
grant that, as he came to share in our humanity,
so we may share the life of his divinity;
who is alive and reigns with you,
in the unity of the Holy Spirit,
one God, now and for ever.

Psalm **102**
Jonah 3 – 4
Colossians 1.24 – 2.7

Jonah 3 – 4

'Is it right for you to be angry?' (4.4,9)

Arriving in Nineveh, Jonah preaches a short sermon with a bad attitude. It is remarkably effective (input: five Hebrew words, outcome: 120,000 penitents), but this is a cause of dismay rather than joy. 'I knew you'd let them off', he complains (4.1-2).

One of the hardest things to swallow about the nature of grace is that it means God can, and will, show mercy to our enemies. It deconstructs our fantasy that actually God likes the people we do and dislikes those we dislike. Unfortunately, becoming a mature Christian is about grasping what it means in practice to say that God loves all people – and that can be quite painful! For Jonah it manifests itself in the kind of petulant behaviour we would normally expect from a teenager: 'Yes, I'm right to be angry. Angry enough to die!' The way out of this standoff is the route we all have to take if we are to escape a narrow self-referential view of God: seeing things through another pair of eyes. God encourages Jonah to assume the divine perspective with his penetrating challenge: 'Should I not be concerned about 120,000 persons who do not know their right hand from their left, never mind all those animals?'

How might we enhance our understanding of grace and soften our hearts by assuming a different standpoint to look at those we find difficult?

God in Trinity,
eternal unity of perfect love:
gather the nations to be one family,
and draw us into your holy life
through the birth of Emmanuel,
our Lord Jesus Christ.

COLLECT

Wednesday 1 January

The Naming and Circumcision of Jesus

Psalms **103**, 150
Genesis 17.1-13
Romans 2.17-end

Genesis 17.1-13

'No longer shall your name be Abram, but your name shall be Abraham' (v.5)

What's in a name? Quite a lot usually. Names help to define identity and may indicate nationality, religion or class. You may be fond of your name, or you may feel it doesn't 'fit' you at all. Few, though, will go to the lengths of changing it.

For the Jews, names were of great significance, signifying a person's character or role. We have it time and again: Esau means 'ruddy' while Jacob means 'he supplants'. And throughout Scripture, God himself names those with an important role in salvation history: Abram to Abraham, Simon to Peter. How important, then, is the name of God's own son. He is given the name that signifies the character and role of God himself: Jesus, 'God saves'.

When we say the name of Jesus, we connect with the core message of our faith. God has come to us in a tiny baby and will save us. One day every knee will bow at the name of Jesus because it is the name of the One in whom the fullness of God was pleased to dwell. And whatever our feelings about our own name, we know that God has it inscribed on the palm of his hand, and has written it in the book of life, because through the name of Jesus we have been redeemed.

COLLECT

Almighty God,
whose blessed Son was circumcised
in obedience to the law for our sake
and given the Name that is above every name:
give us grace faithfully to bear his Name,
to worship him in the freedom of the Spirit,
and to proclaim him as the Saviour of the world;
who is alive and reigns with you,
in the unity of the Holy Spirit,
one God, now and for ever.

Psalm 18.1-30
Ruth 1
Colossians 2.8-end

Ruth 1

'Where you go, I will go' (v.16)

There's a good reason why Ruth's words to Naomi are often used for weddings and commitment ceremonies. It is difficult to think of a vow made to another person that could express a deeper level of commitment. Instead of accompanying Orpah back to the relative safety and familiarity of Moab, Ruth embraces an uncertain future for the sake of Naomi. She clings (or 'cleaves') to her, pledging to adopt Naomi's home, people and God; to remain with her until death, indeed *beyond* death, for even death will not part Ruth from her. For those who want to say more than 'till death us do part', this is the text to choose.

Naomi does not know what to make of Ruth's fulsome and ardent expression of fidelity. The text tells us she was silent in response. Ruth's words make no difference to Naomi's perception of her situation: the love of a foreign woman is of little consequence in the face of her bitterness, emptiness and resentment over the Lord's 'harsh treatment'. But Ruth has given herself to Naomi expecting nothing in return. Her promise to accompany and support Naomi is not a contract, which demands reciprocity, but a free gift offered regardless of response. Such is the way of true love, for true love mirrors the self-giving love of Christ

Almighty God,
who wonderfully created us in your own image
and yet more wonderfully restored us
through your Son Jesus Christ:
grant that, as he came to share in our humanity,
so we may share the life of his divinity;
who is alive and reigns with you,
in the unity of the Holy Spirit,
one God, now and for ever.

COLLECT

Friday 3 January

Psalms **127**, 128, 131
Ruth 2
Colossians 3.1-11

Ruth 2

'May I continue to find favour in your sight' (v.13)

The second instalment of the story of a Moabite woman abroad could be seen as the outworking of that oft-toted aphorism 'God helps those who help themselves'. While pessimist Naomi sits at home, Ruth is optimistically proactive; after all, someone has got to put food on the table. She proposes gleaning in the fields with the other poor folk, but her aim is to do more than simply glean; she aims to 'find favour'. Ruth is canny: gleaning is tough work for slim pickings and, while she is prepared to work from early morning without resting, she knows that a change in their fortunes requires more than just hard work. And so she is alert to opportunities, to 'finding favour' with someone who will give her a break.

The word for 'favour' here is the Hebrew term for grace. It is a word Ruth uses three times in this chapter, on seeking (v.2), identifying (v.10) and receiving it (v.13). As is so often the case with grace, when we open ourselves to its workings, it can surpass our imaginings. We never earn or deserve the grace of God; it is a gift freely given. But we may be proactive in seeking and finding 'favour', and surprised by the generosity of God in Christ and our neighbour.

COLLECT

Almighty God,
who wonderfully created us in your own image
and yet more wonderfully restored us
through your Son Jesus Christ:
grant that, as he came to share in our humanity,
so we may share the life of his divinity;
who is alive and reigns with you,
in the unity of the Holy Spirit,
one God, now and for ever.

Psalm **89.1-37**
Ruth 3
Colossians 3.12 – 4.1

Ruth 3

'All that you tell me I will do' (v.5)

Desperate times call for desperate measures. The harvest is over and Ruth and Naomi can no longer rely on food gleaned from the fields: a more permanent solution is required. Naomi has a plan, but it is a dangerous one for Ruth. Whatever the exact meaning of 'uncover his feet' – and scholars disagree – it is clear that the plan contains definite sexual overtones. Ruth does not question it but is obedient to Naomi. Is this because she too seeks security for herself (v.1), or rather that her concern for Naomi, to whom she has bound herself unto death, is stronger than the possibility of 'a fate worse than death'?

Boaz is receptive to Ruth's actions, but in a kindly and responsible manner. He reassures her and, further, is mindful of the risks involved in her visit to the threshing floor – not a place for respectable women. He will fulfil his obligation as next-of-kin if a closer relative does not. The actions of Ruth and Boaz are motivated by this sense of duty. Ruth aims to fulfil her duty to Naomi, to whom she has committed herself. Boaz accepts his responsibilities as a kinsman, but clearly also has regard for Ruth.

Duty is a strange beast: it can be positive, negative, risky or tedious, but delivers its best rewards when motivated by concern for another. What motives lie behind the duties to which we have committed ourselves?

God in Trinity,
eternal unity of perfect love:
gather the nations to be one family,
and draw us into your holy life
through the birth of Emmanuel,
our Lord Jesus Christ.

COLLECT

Monday 6 January

Epiphany

Psalms 132, 113
Jeremiah 31.7-14
John 1.29-34

John 1.29-34

'I came baptizing with water ... that he might be revealed to Israel' (v.31)

Though he 'did not know him' (v.31), John the Baptist recognizes Jesus for the second time on the banks of the Jordan. The first recognition took place when they were in another watery environment: their mothers' wombs (Luke 1.41). This time, the sign John is waiting for is the descent of the Spirit from heaven; by this sign, Jesus is revealed as the one for whom Israel has been waiting. Today, on the Feast of Epiphany, we remember others who identified Jesus as King of the Jews by way of a celestial sign. Together, John the Baptist and the Magi enable us to look backwards and forwards through salvation history. Backwards through John, whose vocation as the last prophet of the old covenant is to reveal the Messiah to Israel (v.31). Forwards through the wise men, whose encounter in the stable is the first manifestation, or epiphany, of the Christ child to the gentiles. The Greek words for 'reveal' and 'epiphany' have the same root, meaning 'to show'. It reminds us that, though John and the Magi could hardly be more different as characters, they are bound together by the common thread in their narratives: the showing of Christ to others. It is the thread that binds us too. How will we reveal, manifest and show forth the love of Christ today?

COLLECT

O God,
who by the leading of a star
manifested your only Son to the peoples of the earth:
mercifully grant that we,
who know you now by faith,
may at last behold your glory face to face;
through Jesus Christ your Son our Lord,
who is alive and reigns with you,
in the unity of the Holy Spirit,
one God, now and for ever.

Psalms **99**, 147.1-12 *or* **73**
Baruch 1.15 – 2.10
or Jeremiah 23.1-8
Matthew 20.1-16

Matthew 20.1-16

'... no one has hired us' (v.7)

We may feel that those 'idlers' who only worked one hour but got paid for the whole day were lucky, but I wonder how lucky they really were? The word for 'idle' here can simply mean unemployed. Were they lazy or just unfortunate men without work? Perhaps they weren't hired because they had a reputation as slackers, or maybe there was another reason: they were older, or slightly infirm, or disadvantaged in some way. One thing is certain: they want to work. When the landowner tells them to go to the vineyard, they go. They don't say 'There's only an hour left – we can't be bothered', or 'We'll get paid so little, it's not worth getting dirty for'. They go because they are desperate and they want to be employed, even if only for one hour.

Work gives us dignity and security, challenge and purpose, and to be without work can be soul-destroying. While those hired at first light have had to bear the heat of the day, those hired in early evening have borne the misery of unemployment and the insecurity of not knowing whether they would receive a wage at all. Seen from this perspective, the complaints of those who worked all day, secure in knowledge of a guaranteed income at the end of it, take on a different light.

Creator of the heavens,
who led the Magi by a star
to worship the Christ-child:
guide and sustain us,
that we may find our journey's end
in Jesus Christ our Lord.

COLLECT

Wednesday 8 January

Matthew 20.17-28

'Are you able to drink the cup that I am about to drink?' (v.22)

What on earth were James and John thinking of when, in response to Jesus' question, they confidently proclaimed 'We are able'? Clearly they have no idea what is in said cup, despite Jesus' words about the fate that awaits him. Perhaps they imagine themselves seated next to him at a great banquet in the new kingdom, sharing a celebratory goblet of the finest wine. Jesus, however, is not thinking about the joys of the messianic banquet; his cup has not the best, but the bitterest contents. It is the cup of suffering referred to by the psalmist and prophets: a cup of wrath, of 'horror and desolation' (Ezekiel 23.33). This is the cup Jesus puts to his lips at Gethsemane. He drinks it for us, and he offers it to us.

It is always enjoyable to raise a glass in the company of friends or family to celebrate an occasion or a piece of good news. But the real test of our love for others is our readiness to share their cup of suffering: to sit alongside them in their agony or grief and help them drain its bitter dregs. This cup is our sharing in the blood of Christ, but, as Paul notes, it is also the cup of blessing (1 Corinthians 10.16).

COLLECT

O God,
who by the leading of a star
manifested your only Son to the peoples of the earth:
mercifully grant that we,
who know you now by faith,
may at last behold your glory face to face;
through Jesus Christ your Son our Lord,
who is alive and reigns with you,
in the unity of the Holy Spirit,
one God, now and for ever.

Psalms 2, **148** *or* **78.1-39***
Baruch 3.1-8
or Jeremiah 30.18 – 31.9
Matthew 20.29-end

Matthew 20.29-end

'What do you want me to do for you?' (v.32)

Today's gospel story is small but perfectly formed. The encounter is brief, the exchange of words sparse, but the level of emotion profound and the connection complete. At the centre is Jesus' response to that desperate shout 'Have mercy on us!'. Amidst the noise and chaos he creates a moment of stillness. Within this moment there is sufficient space for a penetrating question and a simple, honest response. The two blind men have no idea what Jesus could actually do for them. They don't know what he can and can't, will or won't do, and so they don't limit his power with their expectations. They simply ask for what they want most. Their request from the heart elicits a response from the heart of Jesus, and they gain not just their sight, but a whole new way of looking at the world.

Even in situations where the right course of action seems blindingly obvious, the discipline of deliberate stillness, the creation of a moment of calm to come before Christ and tell him what we really want, can mean that the result is far more profound than we ever anticipated.

Creator of the heavens,
who led the Magi by a star
to worship the Christ-child:
guide and sustain us,
that we may find our journey's end
in Jesus Christ our Lord.

COLLECT

Friday 10 January

Psalms 97, **149** *or* **55**
Baruch 3.9 – 4.4
or Jeremiah 31.10-17
Matthew 23.1-12

Matthew 23.1-12

'... they do not practise what they teach' (v.3)

Such is the level of scrutiny to which public figures are subjected in our media-hungry age that their eventual unmasking as 'hypocrites' for one thing or another is inevitable. Peter Schweizer's 2006 publication *Do as I say, not as I do: Profiles in Liberal Hypocrisy* became a bestseller on the back of revelations about covert personal behaviour that entirely contradicted the overt liberal values of various prominent political figures on issues such as investment, racism and sexism. Though the risks associated with not practising what you preach are higher for those who live in the public eye, the challenge is the same for us all: live an authentic life or there will be consequences. It is easy to see those consequences merely in personal terms, such as embarrassment and loss of face; Jesus, however, makes it clear that such hypocrisy has consequences for others, laying heavy burdens on their shoulders.

Many of us struggle against hypocrisy in our lives but it is helpful to remember that this is not the work of a moment but of a lifetime. Authenticity is not a box-ticking exercise but the continual and costly work of aligning belief with behaviour as we become conformed to the pattern of the one who is full of grace and truth.

COLLECT

O God,
who by the leading of a star
manifested your only Son to the peoples of the earth:
mercifully grant that we,
who know you now by faith,
may at last behold your glory face to face;
through Jesus Christ your Son our Lord,
who is alive and reigns with you,
in the unity of the Holy Spirit,
one God, now and for ever.

Psalms 98, **150** or **76**, 79
Baruch 4.21–30
or Jeremiah 33.14-end
Matthew 23.13-28

Matthew 23.13-28

'... woe to you!' (v.13)

Sometimes biblical language seems particularly archaic. The use of the word 'woe' certainly falls into that category. You might encounter it when reading Hamlet, or hear its modern equivalent *oi vey* ('woe is me!') in Brooklyn, but it is hardly part of modern parlance. In using this term, Jesus is drawing on the language of prophetic denunciation. It is not quite the equivalent of 'cursed be', but it is not far off, signalling how seriously the scribes and Pharisees will be judged for the hypocrisy that results in a misplaced hierarchy of values. Though their behaviour seems ridiculous when exposed by Jesus – a greater concern over tithing herbs than pursuing justice – it is actually rather easy to fall into the trap of prioritizing the wrong things because they are simpler and more convenient to achieve. We all do it: cleaning the outside of the cup is a straightforward task; attending to internal cleanliness is challenging on every level.

An effective guard against the charge 'woe to you' is the ability to say 'woe is me'.

This happens when we are exposed to the pure holiness of God and the result is honest self-examination and humility. 'Woe is me!' exclaims Isaiah, '... for I am a man of unclean lips' (Isaiah 6.5). It is at this point that real cleansing can occur.

Creator of the heavens,
who led the Magi by a star
to worship the Christ-child:
guide and sustain us,
that we may find our journey's end
in Jesus Christ our Lord.

COLLECT

Monday 13 January

Psalms **2**, 110 *or* **80**, 82
Genesis 1.1-19
Matthew 21.1-17

Matthew 21.1-17

'Hosanna to the Son of David!' (v.9)

The season of Epiphany allows us to explore a reading more usually associated with Palm Sunday through a slightly different lens. After the intimate wonder of the nativity narratives, the scene opens out as glimpses of the Christ begin to be manifested in the wider world.

And this account of Jesus' entry into Jerusalem at the beginning of the passion narrative bears witness to a very particular kind of epiphany. By choosing to enter Jerusalem as he did – humbly, on a donkey, in fulfilment of the words of the prophet (v.5; from Zechariah 9.9) – Jesus' actions offered an active parable. 'Hosanna to the Son of David! Blessed is the one who comes in the name of the Lord!' cried the crowd in welcome, recognizing Jesus as the divinely appointed successor to David.

But as we know all too well, there was a clear gap between the crowd's inspired words of welcome and their subsequent failure to grasp the full implication of those words as events unfolded. Shouts of welcome all too quickly turned into ugly demands for Jesus' death (Matthew 27.23-25). As Jesus enters Jerusalem, the crowd's words may well be correct theology – but they still miss the point.

The American theologian M. Eugene Boring writes of the crowd: 'They have all of the notes and none of the music.' In respect of our Christian faith – to what extent do we too have the right notes, but miss the music?

COLLECT

Eternal Father,
who at the baptism of Jesus
revealed him to be your Son,
anointing him with the Holy Spirit:
grant to us, who are born again by water and the Spirit,
that we may be faithful to our calling as your adopted children;
through Jesus Christ your Son our Lord,
who is alive and reigns with you,
in the unity of the Holy Spirit,
one God, now and for ever.

Psalms 8, **9** or 87, **89.1-18**
Genesis 1.20 – 2.3
Matthew 21.18-32

Matthew 21.18-32

'May no fruit ever come from you again!' (v.19)

In yesterday's reading, Jesus defied general Messianic expectation by entering Jerusalem on a donkey; today, Christ continues his manifestation to the world in new and disturbing ways. In that part of yesterday's text which told of the cleansing of the Temple (vv.12-13), Jesus took that challenge to the very heart of Israel's institutional religion.

Today's text offers a cascade of images that continue that challenge. The first relates to Jesus' cursing of the fig tree (vv.18-20), condemning it to perpetual barrenness for failing to produce fruit that would satisfy his hunger. This incident disturbs because it forms the only instance in the Gospels where Jesus uses his power to destroy rather than to heal or create. The feeling of petulance is even more marked in Mark's Gospel with its additional comment that 'it was not the season for figs' (Mark 11:13).

But when the incident is examined symbolically, a deeper meaning is revealed. Like the cleansing of the temple, it is an acted parable. Figs and fig trees appear frequently in the Old Testament as symbols for the nation of Israel (Hosea 9.10; Jeremiah 24.5). Coming so soon after the temple cleansing, this blasting of the fig tree would have served as a powerful reinforcement of the sterile, barren heart of Israelite religion. It is a cautionary tale, warning believers of all times and places that they shall be known, and judged, by their fruits (Matthew 7.16, 20).

Heavenly Father,
at the Jordan you revealed Jesus as your Son:
may we recognize him as our Lord
and know ourselves to be your beloved children;
through Jesus Christ our Saviour.

COLLECT

Wednesday 15 January

Psalms 19, **20** *or* 119.105-128
Genesis 2.4-end
Matthew 21.33-end

Matthew 21.33-end

'... this was the Lord's doing, and it is amazing in our eyes' (v.42)

Jesus continues to scatter clues to his true identity like seeds on the soil, and still the religious leaders are slow to understand. At the climax to the parable of the tenants, Jesus quotes words from Psalm 118 (vv.22-23), beginning 'The stone that the builders rejected has become the cornerstone ...'. And – at last! – 'When the chief priests and the Pharisees heard his parables, they realized that he was speaking about them' (v.45).

But this teaching is not just for the chief priests and the Pharisees. Throughout his ministry, Jesus has used both teaching and action to give clues to the true nature of his identity and mission, and most people – not just the religious leaders with their certainty and their vested interests – continued to misunderstand. Even those closest to Jesus, who most *wanted* to believe and understand – his disciples – Jesus chided for their inability to grasp his teaching (Matthew 15.16).

Throughout history, the Christian creeds have provided verbal snapshots, concise summaries of the content of our faith. But we have a problem if our use of them leads us to think that we know it all – in the way that the religious leaders of Jesus' time thought they knew – and that there is nothing more to be discovered about God and his dealings with humanity. Jesus' teaching continually urges his hearers to allow the boundaries of their thinking to be challenged and extended. How open are we to being surprised – 'amazed' – by God?

COLLECT

Eternal Father,
who at the baptism of Jesus
revealed him to be your Son,
anointing him with the Holy Spirit:
grant to us, who are born again by water and the Spirit,
that we may be faithful to our calling as your adopted children;
through Jesus Christ your Son our Lord,
who is alive and reigns with you,
in the unity of the Holy Spirit,
one God, now and for ever.

Psalms **21**, **24** *or* **90**, **92**
Genesis 3
Matthew 22.1-14

Thursday 16 January

Matthew 22.1-14

'Friend, how did you get in here without a wedding robe?' (v.12)

The connection may not be immediately obvious, but Jesus here continues with the same thread of teaching begun in yesterday's passage. On a superficial reading, the story in this parable seems monstrously unfair: why go to the trouble of inviting someone to a wedding banquet, and then not simply turn them out, but condemn them to punishment – simply because they were inappropriately dressed? We will probably find ourselves stumbling awkwardly over this parable, wishing it had been composed slightly differently!

Yet had it been so, a vital point would have been lost. Jesus is saying that it is not enough simply to accept an invitation and 'turn up'. The religious leaders of Jesus' time believed that they knew it all and there was nothing further to learn; they had 'turned up'. But Jesus' words also act as a warning to Christian readers not to fall into the same trap.

Much of Jesus' teaching points towards this end, and expresses the same truth in a variety of ways. Some seeds fall in shallow soil, where they shrivel because they have no root (Luke 8.6,13); the branches of the vine need pruning in order to bear fruit, but those that remain barren are removed and burned (John 15.1-10); the person who buries his talent loses even the little he originally had (Matthew 25.25,30). Yes – all are invited to the banquet, but the invitation is not to stagnation, but openness and growth.

Heavenly Father,
at the Jordan you revealed Jesus as your Son:
may we recognize him as our Lord
and know ourselves to be your beloved children;
through Jesus Christ our Saviour.

COLLECT

47

Friday 17 January

Psalms **67**, 72 *or* **88** (95)
Genesis 4.1-16, 25-26
Matthew 22.15-33

Matthew 22.15-33

*'Give ... to the emperor the things that are the emperor's, and to
God the things that are God's' (v.21)*

Some commentators have pointed to this passage as giving an indication that Jesus advocates a separation of Church and state. But this apparent dualism is occasioned by a very specific context; for Matthew, the kingdom of God represented by Jesus embraces the whole of life and does not split it into factions. The specific occasion here forms part of a series of controversies initiated by the Pharisees in the hope of trapping Jesus into saying something that could be judged to be either blasphemous or heretical. They have already decided to kill him (Matthew 12.14); a successful entrapment here would give that decision a veneer of justification.

But, as with everything that Jesus said, his words here point to levels of meaning beyond their original purpose. They succeed in providing an unanswerable response to the guile of the Pharisees, but they also give his hearers a further indication of the truth of his identity and mission. These are *not* the words of a revolutionary who intends to restore the kingdom of Israel by force, as so many of his followers wanted and expected him to do. Rather, Jesus speaks as one content to give the authorities their due, and to preach his subversive message of God's love and forgiveness within the established social order. It poses a challenge equally valid today, encouraging us to seek God in and through *all* our relationships: within families, communities, and in society as a whole.

COLLECT

Eternal Father,
who at the baptism of Jesus
revealed him to be your Son,
anointing him with the Holy Spirit:
grant to us, who are born again by water and the Spirit,
that we may be faithful to our calling as your adopted children;
through Jesus Christ your Son our Lord,
who is alive and reigns with you,
in the unity of the Holy Spirit,
one God, now and for ever.

Saturday 18 January

Matthew 22.34-end

'You shall love the Lord your God with all your heart ...' (v.37)

The Pharisees' challenge to Jesus continues. In response, Jesus takes the love principle first expounded in the Sermon on the Mount (Matthew 5) and stresses again its central importance to the life of discipleship. And, as so often happens with Jesus, his answers are double-hinged. As Tom Wright puts it: 'Jesus' answer was so traditional that nobody could challenge him on it, and so deeply searching that everyone else would be challenged by it' (*Matthew for Everyone, Part 2*, p. 93).

So where is the challenge for us? The Greek word for 'love' (*agape*) is here used to refer to both love of God *and* love of neighbour. The priority is to love God with all the deepest God-given capacities of our being, but there is to be no either/or about this love. From a true love of God *must* flow love of neighbour: it cannot be otherwise, because both 'loves' are of the same substance. Any supposed love of God that denies or despises the neighbour has no place in this understanding, in which Jesus has extended the interpretation of 'neighbour' to include our 'enemy' (Matthew 5.43-44). It is up to each one of us, under God and in the particular life circumstances in which we find ourselves, to work out how best this dual commandment can be lived. But only if the love of God has priority will it then be possible to love our neighbour as ourselves.

Heavenly Father,
at the Jordan you revealed Jesus as your Son:
may we recognize him as our Lord
and know ourselves to be your beloved children;
through Jesus Christ our Saviour.

COLLECT

Monday 20 January

Psalms 145, **146** *or* **98**, 99, 101
Genesis 6.11 – 7.10
Matthew 24.1-14

Matthew 24.1-14

'What will be the sign of your coming and of the end of the age?'
(v.3)

The fascination of the disciples with the temple buildings and Jesus' alarming observation concerning their fate usher in a section of Matthew's Gospel known as the 'Little Apocalypse', climaxing with the coming of the Son of Man (vv.30-31). It should perhaps be no surprise that the disciples' first concern, on hearing Jesus' prediction of the temple's destruction, should be about how and when this would be fulfilled. Rather than give them a direct answer, Jesus responds with a warning: 'Beware that no one leads you astray. For many will come in my name, saying, "I am the Messiah!" and they will lead many astray' (vv.4-5).

Jesus' catalogue of 'wars and rumours of wars' (v.6) has struck a consistent note of alarm in the human psyche from Jesus' time right up to the present day. Despite Jesus' warnings that 'the end is not yet', every historical epoch including our own has produced its own crop of end-time prophets declaring that theirs was the age in which these things were finally to be fulfilled.

Our awareness of these resonances can leave us in an uncomfortable place of tension. Aware of the turmoil in our world, we are asked to note the working-out of the pattern of events Jesus describes as they evolve in our own time. But we are warned against using them as any kind of accurate predictor of that which still remains hidden within the mystery of God.

COLLECT

Almighty God,
in Christ you make all things new:
transform the poverty of our nature by the riches of your grace,
and in the renewal of our lives
make known your heavenly glory;
through Jesus Christ your Son our Lord,
who is alive and reigns with you,
in the unity of the Holy Spirit,
one God, now and for ever.

Psalms **132**, 147.1-12 *or* **106*** (or 103)
Genesis 7.11-end
Matthew 24.15-28

Tuesday 21 January

Matthew 24.15-28

'Wherever the corpse is, there the vultures will gather' (v.28)

Today we hear both the echoes of history (the appearance of the 'desolating sacrilege' in the holy place when the temple was desecrated in 167 BC by Antiochus IV Epiphanes) and an ominous prediction of future events (the desecration of the temple when Jerusalem was destroyed by the Romans in AD 70). Jesus' words create an atmosphere alive with fear and foreboding. He knew that in such times of peril and anxiety, the longing for a Messiah would be especially acute, with any number of potential 'saviours' declaring themselves and trying to command a following. Jesus' advice both then (and now) is the same as previously (vv.4-5) – 'do not believe it!' (vv.23, 26).

The enigmatic reference to the corpse and the vultures has given rise to much critical speculation. The Greek term for 'vulture' (*aetos*) also means 'eagle'. Tom Wright comments that this may have referred to the eagles on the Roman standards as the army closed in on Jerusalem. But the deeper meaning is eschatological – that is, directly related to the future return of the Son of Man (v.27).

When the women visited Jesus' tomb the angels asked them, 'Why do you look for the living among the dead?' (Luke 24.5). In Matthew's understanding here, those who follow false messiahs are chasing 'the dead', and the Son of Man is not to be found there. He is alive, and when he returns, there will be no mistake about it.

Eternal Lord,
our beginning and our end:
bring us with the whole creation
to your glory, hidden through past ages
and made known
in Jesus Christ our Lord.

COLLECT

Wednesday 22 January

Psalms **81**, 147.13-end
or 110, **111**, 112
Genesis 8.1-14
Matthew 24.29-end

Matthew 24.29-end

Blessed is that slave whom his master will find at work when he arrives' (v.46)

In the readings for the next three days, Jesus uses a variety of parables to further communicate the urgency of the need to be actively prepared for the return of the Son of Man. Learn from the fig tree: you can tell the season from its leaves (vv.32-35). Don't be like the people in the time of Noah: they ignored the warnings and were swept away by the flood (vv.37-39). Take warning from the householder: he slept and let his house be burgled (vv.43-44). Then Jesus offers the parable of the wise and unwise slaves, who reacted so very differently to the work their master gave them to do while he was away (vv.45-51). The scenery changes at a breathtaking speed, but each shift in perspective underlines the same message – be ready!

A friend suffering from illness once told me that it was supremely important to carry out tasks when the need arose, and not to put them off until later. The reason was that he wasn't sure from day to day what his energy levels would be, so it was vitally important that everything was kept up to date. This is surely a useful lesson for everyone – even without the incentive of an illness. And could it be that Jesus was also warning his disciples that he was going to be leaving them? How faithfully would they carry out the work he had entrusted to them?

COLLECT

Almighty God,
in Christ you make all things new:
transform the poverty of our nature by the riches of your grace,
and in the renewal of our lives
make known your heavenly glory;
through Jesus Christ your Son our Lord,
who is alive and reigns with you,
in the unity of the Holy Spirit,
one God, now and for ever.

Matthew 25.1-13

'… but the wise took flasks of oil with their lamps' (v.4)

The parable of the wise and foolish bridesmaids is not the only context in which Jesus refers to himself as a bridegroom. Earlier in Matthew's Gospel Jesus makes a direct self-identification, when he is asked by the disciples of John the Baptist why his own disciples do not fast (Matthew 9.15). The link with the coming of the Son of Man referred to in the previous chapter is clear, and we are viewing the final return of Jesus through yet another lens.

So the parable is about the coming of the kingdom of God and the return of Jesus. The bridesmaids represent the Church. All have lamps and oil; all sleep when the coming of the bridegroom is delayed. But only five have equipped themselves with sufficient oil to last until his arrival; the others are insufficiently prepared. There is a potential for confusion here, as elsewhere Jesus tells his hearers not to worry about the future – what they will eat, drink or wear – 'for tomorrow will bring worries of its own' (Matthew 6.34).

But the contradiction is apparent, rather than real. In Matthew 6, Jesus was concerned with the kind of anxious hoarding and fretting about the future that reveals a basic lack of trust in God's ability to provide. But here, he is addressing the need for Christians to 'keep calm and carry on' – to persist doggedly in faith, hope and trust, year after year, however long the 'bridegroom' is delayed.

COLLECT

Eternal Lord,
our beginning and our end:
bring us with the whole creation
to your glory, hidden through past ages
and made known
in Jesus Christ our Lord.

53

Friday 24 January

Psalms **27**, 149 *or* **139**
Genesis 9.8-19
Matthew 25.14-30

Matthew 25.14-30

'...I was afraid, and I went and hid your talent in the ground' (v.25)

As with so many of Jesus' parables, this tale of the talents is open to several layers of interpretation. On one level, it is of a piece with the other passages we have been reflecting on this week, referring to the need for believers to be alert and watchful, engaged in the work of the kingdom and ready for Jesus' return.

On another level, the parable would have had contemporary application, implying that the scribes and Pharisees – the custodians of the law of Moses – were behaving like the lazy slave who had simply buried his talent in the ground.

But the tale also has an immediate relevance, one easily demonstrated from our own experience. Anybody with a particular talent – piano playing, painting, running, or whatever – knows just how much daily practice over many years is needed for that talent to be maintained and developed. Any relaxation in the intensity of practice means that the level of skill will inevitably diminish.

God's gift of love to us is just such a 'talent', and we too need to practise constantly if that gift is to grow and thrive in us. As we read in an earlier parable, 'many are called, but few are chosen' (Matthew 22.14), and with these words, we come full circle. Though the delay may last a lifetime, the 'chosen' refer to all those who persist in alert watchfulness, preparing and working for the kingdom in faith, hope and trust.

COLLECT

Almighty God,
in Christ you make all things new:
transform the poverty of our nature by the riches of your grace,
and in the renewal of our lives
make known your heavenly glory;
through Jesus Christ your Son our Lord,
who is alive and reigns with you,
in the unity of the Holy Spirit,
one God, now and for ever.

Saturday 25 January

The Conversion of Paul

Philippians 3.1-14

'... as to zeal, a persecutor of the church' (v.6)

On 22 July 2011, Anders Breivik, a far-right militant extremist, murdered 77 people in two separate atrocities in Norway. As I write, the trial has just concluded; Breivik has been declared sane and sentenced to 21 years in prison. After the verdict, he expressed his regret that he had not been able to kill more people.

Breivik is the latest in a long line of people throughout history who fervently believed that their political or religious beliefs somehow gave them the licence to kill. It's easy enough for us to condemn the monstrous – to see them somehow as belonging to a different species to the rest of humanity – and to set ourselves at an appalled distance from them. Paul himself knew that he had once been such a monster – his zealous Pharisaic upbringing leading him to persecute Christians and send them to their deaths (v.6). His conversion dramatically changed his life, but not to the extent that he went into denial about his past.

But what happens when the issue comes much closer to home? Paul writes of those who live 'as enemies of the cross of Christ', saying that 'their god is the belly ... their minds are set on earthly things' (v.19). As Christians, we rightly recoil from the warped thinking and monstrous actions of a Breivik, or a pre-conversion Paul, but can we honestly say that our minds and attitudes are always set on the things of God?

Almighty God,
who caused the light of the gospel
to shine throughout the world
through the preaching of your servant Saint Paul:
grant that we who celebrate his wonderful conversion
may follow him in bearing witness to your truth;
through Jesus Christ your Son our Lord,
who is alive and reigns with you,
in the unity of the Holy Spirit,
one God, now and for ever.

COLLECT

Monday 27 January

Psalms 40, **108**
or 123, 124, 125, **126**
Genesis 11.27 – 12.9
Matthew 26.1-16

Matthew 26.1-16

'... an alabaster jar of very costly ointment' (v.7)

A television advert for perfume presents a beautiful young woman in the style of a modern Marilyn Monroe. She tells us that she does all her own stunts, even making love. We are meant to see her as an enchantress made more alluring by the scent. The gospel has a different take on the place of perfume. Our passage introduces another woman shaped by the power of men's sexual demands. She has broken out of society's condemnation and offers a radical alternative to the scheming of the male, religious establishment.

She does not wear the scent herself. She enters the house to anoint Jesus with expensive perfume. We are back in Bethlehem, where wise men brought gold, frankincense and myrrh to the infant king. We recall the anointing of Aaron the priest and of David the king. The woman anoints our Priest and our King for burial. This is no morbid ritual but rather the making of supper into a true celebration. The fragrance of the perfume fills the house, underlying the fullness of Christ's self-offering.

The poor will always be with us in Jesus – the poor who will always be the recipients of God's extravagant love. The woman's anonymity makes her our forebear. We do not need to know the names of the countless poor and outcast who have served Jesus with the fragrance of their offering, only that we are numbered among them.

COLLECT

Almighty God,
whose Son revealed in signs and miracles
the wonder of your saving presence:
renew your people with your heavenly grace,
and in all our weakness
sustain us by your mighty power;
through Jesus Christ your Son our Lord,
who is alive and reigns with you,
in the unity of the Holy Spirit,
one God, now and for ever.

Psalms 34, **36** *or* **132**, 133
Genesis 13.2-end
Matthew 26.17-35

Matthew 26.17-35

'You will all become deserters because of me this night' (v.31)

In Robert Bolt's *A Man for All Seasons*, originally a 1954 radio play for the BBC, we are invited to explore the integrity and courage of Sir Thomas More, Henry VIII's Lord Chancellor, who could not in conscience accept the King's divorce from Katherine of Aragon and his break from Rome.

Sir Thomas is portrayed as a loving family man who runs a generous and open household. He loves the law and his king, but he loves God and his hold on what is true above all else. He knows that his conscience puts him on a collision course with power, as represented by his nemesis, Thomas Cromwell. More would like to live and uses the protection of the law to forestall his enemies; but he is betrayed by someone weak whom he considered a friend, Richard Rich, who perjures himself to bring about More's downfall.

Jesus knows that he will be betrayed by a friend at a depth which is nothing like paid false witnesses whom no one believes at his trial. This betrayal by Judas will have consequences beyond the personal – it will lead to the un-making of friendship and the spread of betrayal to Peter.

Our continuing sin is false witness to Jesus' gospel of love. Nonetheless, he continues to gather us at his table to forgive us and feed us. The Eucharist is not a reward for good behaviour; it is the transforming place for those praying to be reliable witnesses.

God of all mercy,
your Son proclaimed good news to the poor,
release to the captives,
and freedom to the oppressed:
anoint us with your Holy Spirit
and set all your people free
to praise you in Christ our Lord.

COLLECT

Wednesday 29 January

Matthew 26.36-46

'He ... began to be grieved and agitated' (v.37)

Pilgrims flock to the olive grove full of gnarled and ancient trees on the Mount of Olives, which is the site of the Garden of Gethsemane, the garden of the olive press. Next to it is the modern Church of the Agony. In the 1973 movie version of *Jesus Christ Superstar*, we are treated to a vivid portrayal of Jesus in the Garden, experiencing the full press of agony. The disciples are literally in an untidy pile, asleep. The waking reality of fear and danger is too much for them, so their unconscious draws them into protective oblivion. Jesus, however, moves among the real and figurative rocks and hard places as he contends with the fact of his imminent suffering and death.

When we read that Jesus sweated blood (Luke 22.44), we can only imagine the anguish that he feels; but the Jesus of the movie sings *I Only Want to Say*. This is the very human Jesus who is worn out and alone, contending with futility while still engaged in dialogue with his heavenly Father. Every skilled interrogator of the innocent seeks to seed doubt and futility in the mind of the innocent prisoner.

This is the anguish of Jesus that produces tears of blood. We know that he did not change his mind. He trusted and was obedient to the Father's will. No one but the Son of God going to the cross makes meaning out of meaninglessness.

Almighty God,
whose Son revealed in signs and miracles
the wonder of your saving presence:
renew your people with your heavenly grace,
and in all our weakness
sustain us by your mighty power;
through Jesus Christ your Son our Lord,
who is alive and reigns with you,
in the unity of the Holy Spirit,
one God, now and for ever.

Psalms **47**, 48 *or* **143**, 146
Genesis 15
Matthew 26.47-56

Matthew 26.47-56

'the betrayer ...' (v.48)

On 4 August, 1944, Anne Frank and her family were betrayed in their hiding place within her father's former warehouse office in Amsterdam. We are not certain who betrayed them; but there must have been a tip-off to the Gestapo. The Franks and the other Jews hiding with them had been there for the two years in which Anne recorded her life in her diary. The betrayer is likely to be someone who knew them all that time, rather like those who witnessed Jesus teaching in the temple and who did nothing.

Her arrest, like that of Jesus, led to torture, separation and death, in her case in Bergen-Belsen in 1945. The only survivor of the whole family was Anne's father, Otto Frank. Males and females were separated at the first camp and Otto never got over the look in the eyes of Margot, his elder daughter, as they saw each other for the last time.

Anne wrote in her diary: 'How wonderful it is that nobody need wait a single moment before starting to improve the world.' Anne encouraged others in the camp. She continued to live by her own words: 'Everyone has inside of him a piece of good news. The good news is that you don't know how great you can be! How much you can love! What you can accomplish! And what your potential is!' Jesus was to die for this. No one knew at that time that Anne Frank's diary had survived her arrest and death. Everything seemed empty. Jesus knows that this is prophecy fulfilled; but the disciples fled, preferring to cower rather than look to new creation.

God of all mercy,
your Son proclaimed good news to the poor,
release to the captives,
and freedom to the oppressed:
anoint us with your Holy Spirit
and set all your people free
to praise you in Christ our Lord.

COLLECT

Friday 31 January

Matthew 26.57-end

'At that moment the cock crowed' (v.74)

The American poet, Elizabeth Bishop, was a pacifist. She wrote a powerful anti-war poem in 1940, entitled *Roosters*. She writes about hens rustling around, proud of their fighting cocks. She is also very aware that the rooster is also a symbol of betrayal and crucifixion, another form of violence.

Peter is the disciple who first declares Jesus' identity as the Messiah, the Son of the living God. He is a big-hearted, intuitive enthusiast. He does not understand what he has said, really. He objects to all Jesus' references to his suffering. The gap between intuition and wisdom leads to this inconstancy. Peter's betrayal could not be more dreadful in the light of his declaration that he would never desert Jesus. Yet, in spite of his claims to courage, he was human. The rooster stands for Peter's not having superhuman resolve and, paradoxically, it is this humanity that led Jesus to forgive him, and to forgive us all: Peter's 'dreadful rooster come to mean forgiveness', to quote Bishop's poem.

This is all in the future, however. Peter is still cast as the brassy cockscomb who makes the grating noise of betrayal that gets under our skin because it could be – has been – us. Like the strutting cock, Peter looks ready for a fight, but his courage ends up on the dung heap like the failed rooster. Peter is blown like the weathervane and spins into sadness.

COLLECT

Almighty God,
whose Son revealed in signs and miracles
the wonder of your saving presence:
renew your people with your heavenly grace,
and in all our weakness
sustain us by your mighty power;
through Jesus Christ your Son our Lord,
who is alive and reigns with you,
in the unity of the Holy Spirit,
one God, now and for ever.

Psalms **68** or **147**
Genesis 17.1-22
Matthew 27.1-10

Matthew 27.1-10

'I have sinned by betraying innocent blood' (v.4)

Judas is a plausible disciple, concerned to serve the poor from the common purse, but he is possessed of his own ideas and ambitions, for which Jesus has to be sacrificed, only to discover that all love and meaning are destroyed for him. Shakespeare's tragic figures – Macbeth, Hamlet, Othello – often have a decisive fault that brings about their ruin, like ambition or a refusal to bend to the will of others.

In our society it is tempting to be over-interested in the psyche of the villain. Among the flaws of Martin Scorsese's film, *The Last Temptation of Christ,* is its greater interest in the motives of Judas than in the call of Christ. Judas is not a tragic figure who somehow claims a stake in the tragedy as well as the victory of the cross. He is the person who is revealed to be one who has a howling wilderness with him, succumbing to the temptations that Jesus resisted and finding them so completely false that he despairs. His 'reward' pays for a place of death – 'a place to bury foreigners' (v.7). His suicide is a dead end and a determined refusal to take responsibility for his own actions. Here is a cul-de-sac in contrast to the open road from the cross, from which Christ wins life for all by taking responsibility for the cost of the actions of all.

God of all mercy,
your Son proclaimed good news to the poor,
release to the captives,
and freedom to the oppressed:
anoint us with your Holy Spirit
and set all your people free
to praise you in Christ our Lord.

COLLECT

Monday 3 February

Psalms 1, 2, 3
Exodus 22.21-27; 23.1-17
Philippians 1.1-11

Exodus 22.21-27; 23.1-17

'You shall ...' (passim)

The Human Rights Act came into force in Britain in 2000. It brought into British statutory law principles that we had already adhered to in the Articles of the European Convention on Human Rights since 1953.

Modern approaches to human rights have their immediate roots in the seventeenth and eighteenth centuries, the most famous being the American Declaration of Independence. Its second sentence reads: 'We hold these truths to be self-evident, that all men are created equal, that they are endowed by their Creator with certain unalienable Rights, that among these are Life, Liberty and the pursuit of Happiness.'

The important thing to remember is that these 'unalienable rights' are from God. Caring for the poor and the outsider and living with integrity and generosity is what God expects of Israel and of us. This is all grounded in *shalom*, in God's rest and peace and in the regular call to worship and pilgrimage. Our human rights are non-negotiable because we are children of the one heavenly Father. We are uniquely valued as human beings because we are made in the image and likeness of the God who loves us uniquely and personally. Those who are strangers to us are welcome because they are never strangers to God and we must look for Him in them.

The Human Rights Act guarantees our freedom of religion as a basic human right. The practice of this freedom is meant to energize us to rejoice and serve all the above in the name of Him whose loving purpose is that all shall flourish.

COLLECT

Almighty God,
by whose grace alone we are accepted
    and called to your service:
strengthen us by your Holy Spirit
and make us worthy of our calling;
through Jesus Christ your Son our Lord,
who is alive and reigns with you,
in the unity of the Holy Spirit,
one God, now and for ever.

Psalms **5**, 6 (8)
Exodus 29.38 – 30.16
Philippians 1.12-end

Tuesday 4 February

Exodus 29.38 – 30.16

'... to serve me as priests' (v.44)

The Australian novelist, Morris West, wrote a series of novels about successive fictional modern popes. In the first, *The Shoes of the Fisherman* (1963), the Conclave elects a Russian, styled Kiril I. He has spent 20 years in a Soviet gulag and he becomes pope at the height of the Cold War. The world is on the brink of nuclear war and China is starving. At his coronation, Kiril lays aside his papal tiara and pledges the resources of the Catholic Church to feeding the hungry and averting war.

In a subsequent novel, *The Clowns of God* (1981), a French pope, Gregory XVII, is given a vision of the imminent end of the world and of Christ's return. He abdicates as pope better to serve the vision. Christ does appear, but he defers judgement and tells Gregory and others to grow in humanity in the love they learn from God's clowns, a group of children with physical handicaps and learning difficulties.

While Moses is on the mountain with God for 40 days, the Israelites seek to create order and patterns of sacrifice before God. Aaron and his sons are inaugurated as an order of priests to coordinate the sacrificial system. But before long these same Israelites with their priests will create the Golden Calf and face great rebuke from God through Moses. Those who organize sacrifices and elaborate systems must lay aside their crowns so that people always are led to the vision of God and of God's glory and bear it from the tabernacle to the poor.

God of our salvation,
help us to turn away from those habits which harm our bodies
and poison our minds
and to choose again your gift of life,
revealed to us in Jesus Christ our Lord.

COLLECT

Wednesday 5 February

Psalm 119.1-32
Leviticus 8
Philippians 2.1-13

Leviticus 8

'Thus he consecrated Aaron and his vestments' (v.30)

George Herbert's *The Temple* was published first in 1633, the year of his death. He brought together, in a carefully crafted sequence, poetry that reflects uncertainty and frailty leading to deeper serenity and assurance. He wrestled for a long time with the calling to be a priest, even after he had been ordained a deacon. One of the poems in *The Temple* articulates the struggle and the resolution. It is called 'Aaron' and is directly derived from the content of this passage and the corresponding passages in Exodus.

Vocations advisers regularly encounter people who have a genuine sense of God's call to various forms of lay and ordained ministry. Very commonly they encounter in those same people a profound understanding of their own unworthiness. We all know within ourselves the impulse that holds us back from offering ourselves for a particular office or task because we are not 'up to it'.

Herbert articulates the sharp contrast between the perfection of heart that God desires in those who serve and the darkness in his heart. Using the imagery of Aaron being properly dressed for his role as God's priest, neither Herbert nor we are much of a fashion statement.

We do not need to despair. The one who makes the call of the unworthy both true and useful is Christ, our 'only heart'. What counts for Aaron, for Herbert and for us is not that we first choose, but that we are first chosen. We can step up with confidence and say, 'Come people; Aaron's dressed' because Jesus tells us, 'You did not choose me; I chose you'.

COLLECT

Almighty God,
by whose grace alone we are accepted
    and called to your service:
strengthen us by your Holy Spirit
and make us worthy of our calling;
through Jesus Christ your Son our Lord,
who is alive and reigns with you,
in the unity of the Holy Spirit,
one God, now and for ever.

Psalms 14, **15**, 16
Leviticus 9
Philippians 2.14-end

Leviticus 9

'... sacrifice ... make atonement' (v. 7)

Any talk of sacrifice is unfashionable today. Reference to physical sacrifice conjures those scenes of savage human sacrifice in Mel Gibson's 2006 film, *Apocalypto*, about the end of the Mayan civilization in Mexico. The sacrifices of Aaron and the people were costly because they were the fruits of their toil and material they could have eaten themselves. Like our own costly stewardship, they were offering to God what was his already. There is no doubting that the sacrifices of Aaron as the priest of the people were efficacious in offering expiation for sin and inviting the outcome that God's glory be revealed to all Israel gathered outside the tent of meeting. The work of atonement by the High Priest continued until the final destruction of the temple in AD 70. As we know, however, this was an atonement that had to be endlessly repeated; the atonement wrought by Christ on the cross was once and for all.

The holy places of Israel were steaming with fresh blood and wreathed in the smoke of burnt offerings. Mel Gibson's even more controversial film, *The Passion of the Christ* (2004), shocks us in Technicolor with the graphic bloody suffering of Jesus. Whatever we think of that, and whatever the contrast with beautiful churches lit by stained glass and filled with beautiful music, we must acknowledge the power of offering to God the force of life and growth. Every service of the Church is rooted deeply in the bloody sacrifice of Christ, the only answer to sin in the real world.

God of our salvation,
help us to turn away from those habits which harm our bodies
and poison our minds
and to choose again your gift of life,
revealed to us in Jesus Christ our Lord.

COLLECT

65

Friday 7 February

Leviticus 16.2-24

'The goat shall bear on itself all their iniquities ...' (v.22)

Harper Lee's novel of 1960, *To Kill a Mockingbird*, is a powerful study in racism and courage. Atticus Finch defends the black Tom Robinson in court against a false charge of rape. Although it is patently obvious that Tom is innocent, the jury believes the lies of the town drunk. Tom is shot and killed while trying to escape. Finch's children are later only saved from that same drunk by Boo, a reclusive young man whom the children had previously feared.

Tom is an obvious example of a scapegoat, an innocent blamed for the shame of a community that needs desperately to define itself over against the object of rejection. The devil goat sent into the wilderness had an even stronger spiritual purpose: to bear away the sins of the people and take them to an empty place.

We know that Jesus was innocent and wrongly accused. He had the sins of the whole world laid on him; he took them to the place where he knew our alienation so cruelly that he felt abandoned even by his Father. The philosopher, René Girard, developed the *Scapegoat Mechanism* as a way of explaining human violence. His contention is that God is not only separate from that violence, but, in Jesus, becomes its object deliberately to break the cycle of human violence by his resurrection from the dead. But first he has to die because he refuses to be defined over against anyone, even his despisers, even us, and so brings upon himself the violence of the whole world.

COLLECT

Almighty God,
by whose grace alone we are accepted
    and called to your service:
strengthen us by your Holy Spirit
and make us worthy of our calling;
through Jesus Christ your Son our Lord,
who is alive and reigns with you,
in the unity of the Holy Spirit,
one God, now and for ever.

Saturday 8 February

Leviticus 17

'No person among you shall eat blood ...' (v.12)

Draining the blood from meat is a fundamental part of Jewish law concerning food. What is most significant is that food is not just functional; there is a ritual significance to it. Jews believe that keeping kosher is deeply connected to being holy. Jews live a life enfolded in ritual, and this applies to cleanliness and clothes as well as to food. If a Jew is described as being *frum,* it means in Yiddish that he is devout enough to be keeping all 613 Jewish commandments.

Living this ritual life according to God's commands is primarily intended to bring the person close to God, not to separate the Jew from others. The call to live a ritual life apart has a strong Christian dimension in the call to the religious life. Rumer Godden's novel, *In This House of Brede,* is about a Benedictine community of nuns, one of whom, Dame Philippa, writes: 'There is a story about Newman that I like very much. In his room he had a picture ... of the Blessed in Paradise praising God, and every time he came in and out, he used to smile at it and say, "What! Still at it?" That about sums up life at Brede...'

As Christians in the world, we live the same ritual life in the rhythm of our prayers and, as we come to receive the most important food of all, in the body and blood of Christ.

God of our salvation,
help us to turn away from those habits which harm our bodies
and poison our minds
and to choose again your gift of life,
revealed to us in Jesus Christ our Lord.

COLLECT

67

Monday 10 February

Psalms 27, **30**
Leviticus 19.1-18, 30-end
I Timothy 1.1-17

Leviticus 19.1-18, 30-end

'You shall be holy' (v.2)

For most of this week we are exploring a section of Leviticus known by many as the Holiness Code (Chapters 19–26). Just what the doctor ordered for the second week of February! Holiness doesn't always have a good press. We think it's beyond our reach. People who claim to be holy risk being shown up as hypocrites.

Much of Leviticus chapters 19 to 26 is what we might call 'preached law'. It's not so much a legal code as one long encouragement to put God's commandments into practice in daily life. Many of the commandments found here are not new. The first verses of today's reading contain three of the ten in Exodus 20.

But two things are distinctive here. The first is the reasons given. God's people are called not just to do what God says but to reflect God's very nature: 'You shall be holy, for I the Lord your God am holy' (v.2). The refrain that runs through this needs expanding a little. '(You should be like this because) I am the Lord your God'. Belonging to the Lord creates responsibilities as well as privileges.

The second distinctive element, which I love, are the practical touches that run through the holiness code. These are the bits which call for imaginative interpretation today: not many of us will glean fields or measure cloth today. How are we to fulfil these commandments?

COLLECT

O God,
you know us to be set
in the midst of so many and great dangers,
that by reason of the frailty of our nature
we cannot always stand upright:
grant to us such strength and protection
as may support us in all dangers
and carry us through all temptations;
through Jesus Christ your Son our Lord,
who is alive and reigns with you,
in the unity of the Holy Spirit,
one God, now and for ever.

Tuesday 11 February

Leviticus 23.1-22

'... at the time appointed' (v.4)

Time needs to be marked out in order to make sense to us. We need sensible rhythms in order to live healthy and productive lives and in order to nurture community. To be fully human, there has to be more to life than work, and the way we express that is in the way time is ordered.

The Holiness Code here marks out time in two ways. There is a weekly rhythm and an annual cycle. Both are very simple. The first underlines the importance of Sabbath: one day each week of rest and reflection. For the community envisaged by Leviticus, Sabbath is not an individual event but a corporate one. It's a day to gather together as well as to find space. It's a precious gift that helps make us whole.

The second rhythm is set by marking out the pattern of the year with periods of holy days (or holidays): days of pilgrimage, festival, feasting, gathering and reflection. These holy days in Israel are tied to not one but two patterns of meaning. The first is the agricultural pattern of sowing and harvest shared by every society in the ancient world and by most cultures until modern times. The second is the connection of this annual rhythm in Israel's story of salvation. The feast of the passover and of unleavened bread look back to the Exodus and to what it means to be God's own people.

Lord of the hosts of heaven,
our salvation and our strength,
without you we are lost:
guard us from all that harms or hurts
and raise us when we fall;
through Jesus Christ our Lord.

COLLECT

Wednesday 12 February

Leviticus 23.23-end

'... self-denial' (v.29)

The marking out of time continues. Leviticus strives for a balance, like the great rule of St Benedict, between prayer, rest and work. For most of us, unless prayer and rest are clearly protected by internal boundaries and external markers, then work and the demands of other people can expand to fill every available space.

The feast of weeks in the autumn was called simply 'the festival of the Lord' (v.39). It became the most important of the annual gatherings in ancient Israel. The festival draws together the themes of harvest and prayers for the renewal of the land in the coming year with the exodus and the origins of the nation. It would become the time when the nation came together to learn and rehearse its story; a time when priests and prophets taught the people; a time, eventually, when God's kingship was celebrated and human kingship renewed. Many of the psalms originally found their setting here in the life of the temple.

For those of us who love to work, note the interesting and demanding phrase in 23.29. Keeping Sabbath rest on the day of atonement is deliberately called 'self-denial'. If you are paid by the hour or by what you produce, you have less money if you take a day off. Yet this time off is of immense value both to individuals and community. Its worth cannot be measured. A real challenge to our current values and practice.

COLLECT

O God,
you know us to be set
in the midst of so many and great dangers,
that by reason of the frailty of our nature
we cannot always stand upright:
grant to us such strength and protection
as may support us in all dangers
and carry us through all temptations;
through Jesus Christ your Son our Lord,
who is alive and reigns with you,
in the unity of the Holy Spirit,
one God, now and for ever.

Psalm **37***
Leviticus 24.1-9
1 Timothy 4

Leviticus 24.1-9

'... before the Lord' (vv.3,4,8)

Holiness is partly about what we do. Holiness is partly about discovering God in the ordinary tapestry of life. Here the Code offers two signs and symbols of God's presence in the life of God's people. These are not special or particularly expensive signs and symbols but ordinary, everyday objects – the best that can be provided and invested with a special meaning.

The first is the light burning continuously from evening to morning. God is with us in the night as well as the daytime, to guide, to comfort, to lead. There is an echo of the pillar of fire and a looking forward to the one who will come, the light of the world.

The second sacrament is bread: the twelve loaves set each Sabbath day before the symbols of God's presence in the tent of meeting. There are echoes here, of course, of the manna and God's provision in the wilderness. There is a looking forward to miracles of feeding in the desert, to the one who calls himself the 'bread of life', to Eucharist.

The passage raises for us today the power of physical symbols in communicating God's presence in the midst of our communities and homes and lives. What are the most important physical signs of God's presence as I come 'before the Lord' to pray each day and as I gather 'before the Lord' with God's people?

Lord of the hosts of heaven,
our salvation and our strength,
without you we are lost:
guard us from all that harms or hurts
and raise us when we fall;
through Jesus Christ our Lord.

COLLECT

Friday 14 February

Leviticus 25.1-24

'You shall proclaim liberty' (v.10)

Holiness is not a private and individual matter. Holiness is about how we live together in community, the ways in which we care one for another and tenderly bear one another's burdens. Holiness is also concerned with the way we care for the whole of God's creation and live gently on the earth.

The principle behind the sabbatical year and the jubilee are more important than the law itself. There is little evidence that the law was ever put into practice. But the principles are fascinating. Again, there is a longing for rhythm and for pattern expressed in numbers (seven years and seven times seven years). Ancient commentators draw our attention to the jubilee and the feast of Pentecost (the 50th day after the resurrection).

But there is a deep principle of stewardship here underneath the numerical pattern. Everything we own is entrusted to us by God and must be handed on to those who come after. The way a society is ordered must favour fairness and equality, and prevent both the accumulation of vast wealth and the accumulation of debt that will cripple future generations. There is a principle of grace: depending on and working with the creation rather than exploiting it for short-term gain.

And, finally, there is the principle of freedom: prized throughout history and throughout the world. One person is not meant to be a slave to another either through debt or bondage. Leviticus is a gospel of liberation.

COLLECT

O God,
you know us to be set
in the midst of so many and great dangers,
that by reason of the frailty of our nature
we cannot always stand upright:
grant to us such strength and protection
as may support us in all dangers
and carry us through all temptations;
through Jesus Christ your Son our Lord,
who is alive and reigns with you,
in the unity of the Holy Spirit,
one God, now and for ever.

Saturday 15 February

Numbers 6.1-5, 21-end

'The Lord bless you and keep you' (v.24)

It is a great spiritual and human insight that men and women are created equal but different. Some are helped to grow in one way and others in another. There needs to be space among the people of God for special periods of devotion at particular times for those so called. Hence the provisions of the Nazirite vow. God calls some of us, some of the time, to a particular consecration of our lives. Like fasting in Lent, the abstinence is in part symbolic and in part to check our appetites, a sign of deeper devotion. We know from St Paul's own ministry that the practice of the Nazirite vow persisted into the New Testament period (Acts 21.17 ff.). It's not too early to plan your own discipline for Lent this year.

But while some are called to particular periods of devotion in some seasons, all are called to be blessed. The words of the great priestly blessing are worth learning by heart. They have been found inscribed on two silver plaques in the environs of Jerusalem, dated to the sixth or seventh centuries BC. The three lines consist of three, five and seven words in the Hebrew. Each one begins of course with God's name: the Lord.

The act of blessing is described as putting God's name (and also therefore God's nature) on the Israelites. In your own prayers of intercession, who are you asking God to bless today? In which situation do you pray especially, 'Hallowed be your name'?

Lord of the hosts of heaven,
our salvation and our strength,
without you we are lost:
guard us from all that harms or hurts
and raise us when we fall;
through Jesus Christ our Lord.

Monday 17 February

Genesis 24.1-28

'O Lord ... grant me success today' (v.12)

The charge Abraham gives to his elderly servant is not far short of *Mission Impossible*: to find a wife for his master's son, from among his kinsfolk, and persuade her to come back to live in a far-off country she has never seen.

There are many lessons in a beautifully told tale, not least the way in which practical wisdom and prayer combine in the face of an impossible task. The servant acts with prudence and discretion in clarifying the task, in making preparations and in travelling to the right place in the right city at the right time.

Yet the thread of faith through the story is stronger even than the thread of wisdom. Abraham has faith that the right woman will be provided. The servant walks in the greater faith of his master. His practical preparations are accompanied by prayer and also trust that, as he reaches the limits of what he can do, God's faithfulness will supply all that is needed.

The story reminds us that we are never too old to be entrusted with impossible tasks by God. Indeed, one of life's challenges is to be more, not less, ready to undertake impossible adventures as we grow in wisdom and maturity. But these tasks are not to be undertaken in the light of experience alone but in faith and risk and in prayer.

COLLECT

Almighty God,
who alone can bring order
to the unruly wills and passions of sinful humanity:
give your people grace
so to love what you command
and to desire what you promise,
that, among the many changes of this world,
our hearts may surely there be fixed
where true joys are to be found;
through Jesus Christ your Son our Lord,
who is alive and reigns with you,
in the unity of the Holy Spirit,
one God, now and for ever.

Tuesday 18 February

Genesis 24.29-end

'The Lord, before whom I walk ...' (v.40)

Behind the events of the story lies the faith of Abraham, forged in his call to leave his kindred, rekindled in the conception of Isaac in old age, refined in the encounter on Mount Moriah. Abraham's long journey is one of close friendship with God, one in which his whole household and his descendants share. Faith and friendship come together in the final great crisis of Abraham's life: finding a wife for Isaac and the securing of the next generation of God's people.

This faith and this friendship are enough to overcome practical difficulties and scepticism. They create the right conditions for synchronicity: the coming together of events in remarkable ways, in which God's people discern God's guidance and blessing. The synchronicity here is so remarkable and such an important part of the founding of God's people that the storytellers of Genesis repeat the whole tale to Laban and his family. We glimpse Laban's greed, which will recur later in the story, but it is not enough to divert the main stream of events.

All the way through the stories of the patriarchs, the identity and faith of the mother as well as the father is emphasized. Here Rebecca is shown to be a suitable wife for Isaac through her hospitality and graciousness to a stranger, through her faith, through her courage and trust, and finally through her giving of herself to Isaac.

Eternal God,
whose Son went among the crowds
and brought healing with his touch:
help us to show his love,
in your Church as we gather together,
and by our lives as they are transformed
into the image of Christ our Lord.

COLLECT

75

Wednesday 19 February

Genesis 25.7-11, 19-end

'The children struggled together within her' (v.22)

Abraham blessed his son Isaac, but that blessing does not mean that life is a bed of roses for the family who are to grow into the people of God. Despite Abraham's blessing and despite the faith they share, the way ahead is difficult. The pains, thorns and thistles described in the fallen world of Genesis 3 affect even those who are blessed by God. Progress for God's people is difficult and takes place over generations not days.

Rebecca and Isaac are together for 20 years before Rebecca conceives. Perseverance and prayer are needed. The pregnancy and birth of the twins, Esau and Jacob, are difficult, with conflict and rivalry even in the womb. Rebecca despairs of life itself. The two brothers are radically different by nature, temperament and instinct. The family itself is divided with the mother siding with one son and the father with another. The birthright and blessing come to Jacob, father of the twelve tribes of Israel, but only through cunning and deceit.

In our Christian life today, it is important from time to time to remember that this fallen world is full of thistles, thorns and pain, even now. The progress of God's kingdom is often slow. For Rebecca, for the early Christians and for us, it is through many tribulations that we must enter the kingdom of God (Acts 14.22).

COLLECT

Almighty God,
who alone can bring order
to the unruly wills and passions of sinful humanity:
give your people grace
so to love what you command
and to desire what you promise,
that, among the many changes of this world,
our hearts may surely there be fixed
where true joys are to be found;
through Jesus Christ your Son our Lord,
who is alive and reigns with you,
in the unity of the Holy Spirit,
one God, now and for ever.

Psalms 56, **57** (63*)
Genesis 26.34 – 27.40
2 Timothy 1.15 – 2.13

Thursday 20 February

Genesis 26.34 – 27.40

'Bless me, me also, father!' (27.34)

A deathbed is an uncomfortable place. This whole of chapter 27 is one long deathbed drama. Great tension surrounded Isaac's birth, and now a different tension surrounds his final moments.

Esau and Jacob began their struggle in the womb and their conflict here reaches its crescendo. The preference of one parent for one child and the other for another began, no doubt, in small moments in childhood. It results now in a deep fracture in the family, one that threatens disaster.

With the help of his mother, Jacob tricks his father and twin brother. He lies and cheats his way to an inheritance. There is nothing attractive or admirable in his victory. There is little to be admired in the way any of the four main characters behave. This is the lowest point of the patriarchal narratives. There is no sense of a long friendship with the Lord as there was with Abraham. God is largely absent from the story, mentioned only in Jacob's lie to his father (v.20) and the coveted blessing (v.28).

What lessons do we draw? It is vital to deepen friendship with God and integrity through the whole course of our life, not simply to rely on a good background or beginning to sustain us. But the most important lesson is the power of God's grace to work through the most dysfunctional of families and relationships. Salvation is God's work from beginning to end, not ours.

Eternal God,
whose Son went among the crowds
and brought healing with his touch:
help us to show his love,
in your Church as we gather together,
and by our lives as they are transformed
into the image of Christ our Lord.

COLLECT

Friday 21 February

Psalms **51**, 54
Genesis 27.41 – end of 28
2 Timothy 2.14-end

Genesis 27.41 – end of 28

'All the families of the earth shall be blessed in you' (28.14)

The deep bitterness and long rivalry in the family home drive both sons away in the end. Jacob is sent back to Paddan-aram, following in the footsteps of Abraham's faithful servant and bearing his father's blessing.

Here, at this low point in the story, Jacob the deceiver encounters the living God in his dream at Bethel. Jacob sees in his dream that a deeper spiritual reality lies beneath the physical world we inhabit. Like many who have encountered God since, Jacob is alone, at a low point in his life, and on a journey. In a profound moment of encounter and reality, the faith of his fathers becomes his own faith. The call to his fathers becomes his own call.

The Lord's promise to Jacob echoes the promise to Abraham (compare Genesis 12.3 with 28.14). We see here clearly the missionary purpose of the God of Abraham: in calling one family and nation, the Lord is seeking to bless every family and nation.

God's promise to Jacob, like his promise to Abraham, demands a response of faith. Jacob's faith is shown in his establishing a pillar and an offering and a renaming of the place, later to become a great shrine for the northern kingdom. What promises does God make to us today and how do we respond?

COLLECT

Almighty God,
who alone can bring order
to the unruly wills and passions of sinful humanity:
give your people grace
so to love what you command
and to desire what you promise,
that, among the many changes of this world,
our hearts may surely there be fixed
where true joys are to be found;
through Jesus Christ your Son our Lord,
who is alive and reigns with you,
in the unity of the Holy Spirit,
one God, now and for ever.

Saturday 22 February

Genesis 29.1-30

'He loved Rachel more than Leah' (v.30)

There is a strong theme in Scripture of the sins of one generation being passed on to the next. It's a theme that resonates with modern understandings of psychology. Jacob the trickster now reaps what he has sown. The one who has deceived his father and brother now encounters greedy uncle Laban, who recognizes profit and free labour when he sees it.

Jacob himself is painted now as reformed and sincere. His love for Rachel is genuine and the seven years he serves for her seem but a few days. Yet Laban substitutes his elder daughter Leah for Rachel just as his sister Rebecca had substituted Jacob for Esau. Jacob is deceived but receives the gift of Rachel also. Not surprisingly, he loves one of his wives more than the other.

So the intense rivalry is passed from one generation to another. Laban sets up the situation where his own daughters, Leah and Rachel are in competition for the affections of a single husband. This, in turn, creates the rivalry and jealousy between the twelve sons of Jacob that will result in further evil in the next generation and which, in turn, will only be overcome by Joseph's extraordinary wisdom and willingness to forgive.

A moment to reflect today, then, on the deep patterns in our own families and what we are called to do to change them in our own generation.

Eternal God,
whose Son went among the crowds
and brought healing with his touch:
help us to show his love,
in your Church as we gather together,
and by our lives as they are transformed
into the image of Christ our Lord.

COLLECT

Monday 24 February

Genesis 29.31 – 30.24

'God has judged me, and has also heard my voice' (30.6)

This story of Jacob's two wives, their maids and their children contains traditions about the origins of the twelve tribes of Israel. It is also a very human story of Rachel and Leah's rivalry, and Jacob's working out of his place in the purposes of God. Jacob is still the ruthless younger brother who tricked Esau out of the blessing that was his right. Now he himself has been tricked into marrying Leah when he desired Rachel, and is serving as a hired hand of his brother-in-law Laban.

Jacob's destiny is not an easy one and nor is that of his household. Christian vocation often comes with a cost. We may desire to fulfil God's will for us, but the twists in our personal history and the flaws in our character can still bring unhappiness to ourselves and to others. This does not prevent God working out his will in our lives, but it does mean that we sometimes have to put up with a fair measure of unhappiness and ambiguity. We can get through this if we are able to accept it as the training and discipline that fit us for God's purpose. In the end God's purpose will prevail; it is for us to decide whether it is because of, or in spite of, us.

COLLECT

Almighty God,
you have created the heavens and the earth
and made us in your own image:
teach us to discern your hand in all your works
and your likeness in all your children;
through Jesus Christ your Son our Lord,
who with you and the Holy Spirit reigns supreme over all things,
now and for ever.

Psalm **73**
Genesis 31.1-24
2 Timothy 4.9-end

Tuesday 25 February

Genesis 31.1-24

'So Jacob arose…' (v.17)

Jacob's time of servitude has been long enough, and this part of his life is now coming to an end. His good stewardship of Laban's wealth has caused comment, and Laban is beginning to be anxious about his intentions. He is beginning to acknowledge that he has cheated Jacob and dealt with him unfairly. The decision to leave, though, is not Jacob's alone. He is commanded to depart by God in a dream. From the conversation that follows with Rachel and Leah, it is clear that they are ready to go with Jacob; they too are victims of Laban's dishonesty. Laban pursues the fleeing company, but he is warned by God not to intensify the quarrel with Jacob.

It is not always easy to know when to leave an unpromising and unfulfilling situation. God makes clear to Jacob that he has not abandoned him, reminding him of the dream at Bethel when Jacob saw the heavenly ladder and the angels. Heaven is still interested in Jacob's life and still expects great things from him. We cannot expect the course of our lives to run smoothly all the time, but we need to be alert to those times when God requires us to change course, and then do what we believe we are being asked to do. There are always risks: Jacob and his household lose their security, but God's promises invite our faithfulness.

Almighty God,
give us reverence for all creation
and respect for every person,
that we may mirror your likeness
in Jesus Christ our Lord.

COLLECT

81

Wednesday 26 February

Genesis 31.25 – 32.2

'Jacob went on his way and the angels of God met him' (32.1)

Today's reading concludes the story of Jacob's servitude. Laban pursues Jacob but is commanded by God to refrain from violence. Laban remains aggrieved, though, suspecting that Jacob has stolen the *teraphim*, the household gods that Laban may have used for divination. In fact, it is Rachel who has stolen them and who ingeniously conceals them. Jacob claims that he has fulfilled the terms of his servitude to the letter and more, and that it is God who wants to prevent him from being further exploited by Laban. The outcome of their dispute is that Laban climbs down and proposes a covenant. So, in spite of the differences between the two of them, they agree to refrain from aggression.

There are loose ends to this story. Jacob is never fully vindicated, yet the result is peace – and Jacob's resumption of his quest for the land of promise.

Our lives, like Jacob's are lived within the promise of God. We may find ourselves with all kinds of loose ends that never get sorted out; we may not always receive exact justice or fairness. In the broader picture, this may matter less than we think. Being faithful to God's promise and being ready to meet his guiding angels is usually more important than tidying up the past.

COLLECT

Almighty God,
you have created the heavens and the earth
and made us in your own image:
teach us to discern your hand in all your works
and your likeness in all your children;
through Jesus Christ your Son our Lord,
who with you and the Holy Spirit reigns supreme over all things,
now and for ever.

Psalm **78.1-39***
Genesis 32.3-30
Titus 2

Genesis 32.3-30

'And there he blessed him' (v.29)

During his exile Jacob has learnt self-discipline. Now he learns fear. He is coming to the territory controlled by Esau and realises that he will either have to fight or make peace with the brother he has cheated. He has no resources to fight; making peace is the only option. So he sends extravagant presents to Esau, hoping that his brother will refrain from revenge. Alone at night 'a man wrestles with him until daybreak'. Jacob's inner struggle is worked out in the encounter with the mysterious stranger. Jacob wrestles alone with his past and his future; with his treachery and with the promise of God; with his sin against his brother and with the mercy that God offers him. The fight has a double conclusion: Jacob wins the struggle but he is injured. He is given a new name, Israel, signifying his destiny, but in spite of trying he cannot force a name out of his opponent.

This passage yields profound insight into our relationship with God. It shows us that God takes us on as we are, but does not leave us unchanged. God struggles with the flaws of our nature; we struggle with the contradictions of our experience. God want us to be healed, but we need to be humbled. The blessing that Jacob receives is the blessing of integrity. Mysterious though it is, it is our wounds that make us whole.

Almighty God,
give us reverence for all creation
and respect for every person,
that we may mirror your likeness
in Jesus Christ our Lord.

COLLECT

Friday 28 February

Psalm **55**
Genesis 33.1-17
Titus 3

Genesis 33.1-17

'... to see your face is like seeing the face of God' (v.10)

Jacob is expecting the worst. He prepares for his encounter with his brother with care, hoping that a degree of flattery and self-abasement will turn away Esau's wrath. He seems unprepared for Esau's wholehearted welcome, the warmth of which anticipates the parable of the Prodigal Son. There, the father runs out to meet his wayward child; here, the betrayed brother runs to greet his betrayer. And Jacob too has learnt the value of generosity – he is willing to share his wealth. Whether Jacob is sincere when he speaks of Esau's face as the face of God is difficult to judge, but from our point of view he is speaking the simple truth. Esau has forgiven him and greeted him as his brother; thanks to his spontaneous welcome, their bitter rivalry is set aside. Jacob, who wrestled with the angel, recognizes the hand of God in the encounter. Forgiveness and generosity are divine attributes.

When we struggle with difficult family relationships, we should remember God's desire for the healing of family rifts. The reconciliation of Jacob and Esau should inspire us to hope that conflicts need not be permanent. God can work even through our self-interest if we are willing to see those we find most difficult as messengers sent to us by God.

COLLECT

Almighty God,
you have created the heavens and the earth
and made us in your own image:
teach us to discern your hand in all your works
and your likeness in all your children;
through Jesus Christ your Son our Lord,
who with you and the Holy Spirit reigns supreme over all things,
now and for ever.

Psalms **76**, 79
Genesis 35
Philemon

Saturday 1 March

Genesis 35

'Let us go up to Bethel, that I may make an altar there' (v.3)

Jacob now comes again to Bethel, where he had first encountered God in the dream of the heavenly ladder. Bethel means 'house of God', and it is always a place of promise for Jacob, a threshold between heaven and earth. So, not surprisingly, it is here that Jacob's faith is purified; the gods that his household have worshipped, perhaps including the gods that Rachel stole from Laban, must now be given up. On the way from Bethel, Jacob's much-loved Rachel dies. Jacob's journey, though, does not end, and he eventually reaches Mamre in time for the death of his father. The reconciliation between Jacob and Esau is shown in the way that they bury him together, equals in sonship at the last. Jacob's story has been a winding quest, which begins in selfish desire and ends in worship. The journey goes on; Jacob's sons by his two wives, Leah and Rachel, will form the twelve tribes of Israel.

We rarely understand the full significance of our lives or the lives of those around us. But, like Jacob, we can experience a process of purification through our Christian pilgrimage. We need to return again and again to the sources of our faith, and let go ever more fully of the false gods that captivate us. If we are faithful, we will find life fruitful.

Almighty God,
give us reverence for all creation
and respect for every person,
that we may mirror your likeness
in Jesus Christ our Lord.

COLLECT

Monday 3 March

Galatians 1

'the gospel … is not of human origin' (v.11)

The letter to the Galatians begins in a rush. Even before the usual goodwill greetings (v.3), Paul launches in by insisting that he writes with unique authority, which is not derived from others but comes direct from Christ and God the Father. His intervention in Galatian affairs is a direct consequence of the resurrection faith. Now to the point. The Galatians have turned away from the true faith, seduced by 'a different gospel'. In an attempt to counter this, Paul tells his own story. As a zealous student of the Jewish law, he persecuted the Church. Yet God had another plan for his life and revealed Christ to him so that he should become his emissary among the gentiles.

The anguish in the letter reflects Paul's consternation that his flock have gone astray; those who had received his teaching, which should have liberated them, are now seeking to be enslaved all over again. At his conversion Paul deliberately avoided contact with those who might have threatened or over-influenced him. The Galatians need to recognize that the new teachings they are drawn to are not only confusing but also destructive.

Paul's *cri de coeur* invites us to consider fundamentals. What is our gospel today? How firm is our foundation in Jesus Christ and God the Father who raised him from the dead? What might lead us astray from the faith we have received?

COLLECT

Almighty Father,
whose Son was revealed in majesty
before he suffered death upon the cross:
give us grace to perceive his glory,
that we may be strengthened to suffer with him
and be changed into his likeness, from glory to glory;
who is alive and reigns with you,
in the unity of the Holy Spirit,
one God, now and for ever.

Psalms 87, **89.1-18**
Genesis 37.12-end
Galatians 2.1-10

Tuesday 4 March

Galatians 2.1-10

'... we did not submit to them even for a moment' (v.5)

Paul continues his testimony to his wavering gentile converts. Although he has emphasized the authenticity of the teaching he gave them, he explains that he did eventually seek to discuss his message with the leaders of the Jerusalem Church. This was not because he needed their agreement, but to prove to himself that he was not 'running in vain'. His mission in no way depended on them; it came directly from God. As it turned out, James and Cephas (Peter) and John approved his activities, and they parted amicably with the agreement that the Jerusalem apostles should continue their evangelism among the Jews while Paul continued with his gentile mission. They also agreed to collaborate on relief to the poor.

Paul's explanation of his visit to Jerusalem is important because he is determined to prove to the Galatians that the true gospel does not depend on allegiance to the Jewish law (Titus did not have to be circumcised). He did not go to Jerusalem to submit to anyone, but simply to share what he was doing. Paul, the passionate, vulnerable apostle, has grasped that the outcome of the Galatian crisis will determine the future of the Christian Church. Is the gospel really a gospel for everyone? Does the resurrection faith really transcend race, history and cultural background? We should ask ourselves the same question.

Holy God,
you know the disorder of our sinful lives:
set straight our crooked hearts,
and bend our wills to love your goodness
and your glory
in Jesus Christ our Lord.

COLLECT

Wednesday 5 March

Ash Wednesday

Psalm **38**
Daniel 9.3-6, 17-19
I Timothy 6.6-19

Daniel 9.3-6, 17-19

'O Lord, hear; O Lord, forgive!' (v.19)

At the beginning of Lent, the Church turns back to its origins. Christian life begins in the baptismal font, when we first renounced evil and turned in faith to the Lord. Daniel, the prophet and visionary, shows us the way in today's reading as he repents on behalf of his people, acknowledging their history of sin and rebellion. Repentance is never the outcome of despair, but rather an act of profound hope. Daniel trusts that Jerusalem will be restored. The Lord will shine upon his people once again.

History vindicates Daniel – the book was almost certainly composed long after the time it reflects, when God had brought his people home. As we make confession of our sins this Lent, we do so not as a grovelling act of self-hatred, but as a response to God's mercy. Confession is grounded in clarity about ourselves, a recognition that sin is a consequences of our choices, and that our choices are determined by our desires. So we come home to reality, to the God 'to whom all hearts are open, all desires known, and from whom no secrets are hidden'. God does not lead us to repentance to condemn us but to set us free from all the destructive and acquisitive instincts that crowd in on our lives and erode our faith and humanity. It is an act of trust – our part in the renewal of all creation.

COLLECT

Almighty and everlasting God,
you hate nothing that you have made
and forgive the sins of all those who are penitent:
create and make in us new and contrite hearts
that we, worthily lamenting our sins
and acknowledging our wretchedness,
may receive from you, the God of all mercy,
perfect remission and forgiveness;
through Jesus Christ your Son our Lord,
who is alive and reigns with you,
in the unity of the Holy Spirit,
one God, now and for ever.

Psalms **77** *or* 90, **92**
Genesis 39
Galatians 2.11-end

Galatians 2.11-end

'I have been crucified with Christ; and it is no longer I who live,
but it is Christ who lives in me' (vv.19-20)

We come now to the heart of Paul's despair over his back-sliding converts. He has seen for himself how deep a hold the Jewish law still has on Peter, and how easy it is for gentile converts to be pressured into accepting circumcision and the food laws 'just in case', or to gain approval from others who are doing so.

For Paul, this is a betrayal of the gospel that makes null the saving death of Christ. His language is extreme because something extreme is at stake. Is Christianity another form of Judaism – more open and accessible to gentiles but still requiring the adoption of a distinctly Jewish identity? Or is it something different – a new movement of God to bring the gentiles into the promises God made to the Jews, and yet without requiring conformity to the law? If the second of these is true, then obedience to the law implies radical doubt in the gospel, a sinful abandonment of hope in Christ alone.

In his anguish over the fate of the Galatians, Paul articulates the mystical heart of the gospel. Through his death on the cross, Christ has become the inner life of every believer. Our selfhood is not grounded in our achievements, however worthy, but only in his grace and love.

Holy God,
our lives are laid open before you:
rescue us from the chaos of sin
and through the death of your Son
bring us healing and make us whole
in Jesus Christ our Lord.

COLLECT

Friday 7 March

Galatians 3.1-14

'Did you experience so much for nothing?' (v.4)

Paul is determined to bring the Galatians back to the liberation they initially experienced through his preaching. He now batters them with a series of rhetorical questions. He insists that they review their experience, remembering that it was trust that enabled them to receive the Spirit, and not conformity to the Jewish law. Their former willingness to trust proved that they were genuine children of Abraham, included in the promise God made to him and to all his descendants, even though they were not Jews by birth.

Paul's characteristic theology of grace and faith is drawn out of him by this conflict and crisis; we can see him articulating the principles by which Christians have lived for 2000 years as he struggles to convince his 'foolish' and 'bewitched' converts.

In our time, tolerance is considered a virtue, and Paul's heated argument might be regarded as a form of persuasion close to bullying. Yet there is a challenge for us here. How ready are we to explore our own Christian experience and renew our trust in the fundamentals of our faith? This Lent we have a chance to consider whether the faith we hold is progressively liberating us or imprisoning us. Are we growing in maturity, generosity, charity – or are we becoming embittered, fearful, cynical? Has Christ indeed redeemed us from 'the curse of the law'?

COLLECT

Almighty and everlasting God,
you hate nothing that you have made
and forgive the sins of all those who are penitent:
create and make in us new and contrite hearts
that we, worthily lamenting our sins
and acknowledging our wretchedness,
may receive from you, the God of all mercy,
perfect remission and forgiveness;
through Jesus Christ your Son our Lord,
who is alive and reigns with you,
in the unity of the Holy Spirit,
one God, now and for ever.

Saturday 8 March

Galatians 3.15-22

'Why then the law?' (v.19)

Now comes Paul's most radical theological innovation in this letter. He compares God's promises to Abraham and his offspring to a will that cannot be legally altered. He then suggests, daringly, that God's promise was not directed to the plurality of Abraham's descendants, but rather to the one descendant who sums up in his person the whole of Israel's faith, Jesus Christ. This is startling enough, but the concept of God's promise as a 'will' enables Paul to put the law in a secondary place. The promise came first. The law was added centuries later in the time of Moses as a restraining force, to keep lawlessness under control, until the 'offspring' to whom the promise was made was born.

This argument is more fully stated in the letter to the Romans, but here it enables Paul to reassert the primacy of the gospel over the law without denying that the law was given by God. How are we to understand this? Law is a social good and gives us a moral code. We need constraint and convention. But these have their limits. Even the best laws cannot of themselves set us free from the attitudes and habits that lead to sin. Law cannot save us from death or give us hope in life eternal. But the promise, given originally to Abraham, and vindicated in Christ's death and resurrection, is there for us today and always.

Holy God,
our lives are laid open before you:
rescue us from the chaos of sin
and through the death of your Son
bring us healing and make us whole
in Jesus Christ our Lord.

COLLECT

Monday 10 March

Galatians 3.23 – 4.7

'So you are no longer a slave but ... an heir' (4.7)

Paul wants his listeners to have a grown-up faith. He wants them to move on from being a slave to being an heir, from minor to major, and he uses all sorts of images and arguments in these chapters to make the point. Paul did his theology on the run, but what rings through his writing all the time is the theme of freedom. He has experienced the power of religion to imprison us in small spaces under the control of rulebooks, and he aches for his converts to know the liberation of a Christ-centred life.

Distorted religion can still clip our wings. The big move forward for me was the realization that faith was not about regulating my life but about relishing a relationship. I had many of the pieces of the Christian jigsaw lying around but they had seemed obscure and opaque. What was this piece for, and that one? (I thought the same about maths). When I found the liberating piece of the jigsaw that described a relationship with Christ, everything began to make sense – and what's more, every other relationship was transformed as well. 'There is no longer Jew or Greek ... slave or free ... male and female ...' (3.28). We've been working on that ever since.

How, I wonder, will we claim and live that freedom today?

COLLECT

Almighty God,
whose Son Jesus Christ fasted forty days in the wilderness,
and was tempted as we are, yet without sin:
give us grace to discipline ourselves in obedience to your Spirit;
and, as you know our weakness,
so may we know your power to save;
through Jesus Christ your Son our Lord,
who is alive and reigns with you,
in the unity of the Holy Spirit,
one God, now and for ever.

Psalms **44** *or* **106*** (or 103)
Genesis 41.46 – 42.5
Galatians 4.8-20

Galatians 4.8-20

'... until Christ is formed in you' (v.19)

The strain on Paul is beginning to show. The believers in Galatia were being disturbed by Jewish Christians who wanted to turn the clock back and put the gentile converts back into a cage of rules and regulations 'observing special days, and months, and seasons' (v.10). 'How can you want to be enslaved again?' (v.9) is his anguished retort – 'I am afraid that my work for you may have been wasted' (v.11).

God always has a bigger vision for us to pursue. We always try to limit the gospel, to tame the tiger into a domestic pet. But (to change the image) God constantly gives us clothes that are two sizes too big for us, inviting us to grow into them and to experience the beauty and risk of a world infused with God's life and love. With God there is always more – more hope, more opportunity, more justice, more joy. Always a bigger vision. It's summed up in an extraordinary group of words: the vision is that 'Christ is formed in you' (v.19). That's a staggering image if you think about it: that the character of Christ himself should become a reality in our own confused and divided lives.

And the point Paul wants to make is as important now as it was then: if that's what God wants for us, how can we settle for anything less?

Heavenly Father,
your Son battled with the powers of darkness,
and grew closer to you in the desert:
help us to use these days to grow in wisdom and prayer
that we may witness to your saving love
in Jesus Christ our Lord.

COLLECT

Wednesday 12 March

Psalms **6**, 17 *or* 110, **111**, 112
Genesis 42.6-17
Galatians 4.21 – 5.1

Galatians 4.21 – 5.1

'For freedom Christ has set us free' (5.1)

Paul relentlessly pursues his theme. Nothing will stop his determination to cry freedom. Now he draws in the two mothers of Abraham's sons, Hagar and Sarah, and uses them as an allegory of two covenants, one leading to slavery and the other to freedom. Everything is fair game as Paul uses argument after argument to beseech the Galatians not to give up the freedom they have in Christ.

A member of my family was once told she couldn't have a position of responsibility in a church because of an improbable reading of something Paul had written in a very specific context. The church leader seemed to be suggesting that Paul was establishing another set of rules, having just released the gentiles from the previous set. As if! Paul specifically says: 'For freedom Christ has set us free' (5.1). The freedom of Christ and the new creation is one of the most important interpretative principles to employ when we're trying to understand and work with difficult biblical material.

The gospel continues to be too good to be true for many (perhaps all) of us. We think we really must put in a few health and safety measures to make the teaching of Jesus manageable. The radical nature of the freedom of Christ is a constant challenge, both a golden promise and an alarming threat.

What will this freedom look like for each of us today? Even better, what will it feel like?

COLLECT

Almighty God,
whose Son Jesus Christ fasted forty days in the wilderness,
and was tempted as we are, yet without sin:
give us grace to discipline ourselves in obedience to your Spirit;
and, as you know our weakness,
so may we know your power to save;
through Jesus Christ your Son our Lord,
who is alive and reigns with you,
in the unity of the Holy Spirit,
one God, now and for ever.

Psalms **42**, 43 *or* 113, **115**
Genesis 42.18-28
Galatians 5.2-15

Galatians 5.2-15

'Christ will be of no benefit to you' (v.2)

This is where we reach the high (or low) point of Paul's irritation. He's tried every argument and now decides to throw in a few threats. 'If you let yourselves be circumcised, Christ will be of no benefit to you … [you] have cut yourselves off from Christ' (vv.2,4). He even gets to the point of wishing his opponents would castrate themselves – not a conventional strategy in pastoral care. All of this shows just how important it is that the Galatian believers don't fall back into a legalistic understanding of faith.

We've travelled so far beyond this particular battle over circumcision that the argument seems almost amusingly arcane to us, but to Paul it was deadly serious. The whole integrity of a faith based on grace was at stake. Truth mattered. The ferocity of Paul's concern ought to give us pause and make us ask how much truth matters to us. There is an urgent explanatory task in our culture, and it often seems that as a Church we're not well equipped for it. Questions about belief in God, the nature of reality, science and faith, suffering, other faiths, etc., are all around us, yet often we duck the conversation, fearing our inadequacy.

If the truth isn't something both to defend and to commend, then we slide into a situation where nothing really matters very much – and nothing is worth either living for or dying for. That way lies tyranny and catastrophe. Paul recognized the danger. Do we?

Heavenly Father,
your Son battled with the powers of darkness,
and grew closer to you in the desert:
help us to use these days to grow in wisdom and prayer
that we may witness to your saving love
in Jesus Christ our Lord.

COLLECT

Friday 14 March

Psalm **22** *or* **139**
Genesis 42.29-end
Galatians 5.16-end

Galatians 5.16-end

'If we live by the Spirit, let us also be guided by the Spirit' (v.25)

In trying to demonstrate what's distinctive about the way Christians should live, Paul sets two approaches in clear opposition: the way of the flesh and the way of the Spirit. By 'flesh', Paul doesn't quite mean what we might think; he means more like 'the way of the world', a world without Christ as the touchstone. As ever, Paul pulls no punches: those who live in a worldly way will not inherit the kingdom of God. Your choice, he says.

It's well on occasions to see the contrast laid out starkly, but the practice of 'splitting', if it becomes a habit, can lead to some pretty unpleasant behaviour – condemnation, judgementalism, etc. But Paul shows us the better way – live by the Spirit and be guided by the Spirit. If you're lost in a car in a strange town, what you need isn't a list of complicated instructions but someone who knows the place well and who'll get in the front seat beside you and talk you through the road system. We have such a guide, says Paul, the Spirit of Jesus Christ, who will ensure that we choose the streets that are marked by love, joy, peace, patience, kindness, generosity and so on. So the question is: which navigation system do we use? Are we nudged and guided by the Spirit, or by the compulsions and obsessions of the world?

Will we start each day by inviting the divine Guide to show us the way?

COLLECT

Almighty God,
whose Son Jesus Christ fasted forty days in the wilderness,
and was tempted as we are, yet without sin:
give us grace to discipline ourselves in obedience to your Spirit;
and, as you know our weakness,
so may we know your power to save;
through Jesus Christ your Son our Lord,
who is alive and reigns with you,
in the unity of the Holy Spirit,
one God, now and for ever.

Galatians 6

'May I never boast of anything except the cross of our Lord Jesus Christ' (v.14)

The final chapter of this anguished letter feels like the final rumblings of a volcano that's now dying down. Paul's impassioned warnings still appear every so often – 'Do not be deceived; God is not mocked ...' (v.7), 'they want you to be circumcised so that they may boast ...' (v.13) – but he's beginning to relax and to return to his most compelling themes of the power of the cross and the reality of the new creation (vv.14,15).

And he alludes to the most mysterious sign of his identification with Jesus Christ – the stigmata, for 'I carry the marks of Jesus branded on my body' (v.17). A few saints through history seem to have been marked in this way, Francis of Assisi and Padre Pio among them. If someone dwells on the cross and lives in its shadow for long enough, perhaps they begin to replicate some of its features. It won't be the case for most of us, but when we read this tiny clue at the end of Paul's letter we might begin to understand why he was so passionate about maintaining the distinctiveness and truth of the gospel.

At one time I thought the Christian faith was a 'take it or leave it' option, mainly for the seriously religious. Now I believe it to be the pearl of great price, the most valuable thing that this world affords. But, as Lent gets under way, how close to the cross do I dare get?

Heavenly Father,
your Son battled with the powers of darkness,
and grew closer to you in the desert:
help us to use these days to grow in wisdom and prayer
that we may witness to your saving love
in Jesus Christ our Lord.

COLLECT

97

Monday 17 March

Hebrews 1

'... in these last days he has spoken to us by a Son' (v.2)

If you've got a main point to make, you might as well make it early. That's what the writer to the Hebrews does. He wants to make it clear that whatever other means God has used to reconcile heaven and earth in the past (angels, the sacrificial system, etc.) the full and final word has been spoken through a Son who is 'the exact imprint of God's very being' (v.3). The writer heaps on the superlatives, tossing in as an aside that it was through the Son that God also created the universe.

The main comparison that he makes in the early chapters is between what the angels do and what the Son does. This may not be something that keeps many of us awake at night now, but in the Jewish culture for which Hebrews is written, this was an important comparison. And it asks us how adequate our own understanding of Jesus Christ actually is. Is there a danger that we reduce him to a strolling minstrel, spinning tales of peace and love in the Galilean hills? Do we play down the divinity in order to make him manageable for a sceptical age? If so, reading the letter to the Hebrews is like a face-full of cold water. Prepare to meet an exalted Christ. Prepare to encounter a divine Son worthy of our wonder and allegiance.

And yet he goes with us this very day. Trust him.

COLLECT

Almighty God,
you show to those who are in error the light of your truth,
that they may return to the way of righteousness:
grant to all those who are admitted
    into the fellowship of Christ's religion,
that they may reject those things
    that are contrary to their profession,
and follow all such things as are agreeable to the same;
through our Lord Jesus Christ,
who is alive and reigns with you,
in the unity of the Holy Spirit,
one God, now and for ever.

Psalms **50** *or* 132, 133
Genesis 44.1-17
Hebrews 2.1-9

Hebrews 2.1-9

'... we must pay greater attention
... so that we do not drift away' (v.1)

The writer introduces us to another great theme of his letter – that his Jewish Christian readers must be careful not to drift back into Jewish practice. The message received through angels was important enough; how much more the message received through Jesus, 'who for a little while was made lower than the angels' but is now 'crowned with glory and honour because of the suffering of death' (v.9). Christ is the final word; you'd better believe it, says the writer. Don't drift.

It's very easy for our faith to drift. I was on holiday recently and realized at the end that I hadn't said my daily prayers all week. Not that I felt out of touch with God as I celebrated family, rest, playfulness, nature and more. But I realized that the discipline of prayer by which I put such store had fallen apart almost without my noticing. A professional musician may neglect practice for a day or two but after a week audiences would begin to notice.

'Therefore we must pay greater attention' says the writer (v.1), not because of some blind requirement but because of the damage that neglect of our core relationship with God may cause. As a Christian I'm only as effective as I allow God's Spirit to make me. On my own I'm like a fish left high and dry on the beach, out of my normal habitat and running out of breath.

So beware – problems often start small but grow big.

Almighty God,
by the prayer and discipline of Lent
may we enter into the mystery of Christ's sufferings,
and by following in his Way
come to share in his glory;
through Jesus Christ our Lord.

COLLECT

Wednesday 19 March

Joseph of Nazareth

Isaiah 11.1-10

'They will not hurt or destroy on all my holy mountain' (v.9)

'The wolf shall live with the lamb,' says Isaiah (v.6), but you can guarantee the lamb won't get much sleep. Or not in the world as it is. But Isaiah is looking beyond the violence and dysfunctionality of our present world order to the peaceable kingdom where God's just and gentle rule holds all things in harmony. Isaiah has just been telling Judah and Assyria that their number is up, but he can see through the veil to another order where the world will be full of the knowledge of the Lord, and God's peace will at last soak into everything.

There's a long tradition of secular kingdom-building and an equally long history of utopian dreams that come down in flames. But the Judaeo/Christian tradition is shaped not around flawed humanity but around the perfect character of God. I'm a willing worker for the kingdom, but I'm not trusting my plans to be more than scratches made on the back of an envelope with a blunt stick. God's purpose is beyond anything that the biblical writers, or Bunyan, or Lewis, or Tolkien could have imagined, even with the help of angels. Just occasionally we glimpse what Joseph must have glimpsed as he worked alongside his Son. That young man might have been making furniture, but he was preparing to design heaven.

I want to be in his team.

COLLECT

God our Father,
who from the family of your servant David
raised up Joseph the carpenter
to be the guardian of your incarnate Son
and husband of the Blessed Virgin Mary:
give us grace to follow him
in faithful obedience to your commands;
through Jesus Christ your Son our Lord,
who is alive and reigns with you,
in the unity of the Holy Spirit,
one God, now and for ever.

Hebrews 3.1-6

'Christ ... was faithful over God's house as a Son' (v.6)

You don't have to remember the epic film *The Ten Commandments* to know that Moses was a colossal figure in Jewish history. He faced up to Pharaoh and led the Israelite charge out of captivity in Egypt, and then he guided his awkward people through years of painful learning in the desert. In the meantime he enjoyed the most extraordinary intimacy with God.

But Moses, for all his distinction, was as nothing compared to the Son, the young man from Galilee. Like Moses in the desert, Jesus was 'faithful over God's house', the little band of loyal disciples who were to be the new Israel, the Church. So now we are God's house, the royal household who have the privilege of belonging to the Son. I wonder if we grasp the dimensions of this privilege? Even coming to church on a Sunday is an amazing honour – to be invited to soak in the Spirit of Jesus, to feed at his table, to spend time with friends of the Friend. Sadly, too often we just roll up by habit and expect some passable Christian event called a service.

Moses came out of God's presence with his face glowing. Might not we open ourselves to the same glory?

Friday 21 March

Psalms 40, 41 *or* 142, 144
Genesis 45.16-end
Hebrews 3.7-end

Hebrews 3.7-end

'Today, if you hear his voice, do not harden your hearts' (vv.7-8)

The image of a hard heart is a vivid one. We've probably all seen a heart on TV, fleshy, beating, and very much alive. A 'hard heart' or a 'heart of stone' is the complete antithesis of such a picture. The writer to the Hebrews is concerned that his readers don't suffer spiritual arteriosclerosis, as did the Israelites following God through the desert and wondering if this was all folly.

We too can suffer from heart disease if we allow the gospel's supple grace to slide into the law's hardened requirements. When that happens, people lose faith in religion – they see faith getting trapped in restrictive practices and our small minds fearing the rampant freedom of God. A religion of rules and regulations is hardly going to get people leaping out of bed on a Sunday morning. The answer lies in that evocative phrase: 'Today, if you hear his voice ...' The voice of God is rarely loud but it's quietly persistent, and it always invites us to a faith that's deeper, richer, more liquid and more adventurous than our human religious constructs.

Behind and within every event of today will be that deep voice which we might hear with the warm pleasure of recognition, 'if we do not harden our hearts'.

COLLECT

Almighty God,
you show to those who are in error the light of your truth,
that they may return to the way of righteousness:
grant to all those who are admitted
    into the fellowship of Christ's religion,
that they may reject those things
    that are contrary to their profession,
and follow all such things as are agreeable to the same;
through our Lord Jesus Christ,
who is alive and reigns with you,
in the unity of the Holy Spirit,
one God, now and for ever.

Hebrews 4.1-13

'... the promise of entering his rest is still open' (v.1)

When you're writing Bible reflections late at night – again – you find yourself much attracted to the promise that God's rest is still open. But that rest is much deeper than merely a better organized life. It's the rest of God after the massive work of creation. It's the rest sought by the wandering people of Israel in a land of promise. It's the rest summed up in that beautiful word *shalom*, meaning harmony, peace, fulfilment, wholeness. It's the eternal rest we have in God.

But 'today' that rest is available again. Why? Because of Jesus. There's both tenderness and warning in this passage. The writer is desperate that his readers don't harden their hearts and disobey the heavenly vision, because the opportunity to enter their inheritance, their rest, is right there before them.

We might not live in such fear and trepidation in our day, but this promised rest in God can still be missed if we're not careful. We can be so Christian we fail to follow Christ. We can be so familiar with the good news that we fail to live it. We can be so confident of our faith that we forget to use it. When a small child from our church school saw me in a cassock, she said: 'Mr Pritchard, are you pretending to be a vicar?' The question has gone deep.

God's glorious rest is available today, but will we enter it?

Almighty God,
by the prayer and discipline of Lent
may we enter into the mystery of Christ's sufferings,
and by following in his Way
come to share in his glory;
through Jesus Christ our Lord.

COLLECT

Monday 24 March

Hebrews 4.14 – 5.10

'... so that we may receive mercy and find grace' (4.16)

From cool to warm, today's passage acts like a pivot point for the whole of the letter to the Hebrews, an early (possibly 60s AD) community of Jewish followers of the Messiah Jesus, probably somewhere in the eastern part of the Roman Empire. The writer has been advocating the uniqueness of Jesus with particular reference to the temple system of priesthood and sacrifice – and will develop that argument later in the letter. At times, to our hearing at least, the argument can seem technical, rational and even cool. But here the rational argument gives way to warmth and tenderness.

The humanity of those receiving the letter is recognized. And the high priest Jesus is not just being acclaimed for his sufficiency in the great act of salvation. He is, through it all, revealed to be compassionate and good. He is the One to whom we can come 'with boldness' to receive all the mercy and find all the grace we need. And so today, wherever we are, the gospel – the good news – of Jesus the Christ needs to be experienced exactly as that, as good news, as mercy and grace. However 'correct' or brilliant our understanding of theology, the Jesus path must above all be lived and shared as a life of tenderness and compassion. So may you receive from him all the mercy and grace you need for this day!

COLLECT

Almighty God,
whose most dear Son went not up to joy but first he suffered pain,
and entered not into glory before he was crucified:
mercifully grant that we, walking in the way of the cross,
may find it none other than the way of life and peace;
through Jesus Christ your Son our Lord,
who is alive and reigns with you,
in the unity of the Holy Spirit,
one God, now and for ever.

Tuesday 25 March

Annunciation of Our Lord to the Blessed Virgin Mary

Romans 5.12-end

'... by the one man's obedience the many will be made righteous'
(v.19)

You can help to change the world for good today. In this part of his inspiring letter to the first Church in Rome, Paul is highlighting how the actions of one person can change everything. Specifically, he is contrasting the actions of Adam, the archetypal human from the great Jewish story of beginnings – and, says Paul, the one through whom sin, judgement and death came into the world – with the actions of Jesus the Christ, the One through whom has come grace, justification and life 'abounding for the many' (v.15).

On this Day of the Annunciation, we celebrate the actions of another *one person changing everything*. Mary's brilliant and beautiful 'let it be' to the angel Gabriel's astonishing message both anticipates and makes possible the coming into the world of the One who will bring grace and life. Mary's grace opens up the way for the grace-filled Christ to become one of us, one with us, and so to change everything. This pattern and possibility continues for us now. The decisions we are called to make today, while probably being far more 'ordinary' than that which was asked of Mary, may also change the world! May we have the courage to say with Mary, 'let it be with me according to your word' (Luke 1.38)!

We beseech you, O Lord,
pour your grace into our hearts,
that as we have known the incarnation of your Son Jesus Christ
by the message of an angel,
so by his cross and passion
we may be brought to the glory of his resurrection;
through Jesus Christ your Son our Lord,
who is alive and reigns with you,
in the unity of the Holy Spirit,
one God, now and for ever.

COLLECT

Wednesday 26 March

Psalm **38** *or* **119.1-32**
Genesis 49.1-32
Hebrews 6.13-end

Hebrews 6.13-end

'We have this hope ...' (v.19)

Where we do go when the pressure is on and everything threatens to overwhelm us? The letter to the Hebrews, like most of the letters in our New Testament, is written to a community of Christ-followers who are under some kind of pressure. It's not clear what form the particular pressure was taking in the case of this small church community, but it is clear that those pressures had led some to 'fall away' from the faith. For a movement constantly under suspicion and threat, this was a particularly serious matter.

This is the backdrop to the writer's great declaration of hope in Jesus, who has gone this way before us, undergoing similar trials and emerging faithful to his calling. This hope is, the writer says, 'a sure and steadfast anchor of the soul' (v.19). Anchors may be some way from most of our daily experience, but the picture is clear. Our hope in Jesus will be enough, should we entrust ourselves to it, to hold us when everything gets rough and threatens to overwhelm us, even (and particularly) in the toughness of Lent. Vitally, this is not hope in a concept, a creed or even the Church. It is hope rooted in a person, in the One who promises: 'I am with you always, to the end of the age' (Matthew 28.20). We have this hope!

COLLECT

Almighty God,
whose most dear Son went not up to joy but first he suffered pain,
and entered not into glory before he was crucified:
mercifully grant that we, walking in the way of the cross,
may find it none other than the way of life and peace;
through Jesus Christ your Son our Lord,
who is alive and reigns with you,
in the unity of the Holy Spirit,
one God, now and for ever.

Psalms **56**, 57 *or* 14, **15**, 16*
Genesis 49.33 – end of 50
Hebrews 7.1-10

Hebrews 7.1-10

'... but resembling the Son of God' (v.3)

What words might people choose to describe you in this season of your life? And whom do you resemble? In this passage in the Letter to the Hebrews, the writer is working with connections between Jesus and a famous figure from the beginning of the story of the Hebrew people, the fabled King Melchizedek of Salem, who blessed Abraham when the latter was returning from a victorious battle. There's a technical aspect to the argument that is developed, around greatness, order and rank. But perhaps more interesting from our perspective is the idea that emerges of likeness to another. Melchizedek, says the writer, resembles the Son of God (who we may take to represent the God-man Jesus).

What does this likeness look like? Two words are used to describe the character of the likeness shared between Melchizedek and Jesus the Christ. They are 'righteousness' and 'peace' (v.2) – two words that appear in close proximity in the Jewish Scriptures (Isaiah 60.17). If we are to resemble Jesus at all, perhaps these two words – and the ideas that have emerged around them from our living with the Jesus story – might be very good places to begin. To bring righteousness and peace to others in the name of Jesus, we need first to become people of righteousness and peace ourselves. So what might it look like for us to be people of righteousness and peace today?

Eternal God,
give us insight
to discern your will for us,
to give up what harms us,
and to seek the perfection we are promised
in Jesus Christ our Lord.

COLLECT

Psalm **22** *or* 17, **19**
Exodus 1.1-14
Hebrews 7.11-end

Hebrews 7.11-end

'Now if perfection had been attainable ...' (v.11)

Could anything be better than perfect? In this part of the letter to the Hebrews, the writer suggests that the sacrificial system of the levitical priesthood can only go so far in its making right of what is wrong. Something else is needed. And only the coming of the One who 'through the power of an indestructible life' (v.16) and 'who has been made perfect forever' (v.28) can truly bring salvation (v.25). Perfection clearly means a lot in the context of this letter, its author and the community to whom it was written; in our own context, the idea of perfection may need careful handling.

One of the wonderful characteristics of the Jesus path is the sense that it is not a ladder of achievement. It's not just for the most brilliant and the most committed, nor the most perfect of disciples. Rather, it's a new call each day to every one of us, in all our mess and wonder, to step into the way of Jesus, and to adopt a continual life of orientation towards him, and to move in his direction. Of course we should aim to be as righteous and as peaceful as we possibly can be! And we are made perfect – in the perfection of Christ. In the light of that beautiful gift, our call is to live each day with grace and mercy, peace and righteousness. May that re-orientation resume today!

COLLECT

Almighty God,
whose most dear Son went not up to joy but first he suffered pain,
and entered not into glory before he was crucified:
mercifully grant that we, walking in the way of the cross,
may find it none other than the way of life and peace;
through Jesus Christ your Son our Lord,
who is alive and reigns with you,
in the unity of the Holy Spirit,
one God, now and for ever.

Hebrews 8

'for they shall all know me' (v.11)

Rules or relationship? In today's passage, the writer acclaims the better nature of the new covenant that the coming of Jesus the Christ has brought to the world. This covenant will transcend the keeping of rules and the making of sacrifices. Keeping the laws of the new covenant will become our instinct, not our duty, and the writer portrays God as saying of his people, 'I will put my laws in their minds, and write them on their hearts' (v.10). We'll do the right thing not because we are being forced to, but because it is our deepest, and God-given, intuition.

This picture that the writer gives us of the relationship between God and God's people is one of intimacy. We will be moving away from a behaviour- and rules-based relationship towards a relationship characterized by love. 'I will be their God, and they shall be my people' (v.10) says God and, coming to the intimate core of this new relationship 'they shall all know me' (v.11). This is an encouragement to us to open ourselves up to the possibility of a more intimate and personal relationship with God. So may our prayer and action today be permeated with a sense of the loving presence of the Holy Trinity, as close as breathing. May we come to 'know the Lord' – and to be known ...

Eternal God,
give us insight
to discern your will for us,
to give up what harms us,
and to seek the perfection we are promised
in Jesus Christ our Lord.

COLLECT

Monday 31 March

Psalms 70, **77** or 27, **30**
Exodus 2.11-22
Hebrews 9.1-14

Hebrews 9.1-14

'... this is called the Holy Place' (v.2)

Are there still holy places? In this section of the letter to the Hebrews, the writer is contrasting the elaborate arrangements made for creating a holy place in which sacrifices for sin could be made under the old covenant – with 'cherubim of glory overshadowing the mercy-seat' (v.5) – with the new covenant under which Jesus 'entered once for all into the Holy Place' (v.12) to make the sacrifice that can never be repeated. It's as if Christ himself has become the Holy Place. And he is with us, and he is everywhere.

So are there still holy places? Many of us have an instinct that some places have a tangible feeling of holiness. A medieval church building can feel prayed in. The open moor can seem full of the Creator's presence. And on the holy islands around our shores (including, of course, the Holy Island of Lindisfarne), we can sense the 'thin' quality of the setting and the presence of the saints. So can these places be holy? I think they can – but perhaps what's going on is that their particular holiness is a gift to show us that all places are holy, and that the Christ can be found in every place. So wherever you are today, may you sense the holiness of each place you are in, and the presence of Jesus the Christ, *the Holy Place*.

COLLECT

Merciful Lord,
absolve your people from their offences,
that through your bountiful goodness
we may all be delivered from the chains of those sins
which by our frailty we have committed;
grant this, heavenly Father,
for Jesus Christ's sake, our blessed Lord and Saviour,
who is alive and reigns with you,
in the unity of the Holy Spirit,
one God, now and for ever.

Psalms 54, **79** *or* 32, **36**
Exodus 2.23 – 3.20
Hebrews 9.15-end

Hebrews 9.15-end

'... sketches of the heavenly things' (v.23)

It's understandable to become frustrated and even angry with the way that we behave as a Church. Our mixed motives, worrying hypocrisies and lack of holiness (and our own individual part in all this!) can cause us to lose faith in the community that we call home and which the Christ loves. Our failure so often to be a true sign of the kingdom of God breaking in and breaking out is a thing of deep regret. So what are we to do about the Church (and about us!)? It may be that we can learn from a line in today's passage in the letter to the Hebrews: 'It was necessary' the writer says, 'for the sketches of the heavenly things to be purified with these rites' (v.23).

The initial workings for an artwork are often rough. We and the Church are just 'sketches of the heavenly things'. In the light of this we need to be serious about our discipleship, and to work hard in whichever ways we can to help shape the Church to become more pure in its life, starting of course with ourselves. But perhaps also it's time to give the Church (and ourselves) some breathing space. We are just the first lines of a sketch being drawn for a picture. In the care of the great artist that picture will, in time, become the wonderful artwork it is destined to be.

Merciful Lord,
you know our struggle to serve you:
when sin spoils our lives
and overshadows our hearts,
come to our aid
and turn us back to you again;
through Jesus Christ our Lord.

COLLECT

Wednesday 2 April

Hebrews 10.1-18

'I will remember their sins and their lawless deeds no more' (v.17)

Sin is so boring. In this passage from the letter to the Hebrews, the writer pictures God as saying that the time of sin and sacrifice is over. Actually the writer comes close to indicating that God seems to be tired of the whole business of sin and sacrifice repeating itself *ad infinitum*. The law and its consequences are, says the writer, just a shadow of the good things to come. In the meantime, we seem to be stuck with an endless round of shame and blame. I remember hearing a priest in the tradition of hearing confession once saying that there's nothing quite as boring as people's sins.

Bored with sin and its consequences? Or full of compassion and hope? Either way – or both – God finally says 'I will remember their sins and their lawless deeds no more' (v.17). So how might this shape us today? It may be a reminder to us of the boring nature of our sin. If so, let's become a whole lot more imaginative and start to seek out very good things to do! And if someone has sinned against us (again), perhaps the time has come to enjoy the freedom of remembering their lawless deeds no more.

Sin is so boring. Let's become imaginative – let's start doing good!

COLLECT

Merciful Lord,
absolve your people from their offences,
that through your bountiful goodness
we may all be delivered from the chains of those sins
which by our frailty we have committed;
grant this, heavenly Father,
for Jesus Christ's sake, our blessed Lord and Saviour,
who is alive and reigns with you,
in the unity of the Holy Spirit,
one God, now and for ever.

Hebrews 10.19-25

*'... let us consider how to provoke one another to love
and good deeds' (v.24)*

Time to get provocative? At this point in the letter to the Hebrews,
the writer goes up a gear, urging the readers to redouble their
efforts to be Christ's people, seeking God with boldness – 'let us
approach with a true heart in full assurance of faith' (v.22) – and
making a difference in the world. The writer's suggestion is that we
should 'provoke one another to love and good deeds' (v.24). In the
context of the particular first-century Christian community receiving
this letter, those acts of love and good deeds might have been both
effective and dangerous.

There has perhaps never been a better time to provoke one another,
in Christ's name, to love and good deeds. Our world is as needy as
ever for goodness and love, and the means to do this are at our
fingertips. The presence of social media and the accessibility of the
internet mean that we can very easily play our part in the ushering
in of the peaceful kingdom of Jesus. One challenge may be around
deciding where exactly we get involved. Another might be in
learning to be generous to others who don't share our particular
passion. The vital thing is to be open to the acts of love and
goodness to which we are being called – and in our provocation
itself, to be full of love and goodness.

Merciful Lord,
you know our struggle to serve you:
when sin spoils our lives
and overshadows our hearts,
come to our aid
and turn us back to you again;
through Jesus Christ our Lord.

COLLECT

Friday 4 April

Psalms **102** *or* **31**
Exodus 6.2-13
Hebrews 10.26-end

Hebrews 10.26-end

'Do not, therefore, abandon that confidence of yours...' (v.35)

We are going to focus on the positive ending to this passage from the letter to the Hebrews. But first a thought on the opening part of today's passage, which threatens terrible judgement on anyone who 'willfully persists in sin' (v.26). Context is always important, and in the early Church any abandonment of the faith had implications not just for the individual but potentially for the whole community. This may account for the severity of the warning to the persistent sinner. Of course, the Church of this time had probably yet to hear the long-pondered conclusions of the likes of Jesus' young disciple John, who came to believe that *God is love*. Even so, we need to hear uncomfortable texts like this and let them question us. Lent is a powerful time in which to let these Scriptures do their work.

If the first part of the passage is a (very big) stick, the ending is more encouraging. 'Do not,' says the writer 'therefore, abandon that confidence of yours; it brings a great reward' (v.35). Sometimes we just need to go back to whatever drew us first to the compassionate Christ and his path – and give ourselves to him again. He is the source of our hope and endurance, and he is our reward. The One who says 'follow me' also says 'I am with you always' (Matthew 28.20).

Merciful Lord,
absolve your people from their offences,
that through your bountiful goodness
we may all be delivered from the chains of those sins
which by our frailty we have committed;
grant this, heavenly Father,
for Jesus Christ's sake, our blessed Lord and Saviour,
who is alive and reigns with you,
in the unity of the Holy Spirit,
one God, now and for ever.

Psalm **32** *or* 41, **42**, 43
Exodus 7.8-end
Hebrews 11.1-16

Hebrews 11.1-16

'... and he set out, not knowing where he was going' (v.8)

Joy and fear perhaps, in equal measure. We do not know, of course, what it must have been like to have been part of a Jesus-following community in the 40 years after ascension. We don't know the joy of meeting people who may have known Jesus or his disciples face to face. Nor do most of us experience the kind of fear that went with being part of a persecuted religious sect in the Roman Empire. But the journey through Lent is always a reminder that, like Abraham and the other great figures of faith recorded in this passage from Hebrews, we travel 'not knowing where we are going' (v.8).

The basis for this astonishing faith, as described in the letter, is revealing. The letter-writer meditates on the creation story and sees 'that what is seen was made from things that are not visible' (v.3). So our lives take physical shape as we trust ourselves to the unseen processes of God's creating and sustaining. Whatever you face at this time, may this be an encouragement to you to set out (or to keep on) the path that you sense is your calling from God, especially if the destination seems unclear. It may turn out that the journey will be in itself a gift, producing in you a mature life of faith oriented towards Jesus, who is with you all the way.

Merciful Lord,
you know our struggle to serve you:
when sin spoils our lives
and overshadows our hearts,
come to our aid
and turn us back to you again;
through Jesus Christ our Lord.

COLLECT

Monday 7 April

Hebrews 11.17-31

'By faith the people passed through the Red sea as if…' (v.29)

Two small words – 'as if' – that are used in common parlance to mock what sounds an unlikely idea ('*as if* there could ever be peace in the world') but in the gospel show the attitude of mind that marks the people who follow the God of the promise. Abraham, Isaac, Jacob, Joseph, Moses and Rahab all faced situations where the promise seemed hopelessly unlikely of fulfilment.

How could Abraham's descendants fill the earth without his only son, Isaac? How could Joseph's people inhabit the land that God had promised them when they had made their home in Egypt? How would Rahab escape the sword of the invading army while her city was being destroyed? How do we maintain our faith in God and God's great purposes of love for us when so much around us seems to deny the reliability of the promise and the possibility of its fulfilment?

The people of Israel making their way to the Promised Land show us how to live and act by faith. They passed through the Red Sea 'as if it were dry land' (v.29). When faced with seemingly insuperable obstacles to the fulfilment of God's purposes, we are called to trust that, from the perspective of divine providence, they are not the end of the road to God's kingdom but the route to it.

Most merciful God,
who by the death and resurrection of your Son Jesus Christ
delivered and saved the world:
grant that by faith in him who suffered on the cross
we may triumph in the power of his victory;
through Jesus Christ your Son our Lord,
who is alive and reigns with you,
in the unity of the Holy Spirit,
one God, now and for ever.

Psalms **35**, 123 *or* **48**, 52
Exodus 8.20-end
Hebrews 11.32 – 12.2

Hebrews 11.32 – 12.2

'... looking to Jesus the pioneer and perfecter of our faith' (12.2)

If yesterday we saw some examples of people who kept their faith in the face of denials of the fulfilment of God's promises, today we read of those who held to faith in the face of danger and persecution. There are some horrific stories that lie behind these brief and startling reports of flogging, stoning and other dreadful forms of torture. None more so, though, than the events of the end of Jesus' life to which this first week of Passiontide carries us.

That is why the writer to the Hebrews exhorts us – in the company of the 'cloud of witnesses' (12.1) – to look to Jesus, 'the pioneer and perfecter of our faith' (12.2). The exemplars of faith can inspire us, but only Jesus can save us. He not only shows us how to endure the trials and sufferings that come to God's people; he also blazes a trail through the suffering caused by the sin of the world and the chaos of the cosmos to find that joy in the presence of God for which humanity was created.

When our faith is tested in the face of danger and persecution, as it will undoubtedly be, we will need to look to Jesus both as the most excellent example of earthly faithfulness and as the heavenly Lord whose scars are the sign of God's victory over all the powers of evil.

Gracious Father,
you gave up your Son
out of love for the world:
lead us to ponder the mysteries of his passion,
that we may know eternal peace
through the shedding of our Saviour's blood,
Jesus Christ our Lord.

COLLECT

Wednesday 9 April

Psalms **55**, 124 *or* **119.57-80**
Exodus 9.1-12
Hebrews 12.3-13

Hebrews 12.3-13

'…in order that we may share his holiness' (v.10)

Hebrews has been struggling to resolve a dilemma. How can human beings, with all their failings, enter into the pure and holy presence of God? The answer at which it arrives is that 'we have been sanctified through the offering of the body of Jesus Christ once for all' (Hebrews 10.10).

In the words of chapter 11's great refrain, it is 'by faith' that we receive the gift of sanctified status as we trust that, in the words of the eucharistic prayer, God 'has counted us worthy to stand in his presence and serve him'. At the same time, as we step into the presence of God through faith, clothed in the gift of righteousness, we are called to live out that faith in an obedient life that leads to the 'peaceful fruit of righteousness' (v.11) growing within us and seen through us.

That is where the discipline of which the writer talks comes in. It is not, though, some form of punishment that is being described. Rather, it is the shaping process that comes through facing and bearing the inevitable cost of following the one whom the world rejected. As we meet the challenges of Christian living with obedience, so the character of Jesus begins to form within us.

Faith and obedience, though different, are not opposed because, as Dietrich Bonhoeffer writes in *The Cost of Discipleship*: 'Only the believers obey, and only the obedient believe.'

COLLECT

Most merciful God,
who by the death and resurrection of your Son Jesus Christ
delivered and saved the world:
grant that by faith in him who suffered on the cross
we may triumph in the power of his victory;
through Jesus Christ your Son our Lord,
who is alive and reigns with you,
in the unity of the Holy Spirit,
one God, now and for ever.

Psalms **40**, 125 *or* 56, **57** (63*)
Exodus 9.13-end
Hebrews 12.14-end

Hebrews 12.14-end

'See to it that no one fails to obtain the grace of God' (v.15)

Yesterday we thought about how we are led by the crucified hand of Jesus Christ into the presence of God. Today we see something of the awesome scene around the consuming fire of God's presence. The 'innumerable angels', the 'assembly of the firstborn' and the 'spirits of the righteous' surround God, who is 'judge of all' (vv.22-23). No wonder Moses said 'I tremble with fear' (v.21) even before the earthly mountain, the pale shadow of the heavenly city. Fear though, for us, is cast out by the perfect love of God in the gift of his Son, 'Jesus, the mediator of a new covenant' (v.24).

The pure gift of the grace of God in Christ, proved in the privileges of Christian worship, is also to be practised in the relationships of life. 'Pursue peace with everyone' (v.14), implores the writer. Do not let bitterness take root. Otherwise you will find yourselves, perhaps as unaware as Esau, selling your birthright, disinheriting the blessing and failing to obtain the grace of God (v.15).

What could be a greater tragedy than missing out on the grace of God? Perhaps we could make this our motivation for the Holy Week that lies ahead of us: that we will not allow ourselves or our families, our friends or our colleagues, our communities or our churches to fail to receive the grace of God, the grace that consumes us with the fire of divine love.

Gracious Father,
you gave up your Son
out of love for the world:
lead us to ponder the mysteries of his passion,
that we may know eternal peace
through the shedding of our Saviour's blood,
Jesus Christ our Lord.

COLLECT

Friday 11 April

Hebrews 13.1-16

'Remember those who are in prison, as though you were in prison with them' (v.3)

It is the sort of thing we say as Christians – 'let mutual love continue' (v.1). But the writer takes us very deep into the sort of love that we are to practise and the extent of the mutuality that membership of the body of Christ entails.

The Church to which the letter is written is in a very hostile environment, with many believers imprisoned and some being tortured. Remember those who are *bound* as though you were *bound* with them, implores the writer, playing on the Greek word for prisoners. This is the sort of costly identification with those who are suffering for which the gospel calls, a practical empathy that could in the ancient world, as it can in some places today, involve a literal sharing in the actual conditions of detention.

Lest this sound too demanding, even unreasonable, the writer reminds us that it is 'well for the heart to be strengthened by grace' (v.9). The grace of our Lord Jesus Christ, the grace of the cross was well put by the second century bishop, Melito of Sardis, when he said that 'the Lord who had clothed himself with humanity was bound for the sake of the imprisoned'. For our liberation, Christ bound himself to us in the imprisonment of our sin and in the captivity of all that oppresses us. And so – in the words of the hymn – we sing: 'My chains fell off, my heart was free, I rose, went forth, and followed Thee'.

COLLECT

Most merciful God,
who by the death and resurrection of your Son Jesus Christ
delivered and saved the world:
grant that by faith in him who suffered on the cross
we may triumph in the power of his victory;
through Jesus Christ your Son our Lord,
who is alive and reigns with you,
in the unity of the Holy Spirit,
one God, now and for ever.

Saturday 12 April

Hebrews 13.17-end

'May the God of peace … make you complete in everything good'
(vv.20–21)

On the eve of Palm Sunday, as we prepare to enter Jerusalem with Jesus and relive the cruel events that led to his death, it is good to be reminded that all our commemorations take place in the light of the resurrection. It is heartening as well to have a hint of the great Easter blessing that will resound through our churches on the celebration of the Day of Resurrection, a blessing that follows the wording of verse 20 almost exactly.

At the heart of that blessing is that God will complete in us 'everything good' so that we will live in a way that is 'pleasing in his sight'. That is an extraordinarily bold vision of humanity. Through the power of the resurrection, human life is raised to the full stature of its dignity. We become not only objects and recipients of God's immeasurable grace and mercy but also subjects in the exercise of God's will and givers to God of the infinite joy of divine pleasure.

The glorious reality of Christian faith is that the new, redeemed humanity forged in the life, death and resurrection of Jesus Christ, given to us in word and sacrament, and received by us through faith, is to be lived out in Spirit-empowered, Christ-like lives that are – like Jesus' own life – pleasing in God's sight.

Gracious Father,
you gave up your Son
out of love for the world:
lead us to ponder the mysteries of his passion,
that we may know eternal peace
through the shedding of our Saviour's blood,
Jesus Christ our Lord.

COLLECT

Monday 14 April

Monday of Holy Week

Luke 22.1-23

'So he consented...' (v.6)

Last week we were inspired by some holy lives and holy living. This week we are confronted by a very unholy life and a set of most ungodly decisions. We do not see a life that is being raised to the full stature of human dignity but a person disintegrating before our eyes and being reduced, one choice at time, to a frightening level of inhumanity.

Yes, Judas was caught up in a cosmic conflict of evil against good. Yes, he found himself embroiled in the political manoeuvering of anxious national leaders. Yes, he was even a player in the providential plan in which 'the Son of Man is going as it has been determined' (v.22). Nevertheless, he was not an unwitting pawn. It can still be said of Judas that 'he consented'.

It takes two to tango. It takes an alignment between external pressure and internal permission to become entangled in the briars of sin and to sink into the sand of corruption. That is what is happening to Judas and that is his state of mind and heart as he sits at table with Jesus to share in the supper that, because of Judas' sin, will become Jesus' last.

'Let anyone among you who is without sin be the first to throw a stone' (John 8.7). I am no better than Judas. My consent, my sin, my betrayal would have been enough to send Jesus to his cross. Lord, have mercy.

COLLECT

Almighty and everlasting God,
who in your tender love towards the human race
    sent your Son our Saviour Jesus Christ
to take upon him our flesh
and to suffer death upon the cross:
grant that we may follow the example of his patience and humility,
and also be made partakers of his resurrection;
through Jesus Christ your Son our Lord,
who is alive and reigns with you,
in the unity of the Holy Spirit,
one God, now and for ever.

Psalm 27
Lamentations 3.1-18
Luke 22.[24-38] 39-53

Luke 22.[24-38] 39-53

'Judas ... approached Jesus to kiss him' (v.47)

'Is it with a kiss that you are betraying the Son of Man?' asks Jesus of his 'familiar friend', even his 'bosom friend' in whom he trusted, who ate of his bread (Psalm 55.13; 41.9).

Judas' arrogant, calculating, deceitful attempt of a kiss on the face of Jesus could not be a greater contrast with the impulsive overflow of affection of the woman whose tears bathed the feet of Jesus and whose kisses adored him. She too 'was a sinner' (Luke 7.37) but a sinner who was now keeling before the grace-filled presence of Jesus, 'ransomed, healed, restored, forgiven'.

There were other people in the room at the time. Simon, the Pharisee, was one of them. It was his house and he had invited Jesus to eat with him. When Simon began to question why Jesus, a would-be prophet, allowed *that woman* to act in this way, Jesus said to him, 'You gave me no kiss, but from the time I came in she has not stopped kissing my feet' (Luke 7.45).

The grace of the cross brings us to the point of decision. We are not afforded the luxury of Simon, holding back and observing. The choice is to turn away and betray, like Judas, or to turn towards and follow, like Mary the mother of our Saviour who, in Christina Rossetti's unforgettable words, 'worshipped the beloved with a kiss' at his birth and stood by the cross at his death.

COLLECT

True and humble king,
hailed by the crowd as Messiah:
grant us the faith to know you and love you,
that we may be found beside you
on the way of the cross,
which is the path of glory.

Wednesday 16 April

Wednesday of Holy Week

Psalm 102 [or 102.1-18]
Wisdom 1.16 – 2.1; 2.12–22
or Jeremiah 11.18-20
Luke 22.54-end

Luke 22.54-end

'The Lord turned and looked at Peter' (v.61)

What was it like to be looked at in that way at that moment? Peter had just denied that he was with Jesus, that he knew him and followed him. When Jesus first met Peter, so John tells us, he looked at Peter and saw in him strengths that even Peter had not dared to imagine. Jesus looked at him and knew him as he could be – not just Simon son of John, but *Cephas*, upon whose rock-like qualities Jesus would build his new community.

We do not know exactly how Jesus looked at Peter before the cock crowed. But we do know that 'Jesus Christ is the same yesterday, today and tomorrow'. His character is consistent, he can be relied upon to be faithful. So we can say confidently that Jesus would have looked at him and, even then, *loved him*, just as he had done with the rich young ruler whose spirit was willing but, like Peter, whose flesh was weak.

No wonder Peter 'went out and wept bitterly' (v.62), for to be looked at with that sort of love – the love that knows you and still believes in you even though you have condemned that love to death – was a hard and heavy burden to bear. But the kingdom Jesus promised, when he would eat and drink with his disciples again, was coming. And when it came, Peter said, 'Yes Lord, *you* know that I love you' (John 21.15-17).

COLLECT

Almighty and everlasting God,
who in your tender love towards the human race
    sent your Son our Saviour Jesus Christ
to take upon him our flesh
and to suffer death upon the cross:
grant that we may follow the example of his patience and humility,
and also be made partakers of his resurrection;
through Jesus Christ your Son our Lord,
who is alive and reigns with you,
in the unity of the Holy Spirit,
one God, now and for ever.

Psalms 42, 43
Leviticus 16.2-24
Luke 23.1-25

Thursday 17 April

Maundy Thursday

Luke 23.1-25

'[Pilate] released the one who had been put in prison for insurrection'
(v.25)

Last week we thought about the words of Melito of Sardis, that 'the Lord … was bound for the sake of the imprisoned'. Today we see that spiritual truth in historical reality. Jesus quite literally takes Barabbas' place. This is the substitution of the sinner by the sinless. This is Jesus being given over to the judgement that Barabbas deserved for 'insurrection and murder'.

We have all been involved in the insurrection against God's purposes. We have played our part in the murdering of the love that God has for the world. We have all set ourselves up at some point as enemies of God's state of peace and justice. But, though our 'voices' *against God* 'prevailed' before Pilate's seat, they are deafened by God's voice *for us* before the throne where the Lamb who has been slain is to be found.

'Love', as Austen Farrer, the twentieth-century Anglican philosopher, said, 'is the strongest instrument of omnipotence' and God uses this weapon of love with such a divine power that 'he bears our infirmities and carries our diseases' and is 'wounded for our transgressions, crushed for our iniquities' (Isaiah 53.4-5) in order – as Melito put it – 'to set the condemned free'.

As those who have been acquitted by the love of God, we are enlisted to contend with all that contends against God, armed only with, as the notable theologian and medical missionary Albert Schweitzer described it, 'the most powerful weapon you can use against your enemy' – love.

COLLECT

God our Father,
you have invited us to share in the supper
which your Son gave to his Church
to proclaim his death until he comes:
may he nourish us by his presence,
and unite us in his love;
who is alive and reigns with you,
in the unity of the Holy Spirit,
one God, now and for ever.

125

Friday 18 April

Good Friday

Psalm 69
Genesis 22.1-18
John 19.38-end
or Hebrews 10.1-10

Hebrews 10.1-10

'See, I have come to do your will' (v.9)

God's will is for human beings to reach their full dignity as creatures made in the image and likeness of God. God's will for humanity is to live the pattern of divinity in the sphere of creation. It is God's will to shape our species into a form of life that reflects God's joy and justice, peace and kindness, beauty and truth.

God wills a human life that offers itself obediently to God for God's good purposes. This is the will to which Jesus says 'yes' as he gives himself over to the cross. It is the same 'yes' that he said to the Father's will to send him in love to the world. It is the same 'yes' that he said in every step of his ministry as he gave himself in healing and hope, word and promise, praying each moment:

'Ready for all thy perfect will
My acts of faith and love repeat,
Till death thy endless mercies seal
And make my sacrifice complete.'

(Charles Wesley, 'O thou who camest from above')

Jesus says 'yes' to God's will for a holy humanity. This is the will that Jesus wills. This is the will that Jesus enacts as he offers his body once for all, for love of all. As he does so, the need for any other sacrifice of atonement falls away. For now a human being has been found who is *at one* with God. May we be found in him.

COLLECT

Almighty Father,
look with mercy on this your family
for which our Lord Jesus Christ was content to be betrayed
   and given up into the hands of sinners
   and to suffer death upon the cross;
who is alive and glorified with you and the Holy Spirit,
one God, now and for ever.

Psalm 142
Hosea 6.1-6
John 2.18-22

Saturday 19 April

Easter Eve

John 2.18-22

'But he was speaking of the temple of his body' (v.21)

Jesus' body had been destroyed on Friday, Good Friday. It had been racked by intolerable pain, ruined by slow starvation of oxygen and desecrated by penetration of nails and spear.

On Saturday, Holy Saturday, Jesus' body, destroyed by such an ugly death, lay limp on the cold stone of the dark tomb while his spirit descended to the region of the dead, even there proclaiming the gospel (1 Peter 4.6).

On Sunday, Easter Day, the Day of Resurrection, the prophecy would be fulfilled. The body of Jesus would be raised from the dead and the new, glorious temple of Christ's risen body would beckon all of humanity to step through the open doors of Jesus' wide embrace into the Holy of Holies of God's gracious presence.

So, believe the scripture and the word that Jesus spoke (v.22), and 'come to him, a living stone, though rejected by mortals yet chosen and precious in God's sight, and like living stones, let yourselves be built into a spiritual house, to be a holy priesthood, to offer spiritual sacrifices acceptable to God through Jesus Christ' (1 Peter 2.4-5).

COLLECT

Grant, Lord,
that we who are baptized into the death
of your Son our Saviour Jesus Christ
may continually put to death our evil desires
and be buried with him;
and that through the grave and gate of death
we may pass to our joyful resurrection;
through his merits,
who died and was buried and rose again for us,
your Son Jesus Christ our Lord.

Monday 21 April

Monday of Easter Week

Psalms 111, 117, 146
Exodus 12.1-14
1 Corinthians 15.1-11

1 Corinthians 15.1-11

'... his grace towards me has not been in vain' (v.10)

The early Christian teacher Origen once commented that 'those who believe for a time, and in time of trial turn away, believe to no purpose'. As Paul addresses the Christians of Corinth, he seems to be concerned that some of them have similarly believed 'in vain' (v.2); consequently, it is time to remind them of the heart of the gospel and of the transformation it brings to the community of faith if only they will allow God's grace to work in them. Paul is succinct in outlining his original preaching: Christ died, was buried and is raised. He begins this letter by focusing on the centrality of the cross and now turns to the resurrection. Whatever developments Christian faith undergoes, and through all the twists and turns that shape it and seek to make it fresh in every generation, Paul is resolute – there is no Christian faith if you believe that Christ was not raised and if this reality is not translated into the courage and hope needed for everyday life.

Paul talks about Christ's resurrection in terms of mystical 'appearances', such as he had himself, as if the heart of resurrection truth is seeing and knowing Christ among us. This confirms that resurrection is not something based on our own human faithfulness or piety, but that it is Christ who comes to us in peace and, in effect, saying as he does so: 'you denied me, tortured me, killed me, ran away and are still tempted to forget me, but I am with you still, loving you as never before'. To receive this communication of love is not just good news but provides the ground for a new life. How could such grace, demands Paul, be offered and it not change everything?

COLLECT

Lord of all life and power,
who through the mighty resurrection of your Son
overcame the old order of sin and death
to make all things new in him:
grant that we, being dead to sin
and alive to you in Jesus Christ,
may reign with him in glory;
to whom with you and the Holy Spirit
be praise and honour, glory and might,
now and in all eternity.

Psalms 112, 147.1-12
Exodus 12.14-36
1 Corinthians 15.12-19

1 Corinthians 15.12-19

'... how can some of you say there is no resurrection of the dead?' (v.12)

At a recent clergy seminar I attended, a discussion started up about life after death. It appeared that some had become agnostic about it. How could human identity continue once the body had decayed and human consciousness with it? Was Christian belief in resurrection really about life after death, or was it about life *before* death, an enlarging and intensifying of the value of life and a gratitude for it?

There is nothing new under the Church's sun. Paul is clearly addressing Christians who are doubtful about the resurrection of the dead (v.12). We sometimes forget how shocking the idea of resurrection was to many of his time and, even more so, the idea of the value and preciousness of each life, not just powerful ones, that it witnessed to. Life was cheap in the first-century Middle East and Mediterranean. Christians were preaching that each life was of such embraceable beauty to God that, even through death, he could not be parted from his own beloved creations. Paul preaches this truth believing in the depths of his being that God raised Christ. It follows, he says, that if we think this is only of consequence before death then we are to be pitied as being, literally, hopeless (v.19). Paul urges his readers not to deny the creative power of God to bring life out of death, light out of darkness.

Christians will continue to question how our identity will be maintained after death and have to settle for simply not knowing what happens at that inevitable point in our existence. They will also, however, continue to believe that because of God's fidelity towards us, embodied in Christ's deathless love, 'all shall be well and all shall be well and all manner of thing shall be well' (Julian of Norwich).

God of glory,
by the raising of your Son
you have broken the chains of death and hell:
fill your Church with faith and hope;
for a new day has dawned
and the way to life stands open
in our Saviour Jesus Christ.

COLLECT

Wednesday 23 April

Wednesday of Easter Week

Psalms 113, 147.13-end
Exodus 12.37-end
1 Corinthians 15.20-28

1 Corinthians 15.20-28

'... so that God may be all in all' (v.28)

One of the popular visual images of resurrection is found in the icons of the Eastern Church. In it we find Christ holding out his hands to an elderly man and woman who appear to be coming out of some sort of cave or prison. Padlocks and keys lie around on the ground, implying some release for them, and Christ, standing on a wobbly bridge over a deathly river, extends his arms to lift the couple up to where he is but also, it seems, to introduce them to one another.

The man and woman, of course, are Adam and Eve. Imprisoned in hells of their own making through going their own proud and destructive way, Christ now draws them up and invites them to look at one another again. He re-introduces them. When God exposed their self-obsession in Eden they had, as we all do, turned to blame: Adam blamed Eve, Eve blamed the serpent. In the icon, Christ places them back into relationship with each other, offers them a fresh life together, and as he pulls them up out of darkness so their age seems to slip away. What they are being brought into is eternal.

Paul tells the Corinthians that in Adam, a word meaning 'humankind', all died. Humanity became paralysed in its self-regard and blindness. In Christ, though, 'all will be made alive' (v.22) for Christ offers a new path out of the prison. Humanity is defrosted and comes to life again in him. He is the 'first fruits' of the love of God, a love in which all, in the end, is harvest.

COLLECT

Lord of all life and power,
who through the mighty resurrection of your Son
overcame the old order of sin and death
to make all things new in him:
grant that we, being dead to sin
and alive to you in Jesus Christ,
may reign with him in glory;
to whom with you and the Holy Spirit
be praise and honour, glory and might,
now and in all eternity.

Psalms 114, 148
Exodus 13.1-16
1 Corinthians 15.29-34

1 Corinthians 15.29-34

'... why are we putting ourselves in danger every hour?' (v.30)

There are a couple of perplexing references in today's passage. First, Paul seems to refer to the practice of vicarious baptism where people were being baptized on behalf of those who had died. Second, he speaks of having fought with wild animals in Ephesus. The animals here are probably metaphorical. Paul is unlikely to have survived otherwise and, indeed, would have lost his Roman citizenship by such a punishment. He seems to have still had it though at this time in his life according to the Acts of the Apostles.

What is clear is that Paul's Christian friends and partners were suffering for their faith and that death, faithfulness, suffering and baptism into Christ were not only urgent but vital issues for them. Paul teaches them that with God things are as yet unfinished and that Christian existence can only be fully understood in terms of the future. His own life is founded on the principle of hope, and if the Corinthian Christians don't do the same, they will lapse into a compromised and reckless life.

We must not be lulled by thinking such teaching is only applicable to far-off days and cultures. At the moment, many Christian people are finding themselves at great risk because of their faith. In parts of the Middle East, for instance, they are made refugees or are fearful for themselves and those they love. Hearing Paul today provokes us into prayer for them and some self-scrutiny of our own complacency. How would we respond to such danger for our faith in Jesus Christ, risen from the dead?

God of glory,
by the raising of your Son
you have broken the chains of death and hell:
fill your Church with faith and hope;
for a new day has dawned
and the way to life stands open
in our Saviour Jesus Christ.

COLLECT

Friday 25 April

Friday of Easter Week

Psalms **115**, 149
Exodus 13.17 – 14.14
1 Corinthians 15.35-50

1 Corinthians 15.35-50

'What is sown is perishable, what is raised is imperishable' (v.42)

After a slight discursion, Paul gets back to teaching about our resurrection in Christ. Undoubtedly, as he preached publicly and in private, many would have challenged him about the nature of this resurrection and how it takes place. In this letter he seems to return to some images that he has used before, explaining how, though death is not an end, it does mean change, and that God is in charge of this transformation. It is God's creativity and not the natural continuation of some spiritual self that is the power at work in resurrection.

One of the images he uses is that of sowing seeds. The seed is in a frail form and yet, unseen and miraculously, it dies in the dark to fulfil its potential as a life in a new and startling form. So it is, argues Paul, with the human body. God is at work in Christ ensuring that what is raised out of our brittle and dependent life is glorious, fresh and imperishable. God loves us just the way we are, but he loves us so much that he doesn't want us to stay like that. Life in Christ is not a series of full-stops but commas, a life where, even in death, we are beckoned on into new chapters of love. Physically, we are conceived and first carried in darkness in order for life to be born. Spiritually, says Paul, things are not so different.

COLLECT

Lord of all life and power,
who through the mighty resurrection of your Son
overcame the old order of sin and death
to make all things new in him:
grant that we, being dead to sin
and alive to you in Jesus Christ,
may reign with him in glory;
to whom with you and the Holy Spirit
be praise and honour, glory and might,
now and in all eternity.

Psalms 116, 150
Exodus 14.15-end
1 Corinthians 15.51-end

1 Corinthians 15.51-end

'… be steadfast, immovable, always excelling in the work of the Lord' (v.58)

The Corinthians had showed themselves to be susceptible to wandering away from Christian behaviour and belief. Paul has been putting them right about the resurrection of the body and how the word 'body' can mean different things. He tells them that without faith in Christ's resurrection, they are as a community indistinctive in their lives and merely self-resourcing in hope. What he is doing, he tells them, is showing them a great mystery. This mystery is not just a bit of holy information. It is an invitation to be formed rather than informed, and Paul will move on in his letter to show them the generous shape a Christian community should begin to take.

We are living in a world that mocks what it loves and loves what it mocks. We are endlessly distracted by the superficial and showy. It has been said that we are trapped in a circle of spending money we don't have on things we don't want in order to impress people we don't like, and that even the Church is a swimming pool where the noise comes from the shallow end. It is humbling, then, to hear Paul across the centuries remind us as Christians that we are ambassadors of a different kingdom. He tells us, as he does the Corinthian Church, not to make our faith futile or insignificant. Our lives must be a protest against any worldly Church of our own or others' making. How we are to be steadfast in faith in our own times is a question for very serious thought.

God of glory,
by the raising of your Son
you have broken the chains of death and hell:
fill your Church with faith and hope;
for a new day has dawned
and the way to life stands open
in our Saviour Jesus Christ.

COLLECT

Monday 28 April

George, martyr, patron of England

Psalms 5, 146
Joshua 1.1-9
Ephesians 6.10-20

Ephesians 6.10-20

'Put on the whole armour of God' (v.11)

It has been commented that a Greek-speaking Christian Turk who lived in Palestine and joined the Roman army is a good patron saint for a multicultural society such as today's England. We know little about St George's life, but the tradition that he was a soldier undoubtedly influenced the choice of the reading from the letter to the Ephesians in which one of the most striking portraits of Christian life as a spiritual struggle is to be found.

The author of the letter knows their Bible. The imagery used in chapter 6 is largely based on that found in Isaiah (59.12-18), where Yahweh is dressed in armour as a Divine Warrior ready to see off human sin and restore social justice. We are told that the struggle Christians are engaged in is against 'rulers ... authorities ... and cosmic powers' (v.12), references to those powerful influences that operate in the world when fear, oppression and greed take over. To see these as forces that must be battled with spiritually stops us from understanding them as inevitable, trivial or unstoppable.

Among all the armour listed, the one offensive weapon is a sword. It is of the Spirit and is the word of God. This must be understood as being more than a cutting quotation of Scripture but rather a Spirit-inspired use of language for the sake of God's goodness. We musn't forget the 'belt of truth' (v.14) either, because we too often trip over our own deceit and end up, as one scholar has noted, caught with our pants down!

COLLECT

God of hosts,
who so kindled the flame of love
in the heart of your servant George
that he bore witness to the risen Lord
by his life and by his death:
give us the same faith and power of love
that we who rejoice in his triumphs
may come to share with him the fullness of the resurrection;
through Jesus Christ your Son our Lord,
who is alive and reigns with you,
in the unity of the Holy Spirit,
one God, now and for ever.

Psalms 37.23-end, 148
Isaiah 62.6-10
or Ecclesiasticus 51.13-end
Acts 12.25 – 13.13

Acts 12.25 – 13.13

'... John, whose other name was Mark' (12.25)

I well remember going to see the actor Alec McCowen recite from memory the whole of Mark's Gospel. It was a little strange to break off for a choc ice after the Transfiguration – coming as it does right in the middle – but the impact of hearing the gospel as a whole was extraordinarily powerful. Today is a day to give thanks for the person who wrote the first gospel we know of and for doing it with such passion, momentum and theological ingenuity.

Whether the Mark we hear of in today's reading from the Acts of the Apostles is the evangelist we don't know, but he was certainly evangelizing in the early formative days of the Christian Church. Chapter 13 tells of the refugee Christians in Antioch who had escaped from persecution but who now begin their own missionary endeavours, not in the least dispirited by their own circumstances.

Their journey leads to many notable encounters, such as that with Elymas, who is described as being a *magus* and exposed by Paul as being full of deceit and villainy (13.10). Perhaps when those other *magi* laid down their gold and incense before the child, they were laying down the apparatus of their magical show and acknowledging the end of their deception? The story here seeks to distance the Christian message from one of its fiercest rivals in those times as well as reminding us of Paul's own blindness and subsequent conversion. We are left to wonder whether Elymas similarly converted, for Paul and his companions are already setting sail again to do more work for the gospel.

Almighty God,
who enlightened your holy Church
through the inspired witness of your evangelist Saint Mark:
grant that we, being firmly grounded in the truth of the gospel,
may be faithful to its teaching both in word and deed;
through Jesus Christ your Son our Lord,
who is alive and reigns with you,
in the unity of the Holy Spirit,
one God, now and for ever.

COLLECT

135

Psalms 16, **30** *or* **119.1-32**
Exodus 16.11-end
Colossians 2.1-15

Colossians 2.1-15

'… you were also raised with him through faith in the power of God'
(v.12)

Many of Paul's letters address problems that arose in the early Christian communities, not least, in Paul's view, erroneous beliefs and practices. Part of his reason in writing to the Christians in Colossae seems to be his desire to counter a fashionable religious view that was doing the rounds. While not knowing exactly what this belief was, it would appear that it was mystical, ascetic, fantastical and, in Paul's view, lacking intellectual depth, even though to some it seemed plausible (v.4).

Paul brings his readers back to Christ in whom the fullness of God dwells (v.9). God nails the record of his people to the cross, forgiving them and raising them out of the grave with Christ so that our only authority and joy is in him and nobody else. It is as if Christ is the body language of God, communicating his love in every move, gesture and encounter. Nowhere is that language louder than in the silence of Calvary. At the moment when God seems most absent, God has never been closer. God, says Paul, was making us alive by forgiving us and making us free.

Paul is a servant of this mystery of Christ and wants his brothers and sisters to understand that Christian knowledge is only attained when hearts are united in love (v.2). It is not possible to love God until we love other people. Similarly, God is to be shared before he is ever understood; any spiritual discipline that says otherwise misses the 'treasures of wisdom' (v.3).

COLLECT

Almighty Father,
you have given your only Son to die for our sins
and to rise again for our justification:
grant us so to put away the leaven of malice and wickedness
that we may always serve you
in pureness of living and truth;
through the merits of your Son Jesus Christ our Lord,
who is alive and reigns with you,
in the unity of the Holy Spirit,
one God, now and for ever.

Psalms 139, 146
Proverbs 4.10-18
James 1.1-12

James 1.1-12

'James, a servant of God and of the Lord Jesus Christ' (v.1)

Because a church in Rome was dedicated to both St Philip and St James on the first day of May, these two apostles have been celebrated together ever since. Today's reading is from the letter of St James, which most probably was sent to Greek-speaking Jewish Christian churches to teach and encourage them in their discipleship together.

The themes of the letter are distinct and relevant to our own day. They include the ethics of speech and our use of words for good or ill, the importance of prayer, a criticism of the rich, and lessons in the distinction between temptations of our own making and a testing of our faith by God. The letter also famously argues that we cannot say we are in relationship with God if we fail to have an ethical commitment to our fellow human beings. Faith without good works is dead (James 2.17).

James' attitude to doubters seems a bit harsh. After all, isn't certainty rather than doubt the spiritual enemy if all is in God's hands and not our own? But whereas today we consider religious doubts as honest questions about this or that bit of doctrine or belief, James here is pleading with his readers never to stop trusting God and never to behave as if their Christian faith wasn't of supreme significance and implication. He wants to nurture their stability and maturity so that the world can look at them and see its own shortfall. Let sleeping dogmas lie, he implies, but don't lose your trust and faith!

Almighty Father,
whom truly to know is eternal life:
teach us to know your Son Jesus Christ
as the way, the truth, and the life;
that we may follow the steps of your holy apostles Philip and James,
and walk steadfastly in the way that leads to your glory;
through Jesus Christ your Son our Lord,
who is alive and reigns with you,
in the unity of the Holy Spirit,
one God, now and for ever.

COLLECT

Friday 2 May

Colossians 3.12 – 4.1

'... clothe yourselves with compassion, kindness, humility ... ' (v. 12)

There were tensions in the Church at Colossae. There were also tensions in society: a tribal culture where Jews disliked pagans, who in turn disliked non-Greek speakers, who hated Scythians as the lowest of the low. Into this combative chaos Paul tries to spell out what it means to be 'in Christ' and how living with Christ as your master gives an utterly new set of coordinates by which to live. Christians are to make Christ present in the world by certain virtues 'which reduce or eliminate friction: ready sympathy, a generous spirit, a humble disposition, willingness to make concessions, patience, forbearance' (C.F.D. Moule).

He then makes this teaching more specific by focusing on the three core relationships of his day: those of wife/husband, child/father and master/slave. He sets out guidelines for Christian spouses, children, parents, slaves and slave owners. Countering so much that was taken for granted in a hierarchical society, Paul shows how Christians have a duty towards each other, that when one suffers all suffer, and that no matter what station in life a Christian has, he or she is a brother or sister to all the others. It is, perhaps, hard to see quite how radical this teaching was. It is perhaps harder to see how we have yet to work out its implications in the Church for our own time. His appeal to women here draws an intake of breath in some congregations today, but was probably aimed at those who had non-believing husbands and who Paul wanted to maintain their marital relationships. Likewise, some scholars wonder if his other appeal was to husbands of women who were non-believers not to treat them harshly if they refused to convert.

Almighty Father,
you have given your only Son to die for our sins
and to rise again for our justification:
grant us so to put away the leaven of malice and wickedness
that we may always serve you
in pureness of living and truth;
through the merits of your Son Jesus Christ our Lord,
who is alive and reigns with you,
in the unity of the Holy Spirit,
one God, now and for ever.

Colossians 4.2-end

'Let your speech always be gracious, seasoned with salt … ' (v.6)

In these final exhortations and greetings, Paul is signing off, asking that his readers remember him in their prayers. They are to pray for his freedom from prison so that he can continue serving the gospel in his evangelistic mission to 'declare the mystery of Christ' (v.3).

He knows that verbal bullets of piety or self-righteousness fired off at unbelieving targets will convince nobody and only harm the integrity of the Church. Instead, he encourages Christians to conduct themselves wisely to those not of their faith and to be gracious in the manner of tone of their conversation with them. Prayers are not enough. Their presence in society must attract and not repel. They are ambassadors for Jesus Christ and must be 'mature and fully assured' (v.12). It was in this spirit that Francis of Assisi asked his brethren to preach the gospel at all times and, if they must, to use words.

At a time of global and rapid information, of words fired at us from every angle, furthering agendas we can't always work out, the relationship of a Christian to words and how they are used is as important as ever. Much theology has all the integrity of a bumper sticker, soundbites on God that we honk at if we agree. Paul's teaching is that we are held within a divine mystery and that we are charged to help people live fully within it. The seduction of quick clarity and easy answers is to be resisted. Our words must be 'seasoned', resonant and a rooted, gracious call back to our homeland in God.

Risen Christ,
for whom no door is locked, no entrance barred:
open the doors of our hearts,
that we may seek the good of others
and walk the joyful road of sacrifice and peace,
to the praise of God the Father.

COLLECT

Psalms **96**, 97 *or* 27, **30**
Exodus 19
Luke 1.1-25

Luke 1.1-25

'… to make ready a people prepared for the Lord' (v.17)

Luke sets the stage for the main feature – his good news of Jesus Christ, by showing how God works in the lives of everyday people to bring about wholeness and transformation. The scene is being set for the entrance of the Messiah; a herald is being raised up who will prepare the way.

Zechariah and Elizabeth, ordinary people, find themselves caught up in and touched by the purposes of God. Like their spiritual antecedents Abraham and Sarah, they are to have a son who will play a key role in salvation history. History is about to repeat itself. The unthinkable will happen. Genesis tells how Sarah's disbelief was expressed as laughter; Zechariah finds his scepticism leaves him unable to comment. And the child John has a special calling from the moment he is conceived. His vocation will be to turn the hearts of people back to God, to prepare the people of Israel to receive their Saviour. In order to do this, John will be filled with the Holy Spirit even before he is born. A new era is dawning heralded by the return of prophecy, and the promise of the Holy Spirit.

Luke demonstrates how God acts in the midst of everyday life, bringing surprise, adventure and fulfilment. Being a Christian means being open to God's call and responding even when it all seems somewhat strange and mysterious. This is only the beginning of the story. Greater things are yet to come.

COLLECT

Almighty Father,
who in your great mercy gladdened the disciples
    with the sight of the risen Lord:
give us such knowledge of his presence with us,
that we may be strengthened and sustained by his risen life
and serve you continually in righteousness and truth;
through Jesus Christ your Son our Lord,
who is alive and reigns with you,
in the unity of the Holy Spirit,
one God, now and for ever.

Psalms **98**, 99, 100 *or* 32, **36**
Exodus 20.1-21
Luke 1.26-38

Luke 1.26-38

'For nothing will be impossible with God' (v.37)

Another day, another place – Nazareth – and Gabriel makes an entrance again with startling news. He is visiting Mary, a young woman engaged to Joseph. She too is to have a child in unexpected and surprising circumstances. She will be overshadowed by the power of God. The Holy Spirit will enable the conception of the Son of God in her womb. An impossible occurrence? Gabriel reminds her and us that with God there is no such thing as 'impossible'.

Mary's reaction and response contrasts with Zechariah's. Though she asks for clarification, she doesn't doubt, and she is willing and obedient to God's calling of her for this extraordinary and challenging role in the salvation story. Through the acceptance of this unexpected vocation, Mary allows Christ to grow within her so that she can become more than she could ever be on her own. She risks isolation and rejection by her fiancé, family and community, but God provides for her a confidante, Elizabeth, who is walking a similar path.

Sometimes God calls us to do what seems at first glance impossible, unrealistic or impractical. But the God who calls is also the God who equips and makes possible new and challenging ventures. Obedience requires courage and trust but also opens the way for God to act in us and through us. At such times we are called to say with Mary: 'Here am I ... let it be with me according to your word' (v.38).

Risen Christ,
you filled your disciples with boldness and fresh hope:
strengthen us to proclaim your risen life
and fill us with your peace,
to the glory of God the Father.

COLLECT

Wednesday 7 May

Luke 1.39-56

'When Elizabeth heard Mary's greeting, the child leapt in her womb'
(v.41)

High places in the ancient world were often symbolic of encounters with the divine. With this detail Luke signals to us that Mary's journey up into the hills will be more than just a social call on her cousin. The presence of Jesus inside Mary brings excitement from all quarters. God is in the midst of his people. The Holy Spirit brings about recognition, boldness, declaration and joy.

Because Mary's song, the Magnificat, is so well known and used so often in our liturgy, there is the danger that it can wash over us, or become ossified in tradition. Drawing heavily on Hannah's song from 1 Samuel 2, Mary vocalizes a deep desire for God's topsy-turvy kingdom in which the lowest, the least and the poorest will be raised up and honoured. She recognizes that God has begun that process in his choice of her as the mother of Jesus. Already God's kingdom is breaking in and the old order is being overturned. Liberation is possible. Salvation is imminent.

While God's calling often brings fear and anxiety and requires quite a bit of growing into, it should also be shot through with excitement and joy. The Holy Spirit calls us to new and costly adventures that will take us beyond the familiar and careful, into places of risk and surprise. Obediently following our vocation will also release and empower others to serve and praise God.

COLLECT

Almighty Father,
who in your great mercy gladdened the disciples
    with the sight of the risen Lord:
give us such knowledge of his presence with us,
that we may be strengthened and sustained by his risen life
and serve you continually in righteousness and truth;
through Jesus Christ your Son our Lord,
who is alive and reigns with you,
in the unity of the Holy Spirit,
one God, now and for ever.

Luke 1.57-end

'What then will this child become?' (v.66)

Expectant parents often spend many months thinking through possible names for their child. Often the name chosen has a wealth of thoughts, longings, desires and hopes attached to it. This is important because our name plays a part in helping us define who we are and what we will become. In naming his child, John's father speaks out and takes a risk for God.

Zechariah's song – the Benedictus – praises God who is acting in history to bring about liberation and salvation for the people of Israel. Unlike the crowds, Zechariah knows what his child will become; Gabriel told him in the Temple. Zechariah proclaims it from the rooftops: 'you, child, will be called the prophet of the Most High' (v.76). This child's vocation is to prepare the way for the Messiah. He is destined to help the people of Israel back into a right relationship with Yahweh. He will lead them to a point of repentance so that they can acknowledge their Saviour who is coming. This child, filled with the Holy Spirit, bursts through societal norms – even his name John, breaks with family tradition. He is a new sign from God, and he points the way to God's fresh beginning.

What will you become? Who is God calling you to be for him and for others? Some are called, like John, to be a signpost enabling others to find their way to faith in Christ. Is that your calling?

Risen Christ,
you filled your disciples with boldness and fresh hope:
strengthen us to proclaim your risen life
and fill us with your peace,
to the glory of God the Father.

COLLECT

Friday 9 May

Psalms **107** *or* **31**
Exodus 28.1-4a, 29-38
Luke 2.1-20

Luke 2.1-20

'Mary treasured all these words and pondered them in her heart'
(v.19)

Luke tells the nativity story with great economy. In just seven verses, history is made. The true Saviour of the world is set against the Roman Emperor, a self-proclaimed god. Jesus' origins are humble, and the story human and earthy. However, there are extraordinary elements within the everyday. Labourers meet with angels. The baby is called 'Saviour … Messiah … Lord' (v.11), and the story of his birth brings together the whole of creation. Angels, shepherds, straw, animals and stars are represented. Everyone and everything is there. Heaven comes together with earth, and past, present and future are held in tension. Prophecy, which has been dormant for centuries, bursts forth from both angels and people.

The good news that the shepherds bring causes amazement. Mary treasures the words about her new son. She ponders them, taking them out and turning them over – thinking things through. Jesus, born in the city of David, is the chosen one whom all have been waiting for to come and make all things new. Treasuring Jesus and the words about him makes Mary a new person also.

Mary's obedience to God's calling has led her on an extraordinary adventure, which is far from over. There will be many more words about Jesus for her to treasure and ponder in the years ahead. Vocation is never a one-off event, but a lifelong journey of challenge and discovery. There is always more of Jesus to ponder and treasure.

COLLECT

Almighty Father,
who in your great mercy gladdened the disciples
    with the sight of the risen Lord:
give us such knowledge of his presence with us,
that we may be strengthened and sustained by his risen life
and serve you continually in righteousness and truth;
through Jesus Christ your Son our Lord,
who is alive and reigns with you,
in the unity of the Holy Spirit,
one God, now and for ever.

Psalms 108, **110**, 111 *or* 41, **42**, 43
Exodus 29.1-9
Luke 2.21-40

Luke 2.21-40

'... destined for the falling and the rising of many' (v.34)

Like his cousin John, Jesus is taken to the temple aged eight days for the Jewish birth rites. Two elderly saints, Simeon and Anna, make prophetic pronouncements about this child. He is the one awaited by Israel. He is the one who will bring salvation to the Jewish nation and beyond. Both Simeon and Anna have waited all their lives to see God's promises for Israel fulfilled. They can die happy, knowing that the child they have met and held is the future made secure.

Simeon brings warnings too. While this is a child of peace and light, such things are threatening to those who hold power. Jesus will be opposed. He will bring into the light thoughts and actions that many would prefer to remain hidden. God's plans are for the entire world. Universal salvation is revealed. This is potentially destabilizing to both sacred and secular forces. Many will fall, many will rise, and Jesus will do both in his calling to secure salvation for all.

Tomorrow is Vocation Sunday. As we have rehearsed again the nativity story, so we have looked at how ordinary people are called to step out in faith and obedience to play their part in God's plan of salvation for the world. What is God calling you to do? Who is God calling you to be? Step out in faith, like the characters in Luke, to fall and rise with Christ.

Risen Christ,
you filled your disciples with boldness and fresh hope:
strengthen us to proclaim your risen life
and fill us with your peace,
to the glory of God the Father.

COLLECT

Monday 12 May

Luke 2.41-end

'... all who heard him were amazed' (v.47)

More amazement in the temple. Picture the young Jesus sitting with the teachers, listening, questioning and supplying answers with astonishing skill and understanding. He is at home, about his Father's business, exercising his vocation. However, with all the precocity of a 12-year-old youth, he has forgotten to ask permission of his parents or tell them where he is, and naturally they are anxious and annoyed. Jesus shows surprise that they haven't second-guessed his movements – it is obvious to him that his place is in the temple where his Father dwells.

Mary and Joseph temporarily lost their son. They took it for granted that he was with the party making its way home from Jerusalem. It was some while before they realized he was no longer with them, and when they found him again, he didn't react as they expected, but presented them with still more to ponder and treasure. It's easy for us too, to take Jesus for granted – to expect him to be around and do the things we want and ask for. Sometimes we have to search for him again – prayerfully in worship and in the world around us. When we find him, he may unsettle us with his requests and actions. What he calls us to do and be as we follow him may be surprising and challenging, but we can trust that he is calling us to join him in his Father's business.

COLLECT

Almighty God,
whose Son Jesus Christ is the resurrection and the life:
raise us, who trust in him,
from the death of sin to the life of righteousness,
that we may seek those things which are above,
where he reigns with you
in the unity of the Holy Spirit,
one God, now and for ever.

Psalms **139** *or* **48**, 52
Exodus 32.15-34
Luke 3.1-14

Luke 3.1-14

'What then should we do?' (v.10)

Luke pinpoints an exact moment when John the Baptist exercises his vocation of preparing the way for Jesus. In a particular year, surrounded by named secular and religious leaders, Isaiah's prophecy is enacted. John, out in the desert, prepares the way of the Messiah, calling people to repentance and warning them of what is to come.

He is tough with the crowds who flock to him. It's not sufficient to claim family ties, tribal affinities or famous ancestors. Inherited faith, exercised by proxy, holds little weight. God's salvation is on offer to all, and the days are numbered for those who show little inner or outer commitment to serving God and others. Pruning is necessary if new growth is to occur. Trees that are dead are better cut down and burnt – at least then they will provide warmth for a short while. It's a harsh image for a people who believe they are chosen and set apart by God.

When asked, John shows simple ways to get back on track with God. Baptism leads to a new start, and a change of lifestyle. Straightforward human acts of goodness and kindness will follow. Sharing material possessions, showing hospitality, being honest in financial matters, and treating others with honour and respect are the fruits of a right relationship with God. As we consider what God might be calling us to do, it's vital we keep our relationship with God fresh and fruitful.

COLLECT

Risen Christ,
faithful shepherd of your Father's sheep:
teach us to hear your voice
and to follow your command,
that all your people may be gathered into one flock,
to the glory of God the Father.

Wednesday 14 May

Matthias the Apostle

Psalms 16, 147.1-12
1 Samuel 2.27-35
Acts 2.37-end

Acts 2.37-end

'And day by day the Lord added to their number' (v.47)

Today the Church celebrates St Matthias, chosen by lot to replace Judas Iscariot. What was going through Matthias' mind? Did he want to be an apostle? He was with the believers throughout the three years of Jesus' ministry, but he's not mentioned in the Gospels. He's been faithful – but perhaps content to serve in the shadows. Suddenly he's thrust into the limelight. Sometimes God's calling is very surprising and requires courage and considerable growing into.

The task Matthias and his fellow apostles are called to has become huge. Peter's powerful sermon following the outpouring of the Holy Spirit stirs a vast crowd to repentance and acceptance of Jesus as Lord. Three thousand new converts swell dramatically the emerging Christian community. The promise of God's salvation is not for a select few – but as Peter says, 'for you', 'your children,' 'all who are far away,' and 'everyone the Lord our God calls' (v.39). The forgiveness of God and the gift of the Holy Spirit know no limits.

Living in the new messianic community brings responsibilities. While there is excitement at seeing the Holy Spirit powerfully at work through signs and wonders, there is also a new and challenging lifestyle to inhabit. The apostles have their work cut out nurturing this emerging movement, but the Lord is with them daily, bringing fresh challenge and reward. At times when our calling seems much too challenging, it's good to remember that the Lord who calls also equips and sustains.

COLLECT

Almighty God,
who in the place of the traitor Judas
chose your faithful servant Matthias
to be of the number of the Twelve:
preserve your Church from false apostles
and, by the ministry of faithful pastors and teachers,
keep us steadfast in your truth;
through Jesus Christ your Son our Lord,
who is alive and reigns with you,
in the unity of the Holy Spirit,
one God, now and for ever.

Luke 4.1-13

'... led by the Spirit in the wilderness' (v. 1)

Following his baptism and commissioning for ministry, Jesus enters a time of testing and formation in the desert. Luke uses echoes from the Garden of Eden and the Israelites in the wilderness to link Jesus into salvation history. He is the second Adam, the second Moses, walking in the path of his ancestors and redeeming the past. This journey will lead to the cross and resurrection – and ultimately to the redemption of the world.

The devil tests in subtle and reasonable ways. He sows doubt with his 'If you are the Son of God' (v.3), and quotes from the Scriptures to make his point. He pushes Jesus to grasp at divinity, to put himself in the place of God and reveal who he truly is. But Jesus' vocation is to be fully God and fully man, and in the incarnation he reveals what it means to be a complete human being, serving God faithfully and with humility.

As we pursue our vocation and work out what it means to love and serve God, so we too will be tested. While we're often sure we can discern truth from falsehood, sometimes the difference is very subtle and surprising. The way of Christ is the path of humble service, often in arid and empty places, with no recognition and little reward. Jesus teaches us that shortcuts to glory are to be resisted at all costs.

Almighty God,
whose Son Jesus Christ is the resurrection and the life:
raise us, who trust in him,
from the death of sin to the life of righteousness,
that we may seek those things which are above,
where he reigns with you
in the unity of the Holy Spirit,
one God, now and for ever.

COLLECT

Friday 16 May

Psalms **33** *or* **51, 54**
Exodus 35.20 – 36.7
Luke 4.14-30

Luke 4.14-30

'The Spirit of the Lord is upon me' (v.18)

In his home synagogue Jesus declares his mandate. He has come to fulfil the Scriptures, and this vocation will turn the world upside down. Liberation is here for those imprisoned by poverty, lack of vision, or circumstance. This is not a sudden declaration but the fulfilment of years of preparation, prayer and formation. This local lad who speaks with confidence and grace excites the people. They can't quite believe he is Joseph's son. However, as he continues, their amazement turns to fury and he is in real danger. It is only the quiet determination to go his way that saves his life.

Why are the people so angry? Jesus identifies himself with Elijah and Elisha, but more than this, with Isaiah's servant Messiah (Isaiah 42 to 53). The message he brings is deeply threatening to those who believe their salvation is secure. Jesus shows that God's love and mercy are open to all. He has not come to punish and judge but to bring healing and forgiveness for everyone. For his hearers in the synagogue, he is overstepping the mark and offering to those who are beyond the pale what has always been considered a Jewish inheritance. He is not just the son of Joseph but the Son of God, and therefore what is on offer is much broader, deeper and wider than previously perceived. Sadly, those who thought they were the select few show hostility in the face of God's overwhelming generosity to all.

COLLECT

Almighty God,
whose Son Jesus Christ is the resurrection and the life:
raise us, who trust in him,
from the death of sin to the life of righteousness,
that we may seek those things which are above,
where he reigns with you
in the unity of the Holy Spirit,
one God, now and for ever.

Luke 4.31-37

'… he spoke with authority' (v.32)

Another day, another synagogue: this time in Capernaum, Galilee. Luke gives us a window into the healing, preaching and teaching ministry of Jesus, who continues to amaze and astound his listeners with his authority. When the Son of God speaks, it's like electricity. People sit up and listen. Things happen.

Even though it is the Sabbath, and forbidden in the Pharisaic interpretation of the law, Jesus performs an exorcism. It is one of the signs of the kingdom of God breaking through. An unclean spirit hails Jesus as the 'Holy One of God' (v.34) before being silenced and cast out. The man is restored and made whole. Luke demonstrates that though the crowds might not recognize who Jesus is, those not of this world are certainly aware and bow to his power and authority. News about Jesus spreads like wild fire – there's no keeping it quiet.

Jesus, God's anointed, clearly exercised the kind of authority that makes a difference. This is the Jesus who calls us to follow him into new and exciting ways of being fully human. God's call is often surprising, startling and risky. It regularly leads us out of our chosen, comfortable paths, challenging us to see things in new ways, to make unexpected connections and to rethink our ideas and beliefs. Following Christ and responding to his call means enabling others to connect with God who longs to turn their lives around, bringing healing, wholeness and transformation.

Risen Christ,
faithful shepherd of your Father's sheep:
teach us to hear your voice
and to follow your command,
that all your people may be gathered into one flock,
to the glory of God the Father.

COLLECT

Monday 19 May

Psalms **145** *or* **71**
Numbers 9.15-end; 10.33-end
Luke 4.38-end

Luke 4.38-end

'[Jesus] stood over her and rebuked the fever' (v.39)

I was Portsmouth's Diocesan Healing Advisor, but I was unprepared for a Ghanaian hospital visit. For priests in a British hospital, the bedside is usually quiet: reflection, prayer and a Bible reading – and perhaps a sacrament, communion and/or confession. In Ghana, there's African gusto: after talking to the patient the prayer was loud and the disease or illness was *rebuked*. I felt uncomfortable with this approach but it's biblical, with both Peter's mother-in-law's fever and illnesses in general being rebuked.

In Jesus' time it was common for sickness to be personified as demonic possession that needed rebuking. Logically, if we personify goodness in the Father and Jesus, why should we not personify evil? Our baptism rite calls for the rejection of the devil, although this may be shortened to renouncing evil. But there is also a danger in rushing to see demons in a situation. This approach can easily collude with psychological problems and any exorcism is only ever a last resort, by a specialist, after other avenues have been exhausted.

However, many illnesses have their roots in society's sinful structures. The vast and growing disparity in wealth in this country can lead to feelings of alienation and contribute towards drug and alcohol abuse. The increasing use of airbrushed sexualized images in advertising and media is making an idol of the unattainable perfect body or sexual experience. In our Christian vocation to heal, some things need to be rebuked.

COLLECT

Almighty God,
who through your only-begotten Son Jesus Christ
have overcome death and opened to us the gate of everlasting life:
grant that, as by your grace going before us
   you put into our minds good desires,
so by your continual help
we may bring them to good effect;
through Jesus Christ our risen Lord,
who is alive and reigns with you,
in the unity of the Holy Spirit,
one God, now and for ever.

Luke 5.1-11

'... they left everything and followed him' (v.11)

Nets, boats and servants, the trappings of a middle-class artisan lifestyle are left on the seashore as Peter, the self-convicted sinner, leaves to follow Jesus. Jesus has performed miracles in front of Peter: the healing of his mother-in-law, and now the huge draught of fish. However, it's the word of God that is attracting the crowd. The word of God is Luke's shorthand for the message, the good news, that Jesus proclaims, and it is hearing this and experiencing miracles that brings Peter to his knees.

Peter, or Simon, is called while he is unworthy, and later Paul, or Saul, the unworthy persecutor of the first Christians, will be called. This is the pattern of God's grace. Just as Peter lands a huge draught of fish through no personal ability (he is guided to where the net should be thrown and his own nets are insufficient so that he has to rely on the help of colleagues), so he becomes a follower of Jesus through no personal merit.

Peter the rough fisherman will later painfully experience misunderstanding over the mission of Jesus and fear before the crucifixion. Yet he remains a leader of the early Church. A few years after these events, Saul the persecutor becomes Paul the apostle. We are called not because of our merits but because of our need of grace. The ability to walk away from the trappings of trade or status show the attraction of Jesus' call.

Risen Christ,
your wounds declare your love for the world
and the wonder of your risen life:
give us compassion and courage
to risk ourselves for those we serve,
to the glory of God the Father.

COLLECT

Wednesday 21 May

Luke 5.12-26

'When [Jesus] saw their faith ...' (v.20)

Sola fide, faith alone, was Luther's Reformation cry. It meant that an individual's personal faith defined their standing before God. Personal faith and justification were bound together. Today's reading offers a twist on this – it's not the paralytic's personal faith that brings about his healing but the corporate faith of his friends who lowered him through the roof.

By faith, his friends carry him there, dismantle the roof and drop the stretcher through the hole, and it's their faith that Jesus notices. Jesus' reaction is to ignore the believing friends and to proclaim the paralytic's sins forgiven. We don't know what the friends believed. Probably they believed Jesus was *merely* a healer. What they are shown, by the forgiving of sins, is that he is God in human form. The Church father, John Chrysostom says, 'He discloses... His own Godhead... His equality with the Father'. The crowd understood this and accused Jesus of blasphemy but, to give them the chance of coming to personal faith, the friends' actions are rewarded by physical healing.

I imagine that the friends, who risked charges of criminal damage by dismantling the roof, had their faith challenged by the initial response of the forgiveness of sins. That wasn't their goal. By the end of this encounter their faith is deepened by realizing that Jesus is God. Their corporate faith healed their friend and demonstrated God's presence in Jesus. What does our corporate faith do today?

COLLECT

Almighty God,
who through your only-begotten Son Jesus Christ
have overcome death and opened to us the gate of everlasting life:
grant that, as by your grace going before us
    you put into our minds good desires,
so by your continual help
we may bring them to good effect;
through Jesus Christ our risen Lord,
who is alive and reigns with you,
in the unity of the Holy Spirit,
one God, now and for ever.

Psalms **57**, 148 *or* **78.1-39***
Numbers 13.1-3, 17-end
Luke 5.27-end

Luke 5.27-end

'The old is good' (v.39)

What! Can the old be good when Jesus says that no one sows part of a new garment onto an old one, nor do they put new wine into old wineskins? Is Jesus making a break with the old while simultaneously claiming that the old is good, and, if so, what can he mean?

Two answers may be put forward. Either Jesus is being ironic and mimicking those who cling to the old – the Pharisees and the disciples of John who seem attracted by the disciplines of fasting. Maybe they are attracted by clear guidelines and structures, and struggle with the more open parabolic approach of Jesus.

Alternatively, Jesus is not being ironic at all but is saying that the old is literally good. We need the tradition of the Pharisees, alongside the ground-breaking ministry of John the Baptist and his followers, because Jesus' ministry is built upon them. A near opposite conclusion.

Such is the tension in much of Scripture. When we look for clear guidance, it eludes us as we have only partial knowledge of the culture, and little is said about the specific incident from which the Scripture emerged. What was Jesus' tone of voice? Sarcastic or emphatic? The gospel writer fails to say and, as with much of our Scripture, we are left reflecting on the open-ended teaching of Jesus. The old might be good for clear answers, but maybe Jesus calls us to ponder these things.

Risen Christ,
your wounds declare your love for the world
and the wonder of your risen life:
give us compassion and courage
to risk ourselves for those we serve,
to the glory of God the Father.

COLLECT

Friday 23 May

Psalms **138**, 149 *or* **55**
Numbers 14.1-25
Luke 6.1-11

Luke 6.1-11

'The Son of Man is lord of the sabbath' (v.5)

Keeping the sabbath is a principal mark of Judaism. The sabbath is for all, founded at creation when God rested on the seventh day. It is matched in importance only by the physical sign of circumcision. Christians still keep the sabbath, so the Lutheran Service Book says 'Put aside the work you do, so that God may work in you'.

Jesus' disciples push against the sabbath ritual. In rubbing the heads of grain, they are doing something similar to harvesting and all work is forbidden. When challenged by the Pharisees, Jesus invokes the example of David and the bread of the Presence. Twelve loaves of bread were placed weekly before the Lord. At the end of the week, the loaves were consumed by the priests, and David asks for five loaves for himself and his men (1 Samuel 21.3). This is perhaps a strange example, because that action did not take place on a sabbath, but it shows the letter of the law being broken in a time of need. It's also a symbolic response, which the Pharisees would have understood. David was, at the time, the anointed but unrecognized king of Israel with a band of followers. Jesus is a new David, also anointed but unrecognized, and also with authority to interpret the law.

Jesus brings humanity to the sabbath with the spirit of moral obligation not ritual observance; the sabbath, like God's rest during creation, is about restoring and giving rest.

COLLECT

Almighty God,
who through your only-begotten Son Jesus Christ
have overcome death and opened to us the gate of everlasting life:
grant that, as by your grace going before us
    you put into our minds good desires,
so by your continual help
we may bring them to good effect;
through Jesus Christ our risen Lord,
who is alive and reigns with you,
in the unity of the Holy Spirit,
one God, now and for ever.

Luke 6.12-26

'... surely your reward is great in heaven' (v.23)

In *How God Became King*, the former bishop of Durham, Tom Wright, argues that Christians have incorrectly read the Gospels. He refers to credal Christianity that jumps, as our creeds do, from the birth of Jesus to his death – from 'Born of the Virgin Mary' to 'Suffered under Pontius Pilate'. This jump ignores the gospel message of the life, healing and teaching of Jesus. The credal Christian message details how to get to heaven, whereas the life of Jesus demonstrates how to establish God's kingdom on earth by practising social justice and forgiveness. Many Christians have read Galatians and Romans, and emphasized life beyond this one, and overlooked the radical practice taught in our four Gospels.

The Beatitudes, from the Latin for blessed, have been seen as looking forward to a life beyond this life and a future perfect relationship with God. The 'reward' of the beatitudes for the first-century Jews who heard them was about *this* life. The reward for credal Christians, if they read them, is about heavenly bliss. Jesus' emphasis is on building a just kingdom now. Poverty, especially if caused by oppression, is a scandal that needs to be reversed. Hoarding wealth and status is also scandalous, and the woes predicted for the rich and respected are resonant of prophetic warning of impending distress. This isn't about a future life; this is immanent.

The gospel does proclaim eternal life and eternal life starts now.

Risen Christ,
your wounds declare your love for the world
and the wonder of your risen life:
give us compassion and courage
to risk ourselves for those we serve,
to the glory of God the Father.

COLLECT

Monday 26 May

Luke 6.27-38

'Be merciful, just as your Father is merciful' (v.36)

As the sun set on the British Empire in India, Gandhi, himself a Hindu, was taking inspiration from Jesus. He said that 'Jesus' suffering is a factor in the composition of my un-dying faith in non-violence ... He was one of the greatest teachers humanity has ever had', and with this *Christian* approach, he pursued a non-violent campaign against the colonial power.

Jesus' non-violence is humiliating: if you turn the other cheek, you are inviting a strike with the left hand, which was used for unclean purposes; if you give your shirt, along with your coat, you are reduced to nakedness. The humiliation is mutual both for the oppressed and the oppressor who has to act improperly with the second strike or gaze inappropriately upon nakedness. The humiliation of the oppressed shames the oppressor just as Gandhi uncovered the shame of the empire. Both Jesus and Stephen embody non-violence in their deaths, especially in praying for their executors.

Luke recalls Jesus encouraging us to take God's attribute of mercy. The old covenant tended to emphasize God's holiness, leading to an ethic of separation and suspicion of others. The contemporary Roman ethic was, 'I give so that you give'. Generous Roman behaviour was to be rewarded, and thus the rich and powerful helped each other. The call to mercy is radically generous both to those who are different and those who are poor. Living it out prophetically and peacefully speaks truth to power.

COLLECT

God our redeemer,
you have delivered us from the power of darkness
and brought us into the kingdom of your Son:
grant, that as by his death he has recalled us to life,
so by his continual presence in us he may raise us
    to eternal joy;
through Jesus Christ your Son our Lord,
who is alive and reigns with you,
in the unity of the Holy Spirit,
one God, now and for ever.

Psalms 124, 125, **126**, 127
or 87, **89.1-18**
Numbers 16.36-end
Luke 6.39-end

Luke 6.39-end

'... each tree is known by its own fruit' (v.44)

The Irish writer Peter Rollins, who is now part of the American 'emerging Church' scene, reflects on the self-image that we try to construct. So our Facebook profile becomes a story that we tell ourselves and project to others: the books that we want others to think we have read; the films we want to have influenced our lives. For Rollins, a shocking projection comes in a 1938 edition of *Homes and Gardens*. It is set in a politician's home with art hanging on the walls and describes a party where local children are read stories from the piano bench, and guests are generously entertained with a range of food even though the host himself is a strict vegetarian. The article shows the nice guy image projected by Adolf Hitler; we know him by his monstrous deeds.

It is not enough to cry 'Lord, Lord' without *living* with Jesus as Lord of your life. Jesus often turns on the hypocrite. The word literally refers to an actor speaking from under his mask, acting a part. However, our inner being, or the 'abundance of our heart', is shown by our deeds, be they affirming or destructive.

Homes and Gardens was accurate, but it wasn't true. The truth of Hitler was revealed in the evils he committed. Our core beliefs are not what we confess but the desires that become manifest in our actions. The fruits that we bear reveal the person that we are.

Risen Christ,
by the lakeside you renewed your call to your disciples:
help your Church to obey your command
and draw the nations to the fire of your love,
to the glory of God the Father.

COLLECT

Wednesday 28 May

Luke 7.1-10

'Lord ... I am not worthy that thou shouldest enter under my roof'
(v.6, AV)

Society often constructs barriers. In today's reading these barriers are many: between Jew and gentile (as the centurion will not approach Jesus in person); between occupying army and occupied Palestinian (even though the centurion built the Capernaum synagogue, for him to enter a house would cause defilement); and between the holiness revealed in Jesus and our own sinful nature. The centurion's cry 'I am not worthy' is echoed in our traditional liturgy's use of his words (see above).

It is striking that the centurion erects a barrier of unworthiness while the elders dismantle any such barrier by emphasizing his love and deeds. Is this because it's often easier to see the good in others while we are all too aware of our own sinful nature?

This encounter is a foretaste of the post-resurrection Church where another centurion, Cornelius, is welcomed into the Church (Acts 10), and the Church's mission is understood to embrace all humankind. Barriers, erected by both society and our own internal self-criticism, are broken down. There's the Christian vocation to break down external barriers, but also a vocation to break down internal barriers. The Christian call to holiness is associated with wholeness and an integrated personality. This is achieved when we accept and embrace the damaged parts of our ego, seeing ourselves as Christ sees us. To both us and Christ, our own damaged nature is visible, and still he wants to come under our roof.

COLLECT

God our redeemer,
you have delivered us from the power of darkness
and brought us into the kingdom of your Son:
grant, that as by his death he has recalled us to life,
so by his continual presence in us he may raise us
    to eternal joy;
through Jesus Christ your Son our Lord,
who is alive and reigns with you,
in the unity of the Holy Spirit,
one God, now and for ever.

Thursday 29 May

Ascension Day

Hebrews 7.[11-25] 26-end

'... a Son who has been made perfect for ever' (v.28)

To see why this passage was chosen for the Ascension, you have to take the longer reading from verse 11 and understand the purpose of the Letter to the Hebrews. It was written assuming that the Hebrew law was meant to bring union with God; this it failed to do. Therefore Christ came, who can be understood in terms of the inherited sacrificial law, and he succeeded in this union through his perfect 'once for all' sacrifice.

The longer reading draws upon the enigmatic character Melchizedek from Genesis 14. Melchizedek's death is not recorded, and he is traditionally considered eternal (Psalm 110). Also, unlike the later Levitical priesthood traced to Aaron, and the separate kingship based upon David, in Melchizedek priest and king are combined. He is a pattern for Jesus.

Temple ritual in Jesus' time could not bring sanctification. This was because the priesthood was 'subject to weakness' – priests sinned and they died. Also the sacrifice was imperfect being the blood of animals. However, Jesus 'holds his priesthood permanently', and his perfect sacrifice of himself is not just a past event but an ever-present reality: 'he always lives to make intercession' (v.25). The temple altar has become Jesus' cross. The long line of Levitical priests and anticipated promises of a Davidic king, have become the eternal priest-king Jesus. In time, the *sacrificial* blood of animals becomes the *sacramental* new rites of Baptism and Eucharist with our ever-present intercessor.

Grant, we pray, almighty God,
that as we believe your only-begotten Son
our Lord Jesus Christ
to have ascended into the heavens,
so we in heart and mind may also ascend
and with him continually dwell;
who is alive and reigns with you,
in the unity of the Holy Spirit,
one God, now and for ever.

COLLECT

Friday 30 May

Galatians 5.13-end

'... you bite and devour one another' (v.15)

The Galatian Church was in crisis. They followed Jesus the Jew, and this led to heated debate: how Jewish should his followers be? The keeping of Hebrew laws, which some Jewish Christians observed, was being demanded of gentile converts. Some have called it the Judaizing crisis, and into this situation of partisan strife and bitterness Paul writes his letter.

Paul speaks of following the ways of either the flesh or the spirit. These are not separate places, as some later gnostic Christians would argue as they separated physical and spiritual realities. With his Hebrew background, Paul understood that we are whole people – we are psychosomatic – and the whole person is to be redeemed by God. Flesh and spirit represent different orientations and the lifelong struggle that we each have with our desires. The Galatians 'were called to freedom', but this can be misunderstood as 'self-indulgent'. No wonder many wanted to sacrifice their new-found freedom and follow the certainties of the old law with its clear boundaries to behaviour.

The flesh leads away from the 'kingdom of God' because it is either hedonistic (in satisfying base desires) or misappropriating power (in enforcing the law). The flesh leads to division and a denial of grace. In what may be a reference to baptism, Paul tells the Galatians to crucify the flesh and to 'be guided by the Spirit' (v.25). In a place of division, they are to follow the law of love.

COLLECT

Grant, we pray, almighty God,
that as we believe your only-begotten Son our Lord Jesus Christ
to have ascended into the heavens,
so we in heart and mind may also ascend
and with him continually dwell;
who is alive and reigns with you,
in the unity of the Holy Spirit,
one God, now and for ever.

Psalms 85, 150
1 Samuel 2.1-10
Mark 3.31-end

**Visit of the Blessed Virgin Mary
to Elizabeth**

1 Samuel 2.1-10

'My heart exults in the Lord' (v. 1)

At the Visitation, Mary sang, 'My soul magnifies the Lord' (Luke 1.46), thus echoing the earlier prayer of Hannah. We learn two things from Mary drawing upon Hannah's experience.

First, coming towards God is not an individual's solitary journey in faith. We come to God by reflecting and building upon the experience of those around us and those who came before us. Mary builds upon the experience of Hannah – she embellishes her prayer and learns from her experience of how a child, Samuel for Hannah, Jesus for Mary, is a gift from God. Hannah's prayer could have been written for Mary and for all who rejoice in the Lord. The 'I' of Hannah's prayer is also the 'I' of Israel's experience and Mary's response to God. Because the nation Israel rejoiced in Hannah's prayer, Mary could respond with it. We come to understand the call of God by reflectively revisiting the experience of those who have walked in faith.

Second, we need to be immersed in our tradition, especially the Scriptures. We can only reflect with those who have gone before us if we know them. The Bible, the teaching of Church mothers and fathers, and modern writers are all wrestling with similar questions. How do we understand God in the light of our tradition, and our cultural and personal experiences? To exult in the Lord today, we need to rejoice with Mary and Hannah, with Augustine and Julian, and with contemporary theologians.

Mighty God,
by whose grace Elizabeth rejoiced with Mary
and greeted her as the mother of the Lord:
look with favour on your lowly servants
that, with Mary, we may magnify your holy name
and rejoice to acclaim her Son our Saviour,
who is alive and reigns with you,
in the unity of the Holy Spirit,
one God, now and for ever.

COLLECT

Monday 2 June

Psalms **93**, 96, 97 *or* **98**, 99, 101
Numbers 27.15-end
1 Corinthians 3

1 Corinthians 3

'God's temple is holy, and you are that temple' (v.17)

Jealousies, personal rivalries, quarrelling and factions dominate the Church at Corinth. The Corinthians, for all their perceived wisdom and sophistry, are still spiritual infants requiring basic instruction and nurture. This all-too-human community has a long way to go.

Paul reminds them that it doesn't matter who lays the foundations of faith or encourages spiritual exploration and maturity. Often it's a team effort – God's servants working together. What's important is that the foundation laid is Jesus Christ. Whoever sows and tends, God gives the growth.

Paul likens the Christian community to 'God's field' (the Greek can mean 'farm'), a rural analogy, or 'God's building' for more urban listeners (v.9). Jesus Christ, the foundation is secure, but all should take care over the method and materials of the superstructure. Throw the building up too quickly using second-rate materials, and the shoddy work will soon come to light.

Furthermore, the Christian community is not just any field or building, but the temple itself – the most holy place imaginable. As individuals and as community, we are called to build and become God's temple. The place where God dwells, holy and eternal is to be found among us and within us. It would have sounded unbelievable – blasphemous even – to the first generation of Christians. But all is not as it seems for people moving from the flesh to the spirit. Foolishness has become the new wisdom.

COLLECT

O God the King of glory,
you have exalted your only Son Jesus Christ
with great triumph to your kingdom in heaven:
we beseech you, leave us not comfortless,
but send your Holy Spirit to strengthen us
and exalt us to the place where our Saviour Christ is gone before,
who is alive and reigns with you,
in the unity of the Holy Spirit,
one God, now and for ever.

Tuesday 3 June

1 Corinthians 12.1-13

'... in the one Spirit we were all baptized into one body' (v.13)

One body made up of many members, working together for the good of all, was not a new idea for the ancient Greeks. The Stoics used this metaphor to describe the Greek State in which all were citizens. The Corinthians were familiar with this. Paul adopts and adapts the ideas of the culture. However, for the emerging Church, the body is no longer the State – it is now Christ, into whom the Holy Spirit calls men, women and children to be essential components. The Christian community is to be a living, breathing force for good, made in God's image, incorporated into Christ and animated by the Holy Spirit.

The Spirit distributes gifts – a wide variety, given to each member to build up and strengthen the whole body for its work in the world. The business of transforming lives and communities is a joint enterprise in which all have a valuable role to play. Exercising one's God-given gifts is not for personal fulfilment but for the common good.

In the ancient world great weight was given to spirituality that displayed frenzy and fervour. But Paul tells the Corinthian Church that it is not by ecstatic utterance and dramatic behaviour that the believer demonstrates the Spirit within. Rather the recognition and affirmation that 'Jesus is Lord' (v.3), and the change of lifestyle that such allegiance entails, bear witness to the Holy Spirit's presence in the life of the faithful Christian.

Risen, ascended Lord,
as we rejoice at your triumph,
fill your Church on earth with power and compassion,
that all who are estranged by sin
may find forgiveness and know your peace,
to the glory of God the Father.

COLLECT

Wednesday 4 June

Psalms 2, **29** or 110, **111**, 112
1 Kings 19.1-18
Matthew 3.13-end

Matthew 3.13-end

'This is my Son, the Beloved, with whom I am well pleased' (v.17)

Why does Jesus come to be baptized? John is confused by his cousin presenting himself for public baptism – it seems the wrong way round. Why should the sinless Son of God need to go through this ritual of cleansing and incorporation? Prior to John the Baptist and the ascetic, desert-dwelling Essene community, only converts underwent baptism. This ritual bath, circumcision and sacrificial offering incorporated gentile converts into the Jewish faith and way of life. John's shocking new call to repentance marked a national turning to God in which many Jews flocked to the desert to be baptized in the running waters of the Jordan. A weary and besieged people sought new life and a fresh outpouring of the Spirit.

And Jesus participates too. He identifies with the teaching of John and joins in solidarity with his fellow Jews, those he has come to save. In doing so, he lays the pattern for Christian baptism. During this consecration of his life to God, an epiphany occurs. The heavens open and the Son of God is acknowledged by the voice of God the Father, accompanied by the Spirit of God in the form of a dove. The words spoken are a fusion of two messianic prophecies: Psalm 2.7 ('You are my son; today I have begotten you') and Isaiah 42.1 ('Here is my servant, whom I uphold, my chosen, in whom my soul delights'). Jesus will be the servant whose kingship is marked by the way of suffering. Baptism begins this ministry.

COLLECT

O God the King of glory,
you have exalted your only Son Jesus Christ
with great triumph to your kingdom in heaven:
we beseech you, leave us not comfortless,
but send your Holy Spirit to strengthen us
and exalt us to the place where our Saviour Christ is gone before,
who is alive and reigns with you,
in the unity of the Holy Spirit,
one God, now and for ever.

Psalms **24**, 72 *or* 113, **115**
Ezekiel 11.14-20
Matthew 9.35 – 10.20

Matthew 9.35 – 10.20

'The harvest is plentiful, but the labourers are few ...' (9.37)

Jesus is moved to the core of his being as he travels around proclaiming the kingdom. The people are 'harassed and helpless' (9.36) – the Greek translates literally as 'torn and thrown down'. A rich harvest is waiting to be gathered up and brought home, but leaders are lacking who can make that happen. Calling and commissioning the twelve disciples is the first step.

Given authority by Jesus, the disciples are sent out on a strategic mission. Travelling lightly and working hard, they can expect little reward. They are to deliver messages of peace and salvation to those who will accept them and to move on swiftly when they are not welcomed. The mission of God is urgent and costly, and it requires faith, energy and courage. Walking in the way of Christ with his authority to preach, teach and heal may lead to persecution and rejection by religious leaders, the state and even family and friends. But the disciples are not to worry, because the harvest belongs to the Lord and it is his work they are continuing. When they are not sure what to do or say, the Spirit will equip them.

Today's disciples, you and I, are called to bring hope to people who are equally run down and dejected. The Chief Harvester continues to call labourers into his field: a rich harvest awaits. How will you respond to the call of Jesus today? Which field are you called to harvest?

Risen, ascended Lord,
as we rejoice at your triumph,
fill your Church on earth with power and compassion,
that all who are estranged by sin
may find forgiveness and know your peace,
to the glory of God the Father.

COLLECT

Friday 6 June

Matthew 12.22-32

'… no city or house divided against itself will stand' (v.25)

The healing of a blind and mute demoniac by Jesus causes amazement. Unable to deny his power, the Pharisees distrust its source. They lay a charge of magic against Jesus: it must be by the power of Satan that Jesus exorcises demons. Sorcery is a very serious charge, carrying a capital punishment. Jesus quickly unravels their accusation. Satan would not destabilize his realm in such a way, it would be against his best interests, since a kingdom at war with itself is weakened and will fall. Rather, it is by the Spirit of God that healing, integration and transformation occur in people's lives.

More importantly, if the Spirit of God is working through Jesus, then the long-awaited kingdom of God has arrived. The Pharisees, by their refusal to acknowledge Jesus as the Son of David, the Messiah, are deliberately rejecting the light, and failing to recognize the dawning of God's new age. They prefer to demonize God's work rather than celebrate and publicize it. Matthew concludes this passage by having Jesus say that lack of faith in Jesus himself is redeemable, but denying the great works of the Holy Spirit is unforgivable.

We, as Christians, expend much energy fighting among ourselves. Internal battles lead to a weakened position where our claims of love, forgiveness and hope are undermined and lack validity. Proclaiming the incredible work of the Holy Spirit, now and in the future, is God's rallying cry.

COLLECT

O God the King of glory,
you have exalted your only Son Jesus Christ
with great triumph to your kingdom in heaven:
we beseech you, leave us not comfortless,
but send your Holy Spirit to strengthen us
and exalt us to the place where our Saviour Christ is gone before,
who is alive and reigns with you,
in the unity of the Holy Spirit,
one God, now and for ever.

Psalms 42, **43** *or* 120, **121**, 122
Micah 3.1-8
Ephesians 6.10-20

Ephesians 6.10-20

'Pray in the Spirit at all times in every prayer and supplication' (v.18)

Paul, under house arrest and chained probably to a succession of soldiers, developed a sustained military metaphor for early Christians. He uses the imagery of *panoplia* – a soldier's complete battle-kit – reinterpreted as the 'whole armour of God' (v.13). In order for the early Church to stand firm during persecution, it needed to imagine itself preparing for battle with God's weaponry. Withstanding cosmic powers and all kinds of evil requires dressing oneself for the part with Christian virtues, thus remaining strong in the Lord.

For many, down the centuries, this imagery has remained helpful and inspiring. For others, the military theme with its shields and swords is more difficult to grasp. However, the idea of clothing oneself with truth, righteousness, peace, faith, salvation and the word of God as we go about our everyday lives is a pertinent reminder of being immersed in Christ and part of his body, the Church. We are reminded too that we require God's help and protection for many of the situations we encounter in our world.

Paul urges the Ephesians and us to be faithful in prayer. We are to persevere, and be strong and stable in our faith, praying in the Holy Spirit at all times, and for everyone. Standing firm, remaining watchful and persevering enabled Paul to continue to proclaim Christ, even when imprisoned. The Church today, encountering similar antipathy needs to remain faithful to its bold proclamation of Christ.

Risen, ascended Lord,
as we rejoice at your triumph,
fill your Church on earth with power and compassion,
that all who are estranged by sin
may find forgiveness and know your peace,
to the glory of God the Father.

COLLECT

Monday 9 June

Luke 9.18-27

'But who do you say that I am?' (v.20)

Does Jesus know what the people are saying about him? Why does he quiz the disciples so closely? Is he curious, or is he perhaps trying to get them to work out his identity for themselves. As they work through some possibilities, impetuous Peter hits on the truth: 'The Messiah of God' (v.20).

As the disciples digest this startling revelation, Jesus unpacks what his identity as Messiah entails. Suffering, humiliation, death and resurrection are involved. This is something to keep quiet about, since the time is not yet right to reveal such explosive material to the crowds. What follows from Jesus is a scary and challenging lesson for those who acknowledge his identity: life will never be the same again. Following the Son of Man means suffering alongside him, losing one's life to save it and never being ashamed of this or of Jesus. The prophecy of resurrection on the third day comes from Hosea 6.2, where it refers to the vindication not of one person but of Israel. While Jesus is called to enact this fulfilment, he doesn't intend journeying alone. By calling the disciples to tread the path of suffering, Jesus is pointing to the restoration of the entire people of God.

As part of the body of Christ, we too are called to walk the way of the cross; holding on securely to resurrection hope. But we do not walk this road alone. We are alongside one another and we are all in Christ.

COLLECT

O Lord, from whom all good things come:
grant to us your humble servants,
that by your holy inspiration
we may think those things that are good,
and by your merciful guiding may perform the same;
through our Lord Jesus Christ,
who is alive and reigns with you,
in the unity of the Holy Spirit,
one God, now and for ever.

Psalms **132**, 133
Joshua 2
Luke 9.28-36

Luke 9.28-36

'This is my Son, my Chosen; listen to him!' (v.35)

In the context of prayer, Jesus, Peter, James and John enjoy a mountaintop spiritual experience. Jesus, transfigured before the three disciples, reveals the glory of God, and is flanked by Moses and Elijah. The disciples have identified who Jesus is; now they witness the full extent of that revelation. Peter longs to hold on to the moment, offering to build tabernacles to house the glory of God, just as his ancestors did in the wilderness. But Moses and Elijah aren't staying. The old order is passing away. Jesus is embarking on a new venture, treading an unknown path in uncharted territory, which will lead to another hill, and a far greater revelation.

God speaks in a similar vein as at Jesus' baptism. The words are for the disciples who are commanded to listen to Jesus. Probably they would all like to remain on the mountain experiencing the glory of God, but such experiences are given to fuel daily living in the midst of human messiness. The trip is short lived and the party soon enter back into the fray of broken and disturbed humanity.

None of us can live permanently on a spiritual 'high'. Glimpses of the glory of God are to be treasured when they occur and used to resource day-to-day service, giving us the zest to run with the Spirit and continue Christ's work of faithful witness to God. Listening to Jesus takes commitment and discipline.

O Lord, from whom all good things come:
grant to us your humble servants,
that by your holy inspiration
we may think those things that are good,
and by your merciful guiding may perform the same;
through our Lord Jesus Christ,
who is alive and reigns with you,
in the unity of the Holy Spirit,
one God, now and for ever.

COLLECT

Wednesday 11 June

Barnabas the Apostle

Psalms 100, 101, 117
Jeremiah 9.23-24
Acts 4.32-end

Acts 4.32-end

'… great grace was upon them all' (v.33)

Today the Church celebrates Barnabas the Apostle, whom we meet for the first time in Acts 4. He is Joseph, a Greek-speaking Jew from the tribe of Levi in Cyprus, living in Jerusalem. The early Church, filled with the Spirit and testifying to the resurrection of Christ, adopted a lifestyle in which many things were held in common. This was not a new way of living together; both those Greeks who followed the teachings of Pythagoras and the ascetic Jewish sect called the Essenes developed communal living. What was different was the mixture of people and the way the wealthiest contributed. Those with plenty sold land and possessions to support the poorest.

Luke gives a particular example of this. A man sells his field (or farm) and gives the proceeds to the apostles for distribution. The apostles call him 'Barnabas' ('son of encouragement') because of this action. He is 'Barnabas' not because he speaks helpful words or empowers others; rather, he puts his money where his mouth is. He is filled with a spirit of generosity, which enables him to live out his faith in action as well as proclaim it.

Barnabas is destined to play a special part in the early Church. First, his donation is worthy of mention. Luke then records his travels with Paul, and later John Mark, his assistance at the council of Jerusalem and his work with the Church in Antioch. Tradition has it that this generous apostle was stoned to death in AD 61 in Cyprus.

COLLECT

Bountiful God, giver of all gifts,
who poured your Spirit upon your servant Barnabas
and gave him grace to encourage others:
help us, by his example,
to be generous in our judgements
and unselfish in our service;
through Jesus Christ your Son our Lord,
who is alive and reigns with you,
in the unity of the Holy Spirit,
one God, now and for ever.

Psalms **143**, 146
Joshua 4.1 – 5.1
Luke 9.51-end

Luke 9.51-end

'… go and proclaim the kingdom of God' (v.60)

Jews and Samaritans had feuded for centuries, setting up rival temples in Jerusalem and on Mount Gerizim. Therefore, a party of Jewish pilgrims making their way to Jerusalem would hardly be welcome visitors in a village in Samaria. James and John wish to enter into the age-old hostility by aping Elijah, calling down fire on their enemies. Jesus isn't impressed. He is concentrating on the journey to his destiny; this is not the time for destruction and retribution. Many of those he meets along the way are eager to follow him, but the time is short and complete dedication to the cause essential. Those who follow must be prepared to sacrifice anything that holds them back from single-minded completion of the journey.

Today the words of Jesus in this passage appear harsh as we endeavour to juggle competing demands on our relationships and loyalties. Jesus is not saying that family life doesn't matter and that duty and service to others should be set aside. However, in the kingdom of God, the way of Christ comes first, and other responsibilities will fall into their allotted place if we get that right. If we're in the habit of looking back over our shoulder to see where we've been, we may misjudge the path ahead. Looking to Christ takes precedence over all else. Guided by the Holy Spirit, proclaiming God's kingdom can become a natural and habitual part of our everyday living.

O Lord, from whom all good things come:
grant to us your humble servants,
that by your holy inspiration
we may think those things that are good,
and by your merciful guiding may perform the same;
through our Lord Jesus Christ,
who is alive and reigns with you,
in the unity of the Holy Spirit,
one God, now and for ever.

COLLECT

Luke 10.1-16

'Carry no purse, no bag, no sandals' (v.4)

Jesus appoints and commissions 35 pairs of evangelists to go ahead of him into God's harvest. Why does he choose 70 people? There are several suggestions, all with Old Testament connections. They could represent the 70 gentile nations mentioned in Genesis, or the 70 members of Jacob's family who go down to Egypt representing the people of Israel, or the 70 elders chosen by Moses who receive the Holy Spirit.

The 70 Jesus selects are to travel swiftly and lightly. The message of peace they carry is urgent, and they are not to be weighed down with unnecessary paraphernalia. Nor are they to waste time with those who won't listen. Israel is ripe for harvesting and there's no time to be lost: Jesus won't come this way again. Wolves are already snapping at his heels.

Not only does Jesus call us to follow him, he also sends us out ahead of him to herald his existence and harvest the fruit of his kingdom. It's a task that requires dedication and the ability to travel lightly through life, holding onto what really matters and letting go of the rest. Jesus calls you to proclaim his kingdom. What do you need to let go of for that to happen more effectively? We are reminded again that 'the harvest is plentiful but the labourers are few' (v.2). In your prayers today, ask the Lord to call passionate workers into his abundant harvest.

O Lord, from whom all good things come:
grant to us your humble servants,
that by your holy inspiration
we may think those things that are good,
and by your merciful guiding may perform the same;
through our Lord Jesus Christ,
who is alive and reigns with you,
in the unity of the Holy Spirit,
one God, now and for ever.

Psalm 147
Joshua 6.1-20
Luke 10.17-24

Luke 10.17-24

'... Jesus rejoiced in the Holy Spirit' (v.21)

Inspiration and joy accompany the return of the 70 missionaries. In Jesus' name they have seen wonders happen. Jesus too has had a vision in which he has seen the ancient enemy defeated. God's goodness and love will overcome all that seeks to pervert, overthrow or distort. Those that set themselves up in the place of God will be brought to order. There are echoes here of Ezekiel 28. This is a foretaste of the new age of the Spirit, which we celebrate during this time of Pentecost. Through the power of the Spirit, Christ dwells within and among his people so that deeds done in his name continue his work.

There is a deep sense of joy within Jesus in this passage as his relationship to God the Father is confirmed. He celebrates God's plan for humanity, which is simple and universal. It is not age or learning that qualifies people for the kingdom, but faith and humility. God's secrets are revealed to and grasped by children rather than the wise and intelligent.

If we acknowledge Jesus as Lord, then the Holy Spirit dwells within us. Confident that we are filled with the Spirit and called by God, all manner of things can be accomplished in Christ's name. Rather than bewailing the state of the Church and the nation, let's rejoice with Jesus in the Holy Spirit and continue God's work in his name.

What wonders will you see today?

> O Lord, from whom all good things come:
> grant to us your humble servants,
> that by your holy inspiration
> we may think those things that are good,
> and by your merciful guiding may perform the same;
> through our Lord Jesus Christ,
> who is alive and reigns with you,
> in the unity of the Holy Spirit,
> one God, now and for ever.

COLLECT

175

Monday 16 June

Psalms 1, 2, 3
Joshua 7.1-15
Luke 10.25-37

Luke 10.25-37

'And who is my neighbour?' (v.29)

The lawyer asked Jesus a question to which he believed he already had the answer – 'what must I do to inherit eternal life?' (v.25). Jesus knew that the lawyer was testing him, and he reflected the question back to him according to the man's own belief: 'What is written in the law?' (v.26). Sure enough, the lawyer knew exactly what was written, and Jesus affirmed his answer: '...do this, and you will live' (v.28). But the lawyer wanted Jesus to go further and confirm his understanding of 'neighbour': someone just like me.

Jesus' response broke all the barriers and all the limitations and stereotypes that filled the lawyer's head about the meaning of neighbour. By choosing the Samaritan, the traditional enemy of the Jews, as the example of a good neighbour, Jesus redefined 'neighbour' and, at the same time, 'enemy'. He brought the two to meet in the act of mercy.

We still have our own ideas about those around us and who is 'in' and who is 'out'. We constantly need Jesus Christ to challenge us to break down our own barriers. We must always remember that Jesus Christ, through his cross and resurrection, has already decided that everybody is 'in' and nobody is 'out'. Therefore, as Christians, we have no enemy, and every human being is our neighbour. The great challenge of this parable for us today is to see everyone as a neighbour and to be a neighbour to everyone.

COLLECT

Almighty and everlasting God,
you have given us your servants grace,
by the confession of a true faith,
to acknowledge the glory of the eternal Trinity
and in the power of the divine majesty to worship the Unity:
keep us steadfast in this faith,
that we may evermore be defended from all adversities;
through Jesus Christ your Son our Lord,
who is alive and reigns with you,
in the unity of the Holy Spirit,
one God, now and for ever.

Luke 10.38-end

'... the better part' (v.42)

This reading starts with Martha welcoming Jesus into her home, which tells us that she was the host, whose job – especially in the Middle East – has always been to look after guests and make them feel honoured and welcome.

I remember that when I used to come home from college, my mother would be running everywhere to cook my favourite food, expressing her love through her hospitality, and this is absolutely typical of my Syrian culture. Sometimes even our best customs and practices distract us from experiencing 'the better part'! I am sure that Jesus was touched by Martha's hospitality, but he was even more pleased that Mary had stopped everything to be with him. Of course, I was delighted to see my mother doing everything for me when I came home, but what I really wanted was to spend time with her.

Sometimes we fuss over religion and get 'religiously busy' by being involved in the many mundane tasks at church. If we do that, we can miss the better part: we are there to spend time with the Lord, like Mary.

Spending time with friends, family or God means opening up and being vulnerable, and we can be tempted to avoid this vulnerability through appearing busy. What is important is to spend time with the other, interacting with them and being changed by them – this is especially true in our relationship with God.

Holy God,
faithful and unchanging:
enlarge our minds with the knowledge of your truth,
and draw us more deeply into the mystery of your love,
that we may truly worship you,
Father, Son and Holy Spirit,
one God, now and for ever.

COLLECT

Wednesday 18 June

Luke 11.1-13

'Lord, teach us to pray ...' (v.1)

What Jesus gives us in this text is the framework for our prayers, rather than something to be learned by heart for repetition. Prayer is a relationship with God, not a monologue for us to say from memory. Jesus was clear that prayer is not about just asking God for things; God knows what we need and he is always generous and giving. We should think of prayer as a process whereby we build a relationship with God through Christ. God is not a shopping website where we enter our requirements, press a button and wait for the goods to be delivered. God is in constant communication with us, and we should be in constant, intimate communication with him. Prayer should be a *state of being* rather than a special, discrete event like going to the doctor. We only think of our doctors when we want something from them.

God is different: he talks to us through other people, through events in our lives and through experiences, and we need to hear him and receive him. The framework for prayer that Jesus has given us in this passage includes praise, forgiveness, and asking God to help. Our prayer, like our relationship with God, like our relationships with our family and friends, should be on many, many levels. Prayer is an intimate bond with God, and this can only flourish if it is a two-way conversation: we listen, and we share in true fellowship.

COLLECT

Almighty and everlasting God,
you have given us your servants grace,
by the confession of a true faith,
to acknowledge the glory of the eternal Trinity
and in the power of the divine majesty to worship the Unity:
keep us steadfast in this faith,
that we may evermore be defended from all adversities;
through Jesus Christ your Son our Lord,
who is alive and reigns with you,
in the unity of the Holy Spirit,
one God, now and for ever.

Psalm 147
Deuteronomy 8.2-16
1 Corinthians 10.1-17

Thursday 19 June

Day of Thanksgiving for the
Institution of the Holy Communion
(Corpus Christi)

1 Corinthians 10.1-17

'... is it not a sharing in the blood of Christ?
... is it not a sharing in the body of Christ?' (v.16)

One of the most fundamental elements of the Christian faith is the resurrection of Jesus Christ; this glorious act of the love of God has given us, the believers in his name, the power of the presence of Christ in our lives. As we approach the altar to take part in the celebration of Holy Communion, we are declaring and witnessing to the real presence of Jesus Christ in his body, the Church.

Christian denominations may differ on the doctrinal definition of the broken body of Christ and his shed blood – the bread and the wine – but we do all agree that this act of breaking bread and lifting the cup is the physical and visible sign of our fellowship with the Risen Lord. We are spiritual beings, but we remain flesh and blood, and we need tangible icons such as the bread and the wine in order to share with each other our faith and joy in what Christ achieved in his cross and resurrection. We do this because he himself used these icons of his earthly culture to establish this link between the physical and the spiritual.

Every time we participate in the simple and deep act of receiving Communion, let us never forget that we are not alone; the Risen Lord is our unity and power, especially when we carry our cross in life. The real presence of Jesus Christ in the Communion and in our lives gives us confidence that God is always *Emmanuel* – God is with us.

Lord Jesus Christ,
we thank you that in this wonderful sacrament
you have given us the memorial of your passion:
grant us so to reverence the sacred mysteries
of your body and blood
that we may know within ourselves
and show forth in our lives
the fruits of your redemption;
for you are alive and reign with the Father
in the unity of the Holy Spirit,
one God, now and for ever.

COLLECT

Friday 20 June

Psalms 17, **19**
Joshua 9.3-26
Luke 11.29-36

Luke 11.29-36

'Your eye is the lamp of your body' (v.34)

Here is another flash of Jesus' genius; he uses an ordinary icon from his earthly culture to illustrate a particularly profound idea. This time Jesus chose something that everyone would have used – a lamp – and turns something so commonplace into an extraordinary emblem of inner enlightenment. Without the light, we would live in darkness. In exactly the same way, we look at life, at the world around us; if we look at the world through the light of Christ – Jesus had said 'I am the light of the world' (John 8.12) – then our life changes and the whole world is illuminated with his light. When we treat our fellow human beings with love – which is God himself – then we find that our whole perspective on life has completely changed. Life becomes more positive, more fruitful, and more joyful; this holds true even during times of crisis.

God is love, and God is also light. In God, light and love become interchangeable.

Jesus acknowledges that there is darkness – there will be trouble in life. But he focuses not on the darkness but on the light that can conquer darkness. As St John says, 'The light shines in the darkness, and the darkness did not overcome it' (John 1.5).

We have the choice – we can live in darkness, or we can embrace the light and live in a world bathed with the light of Christ.

COLLECT

Almighty and everlasting God,
you have given us your servants grace,
by the confession of a true faith,
to acknowledge the glory of the eternal Trinity
and in the power of the divine majesty to worship the Unity:
keep us steadfast in this faith,
that we may evermore be defended from all adversities;
through Jesus Christ your Son our Lord,
who is alive and reigns with you,
in the unity of the Holy Spirit,
one God, now and for ever.

Luke 11.37-end

'But woe to you Pharisees! For you ... neglect justice and the love of God' (v.42)

A scandalous Jesus appears in this passage, who breaks the rules of hospitality and whose behaviour is not that of a welcome guest! He launches a fierce attack on the Pharisees and lawyers. In the three years of Jesus' open ministry, we see him as the loving, giving healer, friend and companion to the ordinary people and especially to the outcast and the marginalized. However, when it comes to the leaders of society and religion, we see a different Jesus; suddenly, in the face of the leaders' corruption, Jesus the meek lamb becomes the roaring lion.

We often portray Jesus as soft and 'fluffy', floating along on a cloud of love, but when it comes to the essence of the law – justice and mercy – then his love has no compromise, and he confronts those who come between people and God. It is clear that Jesus hates hypocrisy and the use of power for selfish purposes, and when he encounters this, Jesus becomes a revolutionary. Jesus always fought against the leaders when they abused the law and the covenant with God to gain power for themselves and to control the people. Jesus came to liberate the people from this abuse. Sadly, we still find this abuse in some religious leadership even today.

As Christians learning from our master, we should work to find this fine balance between reflecting the love of God through forgiveness and mercy, and challenging injustice, hypocrisy and corruption.

Holy God,
faithful and unchanging:
enlarge our minds with the knowledge of your truth,
and draw us more deeply into the mystery of your love,
that we may truly worship you,
Father, Son and Holy Spirit,
one God, now and for ever.

COLLECT

Monday 23 June

Psalms 27, **30**
Joshua 14
Luke 12.1-12

Luke 12.1-12

'... for the Holy Spirit will teach you ... what you ought to say' (v.12)

In a religiously and culturally diverse world, exactly like that at the time of Christ, Christians unfortunately can sometimes be the first to compromise on the expression of their faith. Talking about faith is mostly understood as being evangelistic – 'I talk about my faith because I want others to adopt it' – but this is far from true. If we believe that our faith is part of our identity – part of who we are – then expressing it should not be a problem. We can easily talk about our nationality; we can talk about our politics, our job, our favourite TV show, our friends, and our family. Expressing our identity means living and being who we are!

Let's remember that when we express our faith, we should always leave a space for the Holy Spirit to move us; we are not reliant only on our own abilities. Trusting in God is an essential and most valuable element of faith. It is good to be vulnerable, to let go and let the Holy Spirit empower us when we express our faith. When Jesus saw the religion of the Pharisees, he saw a religion totally devoid of the Holy Spirit, one based entirely on façade and control.

The real test of faith is to live it. That determines how much our faith is part of who we are, and how much the Holy Spirit is working in us.

COLLECT

O God,
the strength of all those who put their trust in you,
mercifully accept our prayers
and, because through the weakness of our mortal nature
we can do no good thing without you,
grant us the help of your grace,
that in the keeping of your commandments
we may please you both in will and deed;
through Jesus Christ your Son our Lord,
who is alive and reigns with you,
in the unity of the Holy Spirit,
one God, now and for ever.

Psalms 50, 149
Ecclesiasticus 48.1-10
or Malachi 3.1-6
Matthew 11.2-19

Tuesday 24 June

The Birth of John the Baptist

Matthew 11.2-19

'Are you the one who is to come,
or are we to wait for another?' (v.2)

The lion of righteousness, sitting helpless in jail, was still able to send a message to his cousin, the one the world was waiting for. 'Are you the one who is to come, or are we to wait for another?' The message of John elicited the first manifesto of Jesus, which he declared again when he visited his home town of Nazareth: the leaders gave him the scrolls, and Jesus quoted from Isaiah: 'The Spirit of the Lord is upon me, because he has anointed me to bring good news to the poor. He has sent me to proclaim release to the captives and recovery of sight to the blind, to let the oppressed go free, to proclaim the year of the Lord's favour.' (Isaiah 61.1–2; Luke 4.18-19)

Jesus knew that John would understand his response, based on the words of Isaiah, and that John would rejoice that his mission to prepare the way had borne fruit. John was not the light, but he pointed at the light, who is the Lord Jesus Christ (John 1.8). Every Christian can be like John the Baptist, pointing at and reflecting the light of Christ and repeating to the whole world the same manifesto of Jesus. What is the Church if it cannot reflect the light of Christ and 'proclaim the year of the Lord's favour' – to declare openly that the kingdom of God is with us and to invite everyone to become a part of it?

Almighty God,
by whose providence your servant John the Baptist
was wonderfully born,
and sent to prepare the way of your Son our Saviour
by the preaching of repentance:
lead us to repent according to his preaching
and, after his example,
constantly to speak the truth, boldly to rebuke vice,
and patiently to suffer for the truth's sake;
through Jesus Christ your Son our Lord,
who is alive and reigns with you,
in the unity of the Holy Spirit,
one God, now and for ever.

COLLECT

183

Wednesday 25 June

Luke 12.22-31

'... do not keep striving for what you are to eat and what you are to drink, and do not keep worrying' (v.29)

A loud cry from Christ to free us from the burden of worry! This cry could not be more relevant today as we live in a world consumed by the rush to earn and to spend. Two thousand years since God journeyed to our world and preached in our streets, his words still resonate with our busy-ness to obtain the latest technology, to drive a faster car, to live in a bigger house filled with more of everything – except faith, love and justice. But Jesus is not just talking about material things; he knows that there will always be crises in our lives, but no crisis has ever been averted or ended through fear and worry. If we worry, then we think we are facing life on our own. We are not alone, and this is the message that Jesus wants us to understand. The words of Christ deserve a pause so that we can think about the contrast between what is truly essential and what actually dominates our lives.

To be citizens of the kingdom of God, we need to take a decision – a decision to shed our worry and fear and take on the cloak of Christ, giving him the reign over our lives and freeing us to live an abundant life with him and with each other.

COLLECT

O God,
the strength of all those who put their trust in you,
mercifully accept our prayers
and, because through the weakness of our mortal nature
we can do no good thing without you,
grant us the help of your grace,
that in the keeping of your commandments
we may please you both in will and deed;
through Jesus Christ your Son our Lord,
who is alive and reigns with you,
in the unity of the Holy Spirit,
one God, now and for ever.

Psalm **37***
Joshua 23
Luke 12.32-40

Luke 12.32-40

'... an unfailing treasure in heaven' (v.33)

The ultimate question that Christ puts before us, and which we all must answer, is: 'Where is your heart?' The heart of the matter is our citizenship in the Lord's kingdom, and that is determined by where our hearts lie.

If my heart is with the Lord, then that decides the direction of my life, and this decision affects every aspect of my life. We all know that when we put our hearts into something, then we give it our best. The Lord deserves our best, and he deserves to have our hearts.

The heart of a volcano throws burning magma, not pieces of ice; likewise, a good heart does not produce evil any more than an evil heart radiates goodness. Our relationships, our families, our work, everything flows from where our heart is. When my heart is with Christ, then all aspects of my life will be on the right track, and they will be fruitful and fulfilling, even in the darkest times. The cross is always followed by the resurrection, and the last word of God to humanity was not death upon the cross but life in the resurrection. Our crises are like the cross, and when we ask for God's help then we have the sure and certain hope that we will experience the joy of the resurrection.

God of truth,
help us to keep your law of love
and to walk in ways of wisdom,
that we may find true life
in Jesus Christ your Son.

COLLECT

Friday 27 June

Psalm **31**
Joshua 24.1-28
Luke 12.41-48

Luke 12.41-48

'From everyone to whom much has been given,
much will be required' (v.48)

Jesus makes it clear to us all that no one is left without gifts. We all have the responsibility to use these gifts wisely and diligently. It is extremely important that we first discover these gifts and know the abilities with which God has entrusted us. Then we face the choice of what to do with our gifts. According to this choice, we decide the quality of our lives. If we choose to use our gifts properly and prayerfully, then God will bless our lives richly. If we choose to abuse our gifts, then that will be reflected also in the quality of our lives.

Sometimes it is not easy to act upon our gifts and to use them. But at least we need, with the help of the Holy Spirit, to try to use our gifts. When God calls us to do something, he empowers us to do it. Twelve insignificant people were called by the Lord to be his disciples; by the power of the Holy Spirit these people were able to change the face of history forever. I am sure that Peter would never have imagined that he would stand and speak to a crowd, and that each person there would understand him in his own language! Could Saul, the great persecutor of the early Church, ever envisage that he would become Paul, the Apostle of Christ to the whole world?

Christ calls us, and God empowers us.

COLLECT

O God,
the strength of all those who put their trust in you,
mercifully accept our prayers
and, because through the weakness of our mortal nature
we can do no good thing without you,
grant us the help of your grace,
that in the keeping of your commandments
we may please you both in will and deed;
through Jesus Christ your Son our Lord,
who is alive and reigns with you,
in the unity of the Holy Spirit,
one God, now and for ever.

Psalm 41, **42**, 43
Joshua 24.29-end
Luke 12.49-end

Luke 12.49-end

'... they will be divided' (v.53)

Here we hear the grumpy voice of Jesus, rebuking and warning, showing his rebellious side. How could Jesus the peacemaker, the saviour of the world, be a cause of division? We must understand this passage in Jesus' earthly context. Here, Jesus seems to be attacking the family. Today we hear so much about restoring the family, and returning to 'family values', but things were very different at that time, and Jesus was dealing with a genuine social illness.

Here, he was talking about the unhealthily tight family bonds of the Middle East. As someone from the Middle East, I do know how such bonds can be suffocating. Faith in Christ can lead us in any direction, even to break away from family, as I had to do when I left the warmth of the family home to study in the hell of Beirut during the Lebanese civil war.

Jesus was aware of the limitations and the problems of his society, and we often hear him challenging his earthly community, pushing people to acknowledge, address and overcome these problems. In this sense, Jesus becomes a revolutionary voice in our lives, shaking our complacency and forcing us out of our comfort zones, just as he did in the first century AD.

Today, we need to hear the encouraging message within this text: Jesus is calling us to allow our faith to challenge us and to re-examine our lives.

God of truth,
help us to keep your law of love
and to walk in ways of wisdom,
that we may find true life
in Jesus Christ your Son.

COLLECT

Monday 30 June

Luke 13.1-9

'... unless you repent' (v.5)

People ask Jesus about the murder of Galilean pilgrims, perhaps wondering if he will reinforce the prevailing viewpoint that people suffer because they have sinned. Instead, Jesus points to two causes: the ruthless power of the Roman occupying forces for whom religious rituals provided opportunities for unchecked violence, and the risk of – literally and metaphorically – building structures on flawed foundations. Jesus knows that the people of Jerusalem face annihilation unless they begin to live out his teaching, standing on the firm ground of God's love and justice.

The only thing that could possibly overcome the power of Rome then – or the effects of global financial mismanagement or systemic greed now – is the power of prayer released in ever-increasing circles of influence as more and more people, whom God has named as his own, put God at the centre of their lives.

This transformation from self-centred to God-centred living doesn't happen quickly. The fig tree story reminds us of two things: first, the hope-filled patience of the 'gardener', the Spirit of Jesus who nurtures our souls until we begin to bear that sacred fruit of love, joy and peace (Galatians 5.22); and second, that the consequences of failing to follow Jesus are as withering and inevitable as the axing of a barren tree.

What needs to be transformed in you, in me, in our communities? And what are the consequences if no changes are made?

COLLECT

Lord, you have taught us
that all our doings without love are nothing worth:
send your Holy Spirit
and pour into our hearts that most excellent gift of love,
the true bond of peace and of all virtues,
without which whoever lives is counted dead before you.
Grant this for your only Son Jesus Christ's sake,
who is alive and reigns with you,
in the unity of the Holy Spirit,
one God, now and for ever.

Psalms **48**, 52
Judges 4.1-23
Luke 13.10-21

Luke 13.10-21

'... you are set free' (v.12)

What indescribable joy and relief for this unnamed woman, as she experiences the power of Jesus and embraces physical, emotional and spiritual liberation. Her bubbling, joyful praise is in sharp contrast to the response of the leader of the synagogue who bellows 'oughts' and 'shoulds', bound himself by fear of change and his ego-desire for status, untouched by the needs of those seeking healing.

No wonder the listeners are delighted when Jesus speaks passionately of the woman's right to freedom as a 'daughter of Abraham'. Through her healing they glimpse God's kingdom among them, for this event, though arguably small in the grand scheme of things, demonstrates the 'mustard seed' and 'yeast' principle of the kingdom: each act of love has potential to touch others and turn their hearts towards wholeness, towards God. Any pebble of grace, when thrown into life's great sea, sets in motion a ripple of hope, energy and joy, which gathers momentum each time someone recognizes the Spirit of God and does their part to keep the waves of God's love expanding.

There was shame among Jesus' opponents after he had spoken. Perhaps a ripple of love eventually lapped at the toes of the synagogue official, helping him revisit his way of relating, and releasing him from his need to be centre stage!

In what ways do we constrain or enable the continuing expansion of God's waves of love?

Faithful Creator,
whose mercy never fails:
deepen our faithfulness to you
and to your living Word,
Jesus Christ our Lord.

COLLECT

Wednesday 2 July

Psalm 119.57-80
Judges 5
Luke 13.22-end

Luke 13.22-end

'... you were not willing!'(v.34)

Jesus knows how hard it is for us as human beings to fulfil our potential as children of God. We give God our hearts, then take them back again; we tell Jesus we will follow him, then we divert down the nearest primrose path as something 'other' distracts us from the One who *is* the Way. The door to kingdom life *is* narrow – we can enter fully only if we are prepared to give God our bulky baggage: failures and fears, pride or greed, successes and achievements, the ongoing impact of emotional pain, the defences and masks we've adopted and, most of all, our need to be in control.

Jesus yearns over Jerusalem, longing to save its people from the suffering that is to come, but they have a long history of spurning God's messengers and are not willing to turn and find life.

Jesus yearns over us too. He knows that occasional, superficial connection with God isn't enough to build the deeply trusting relationship that makes possible the dismantling of a lifetime's armour of avoidance of pain so our spiritual life may grow and our service of others deepen.

Just as a mother hen offers her life to protect her young, so Jesus will soon offer himself in an act that will ultimately make possible true spiritual intimacy for all humanity – that we may live with and in him forever.

If we are willing ...

COLLECT

Lord, you have taught us
that all our doings without love are nothing worth:
send your Holy Spirit
and pour into our hearts that most excellent gift of love,
the true bond of peace and of all virtues,
without which whoever lives is counted dead before you.
Grant this for your only Son Jesus Christ's sake,
who is alive and reigns with you,
in the unity of the Holy Spirit,
one God, now and for ever.

Psalms 92, 146
2 Samuel 15.17-21
or Ecclesiasticus 2
John 11.1-16

Thursday 3 July

Thomas the Apostle

John 11.1-16

'Let us also go, that we may die with him' (v.16)

Today we remember Jesus' disciple Thomas. Keeping in mind the familiar story of Thomas' refusal to accept the other disciples' accounts of the resurrection (John 20.24-25), we look at another passage set earlier 'across the Jordan', when Jesus hears of Lazarus' serious illness. Knowing that ultimately this sorry situation will reveal God's glory, Jesus initially delays his response. When he finally suggests going to Lazarus, his disciples, still shaken by the Jews' recent threat to stone Jesus, try to put him off – understandably caught between their loyalty and love for Jesus and their human aversion to risk.

It is not the 'leadership team' of Peter, James and John that finally prompts the disciples to action, it is Thomas who addresses the others and invites their commitment to be Jesus' companion – even if the outcome might be death. Thomas steps up, ready to walk with Jesus wherever that journey might lead.

There is no sign of doubt here, but there *is* quiet courage – just as there is quiet courage in Thomas stating his need to experience *for himself* the truth of the resurrection. He is not content with second-hand God-connection; he wants the face-to-face reality. And later, in an intense encounter, he has that very opportunity and comes to acknowledge Jesus as 'My Lord and my God' (John 20.26-28).

How much of your God-connection is 'second-hand'? Talk to God about what you long for.

Almighty and eternal God,
who, for the firmer foundation of our faith,
allowed your holy apostle Thomas
to doubt the resurrection of your Son
till word and sight convinced him:
grant to us, who have not seen, that we also may believe
and so confess Christ as our Lord and our God;
who is alive and reigns with you,
in the unity of the Holy Spirit,
one God, now and for ever.

COLLECT

Friday 4 July

Psalms **51**, 54
Judges 6.25-end
Luke 14.12-24

Luke 14.12-24

'But they all alike began to make excuses' (v.18)

Jesus reminds his host, a Pharisee, of the blessing gained by giving hospitality to those who are unable to repay it. We can almost see the nods of agreement offered around the table, but the listeners' self-satisfaction is quickly deflated. Jesus begins to draw an unmistakable picture of their rejection of God's invitation – and God's frustrated response: the 'master of the house' orders that the welcome be offered more widely to include those considered on the edges of Jewish society and, when there is still room, to be extended to the gentiles, to anyone who finds the appeal of the love of God compelling.

Matters of material wealth, the distraction of newly acquired assets, and the duties and delights of family ties shaped their excuses – and continue to shape ours. Busy-ness *seems* to be at the centre of modern excuses for squeezing God out of our lives, but what it really boils down to is that we choose to make something other than God our priority. Time and again, God holds out the invitation to come close in prayer, close enough to see the love – and the challenge – in Jesus' eyes. We struggle to sit still long enough to be loved, slow to notice God's grace at work, bringing in the kingdom in the midst of the ordinary stuff of life.

What keeps you, keeps me, from prayer, petition and praise?

COLLECT

Lord, you have taught us
that all our doings without love are nothing worth:
send your Holy Spirit
and pour into our hearts that most excellent gift of love,
the true bond of peace and of all virtues,
without which whoever lives is counted dead before you.
Grant this for your only Son Jesus Christ's sake,
who is alive and reigns with you,
in the unity of the Holy Spirit,
one God, now and for ever.

Psalm **68**
Judges 7
Luke 14.25-end

Luke 14.25-end

'None of you can become my disciple if you do not give up ...' (v.33)

This passage shocks. Jesus confronts his listeners – and us – with the cost of discipleship, the level of commitment required for co-builders of the kingdom. Nothing is to hinder our following the way of Jesus. Not our loved ones, our work, our health, our possessions, nor our desire for a life of ease or power. Not others' expectations, nor our own 'oughts' and 'shoulds', nor our need to make things happen. Nothing.

Jesus invites us to consider the cost – not with business-like analysis and columns of pluses and minuses, but by carefully discerning his unfolding call on our lives, considering the implications of that call, and then bringing our worries and needs to God so that the Spirit is free to work in and through us as we follow Jesus.

Fundamentally, this difficult passage is about whether or not we trust God enough to surrender our lives, our total wellbeing and that of our families to God. Are we able to put God first, to rely on God for *all* that we need, not with a lazy, fatalistic 'leave it to the Big Guy' attitude, but with determined trust and the Spirit's guidance, step by trembling, exploratory step?

The way of Christ may include downward mobility, giving away rather than acquiring, holding everything lightly, being open to the unexpected, being prepared to offer our whole selves for the work of the kingdom. It will also include being truly fulfilled, and infused with joy.

Faithful Creator,
whose mercy never fails:
deepen our faithfulness to you
and to your living Word,
Jesus Christ our Lord.

COLLECT

Monday 7 July

Luke 15.1-10

'Rejoice with me...' (v.6)

Using two examples that would have resonated with the experience of his listeners, Jesus paints a radical picture of a God who actively seeks the lost and celebrates the finding with a party of heavenly proportions.

Years ago we lost our five-year-old son in a crowded shopping mall overseas. The panic, the eternity of waiting and the anxious rehearsal of drastic outcomes in my motherly mind, were replaced by utter joy when he was back in my arms, safe and sound.

How much more does God rejoice over us with singing (Zephaniah 3.17) when we are back in the arms of the One who gives us life, and will not let us go? The God whom Jesus embodies does not give up on us even if we have wandered away or been careless with the treasures of our faith.

Perhaps our spiritual practices are patchy and our connection with God compromised by the burden of the years. Maybe we are labouring under a load of guilt or are beset by gut-wrenching grief. Whatever has moved us further away from God need no longer hold power over us. Even if we have wandered far outside the 'sheepfold', God seeks us, sees us through the lens of compassion, and works and longs for our returning.

What examples of losing, finding and rejoicing are there in your own experience?

COLLECT

Almighty God,
you have broken the tyranny of sin
and have sent the Spirit of your Son into our hearts
    whereby we call you Father:
give us grace to dedicate our freedom to your service,
that we and all creation may be brought
    to the glorious liberty of the children of God;
through Jesus Christ your Son our Lord,
who is alive and reigns with you,
in the unity of the Holy Spirit,
one God, now and for ever.

Luke 15.11-end

'Then he became angry and refused to go in' (v.28)

All his life the older brother has had at his fingertips the benefits of his father's character and resources and yet he is unable to recognize what is rightfully his until his errant sibling returns. He sees their father's joy but does not share it, angered by the welcome, envious of the extravagant celebration, alienated by a false sense of injustice.

The younger son 'woke up' to his need of his father's mercy and made the journey home, rehearsing words of confession and regret that were rendered unnecessary by the father's unequivocal embrace. He knows he is not worthy, yet his father's response sweeps away any sense of shame or failure and instead wraps him round in vestments of delight.

But the older son has yet to 'wake up' to the reality that all the father has is his. He has yet to learn how to ask for what he needs; he has yet to believe that his father's love is truly unconditional. And so, instead of being a participant in the feast, he is a disgruntled observer, held back by his own ignorance of his father's true nature: love in its fullest expression.

Sulking and self-righteous, the older brother in all of us struggles to recognise the grace of God in which we 'live and move and have our being' (Acts 17.28).

Are you, am I, *really* awake to the generous love God lavishes on us here and now?

God our saviour,
look on this wounded world
in pity and in power;
hold us fast to your promises of peace
won for us by your Son,
our Saviour Jesus Christ.

COLLECT

Wednesday 9 July

Luke 16.1-18

'God knows your hearts ...' (v.15)

Business ethics are currently being questioned as global banking systems and entire countries buckle under the dynamics Jesus highlights in this parable: the shrewd and self-interested avoid their responsibilities and create indebtedness, caring nothing about justice or community wellbeing. Meanwhile their superiors, instead of dismissing them for dishonesty, give them bonuses!

When mammon is the god being worshipped, much human ingenuity goes into designing systems that benefit a few at the expense of the many. And we help sustain systemic injustice whenever we avoid tax, tweak an insurance claim, gamble our wages, purchase goods made by exploited workers, turn a blind eye to dubious work practices, make wealth acquisition our life goal and fail to help the poor.

We might try to justify ourselves, but we know – and God knows – that we are reluctant to put all of our resources at God's disposal. Instead we put our energy and time into whatever, superficially, makes us feel safe and successful. Beneath the surface however, we don't trust God's provision; perhaps we just don't know God well enough to believe that God wants us to be eternally rich – now.

True riches are the fruit of God's Spirit flourishing in the hearts of godly men and women of integrity. Love, joy, peace, patience, kindness, generosity, faithfulness, gentleness and self-control (Galatians 5.22-23) cannot be purchased and cannot be sold, but multiply as God works in and among those who follow Jesus.

COLLECT

Almighty God,
you have broken the tyranny of sin
and have sent the Spirit of your Son into our hearts
    whereby we call you Father:
give us grace to dedicate our freedom to your service,
that we and all creation may be brought
    to the glorious liberty of the children of God;
through Jesus Christ your Son our Lord,
who is alive and reigns with you,
in the unity of the Holy Spirit,
one God, now and for ever.

Psalm **78.1-39***
Judges 11.1-11
Luke 16.19-end

Luke 16.19-end

'There was a rich man ...' (v.19)

Through a vivid story we encounter poverty and riches, suffering and serenity, consequences and the hint of conversion, as once again Jesus highlights how hard it is for those who make wealth their goal to connect meaningfully with those at the other end of the scale.

The wealthy man was poor – spiritually poor. There is no compassionate connection with the needy. Instead, self-indulgence and indifference formed the barrier that separated him from the very clear suffering of a fellow human being. Even in post-death extremity, when he first pleads with Abraham, there is no admission of wrongdoing, no genuine statement of regret or remorse but rather a continuation of a lifelong pattern of trying to get others to serve his needs. He doesn't own up to his failure of character and behaviour; nor does he realise that the gulf that separates him from healing and hope can be crossed only by sincere repentance and the grace of God.

Maybe, towards the end, there is a glimmer of possible redemption for the rich man. In asking Abraham to send Lazarus to his brothers, he thinks of someone other than himself, perhaps for the first time. Maybe this is the start of a shift in awareness that will eventually see the chasm bridged by the hand of God reaching out to welcome the image of Jesus, rekindled in the heart of the penitent.

That same hand is extended to you, to me, today.

God our saviour,
look on this wounded world
in pity and in power;
hold us fast to your promises of peace
won for us by your Son,
our Saviour Jesus Christ.

COLLECT

Friday 11 July

Luke 17.1-10

'... if there is repentance, you must forgive' (v.3)

When wronged, many of us seek neither revenge nor compensation; what we look for is repentance – acknowledgement of the transgression, acceptance of responsibility and a genuine expression of remorse, rather than some formulaic legal letter designed to minimize judgement. Biblical gatherings of 'elders' or contemporary Restorative Justice conferences aid this process by bringing the injured party and the offender together in a safe, mediated environment where rebuke is allowed, repentance can be expressed and the stream of forgiveness may begin to flow.

For Jesus tells us that we must forgive ... and keep on forgiving whenever there is repentance.

In this quick-fix world, most of us are accustomed to ready solutions applied to any situation with the expectation of immediate success or results. But forgiving takes time – it can be protracted, messy and contentious. As followers of Christ, if we want to forgive, the Spirit will walk with us through the emotionally tough, s-l-o-w, mercy-journey as we allow ourselves to face the reality of the offence, as we listen and weep, acknowledge our hurt and anger, speak aloud our truth and hear the offender's confession and contrition. And then, if we ask, God will provide the will and the compassion we need to enable our deep, costly and liberating forgiveness as we draw on the faith Jesus speaks of – the faith that can move a mountain of pain and grief and anger, and kindle the fire of transforming love.

COLLECT

Almighty God,
you have broken the tyranny of sin
and have sent the Spirit of your Son into our hearts
    whereby we call you Father:
give us grace to dedicate our freedom to your service,
that we and all creation may be brought
    to the glorious liberty of the children of God;
through Jesus Christ your Son our Lord,
who is alive and reigns with you,
in the unity of the Holy Spirit,
one God, now and for ever.

Psalms **76**, 79
Judges 12.1-7
Luke 17.11-19

Luke 17.11-19

*'Then one of them, when he saw that he was healed, turned back ...
and thanked him.' (vv.15-16)*

We've all neglected to communicate our thanks at times, so we can empathise with the nine lepers. Understandably preoccupied with their healing, perhaps they couldn't wait to be declared 'disease free'. But, by not turning back, they miss the deep shared joy of giving praise to God, and having their lives enriched by Jesus' delight in their wholeness.

The nine Jews should have acknowledged God's goodness, but instead the recognition comes from an unlikely person – a Samaritan. As an outcast, this unclean foreigner is not entitled to anything from anyone. Jesus, however, is interested not in 'entitlement' but in 'gift'. In the Samaritan's loving response we see the rare expression of gratitude as he recognizes that the true source of this gift of healing is God. His gratitude prompts a precious moment of personal encounter with Jesus, for whom his thanks is a gift.

By increasingly acknowledging that all we have and are is God's gift, we start to dismantle the culture of entitlement that subtly undermines our capacity for contentment. Gratitude, welling up from the heart, fosters humility in us and deepens our relationship with God. Scripture reminds us 'in every thing give thanks' (1 Thessalonians 5.18, *AV*). A regular review of the grace of God at work in the events of the day – however small or difficult they may seem – is a valuable spiritual practice available to us all.

Will you turn to Jesus in gratitude at the end of the day?

God our saviour,
look on this wounded world
in pity and in power;
hold us fast to your promises of peace
won for us by your Son,
our Saviour Jesus Christ.

COLLECT

Monday 14 July

Luke 17.20-end

'... the kingdom of God is among you' (v.20)

Deep Impact is a 1998 Hollywood disaster movie, starring Robert Duvall and Morgan Freeman. A meteorite is on target for what is described as 'an extinction level event' by colliding with the earth. It does not spoil the story to say that millions die but that many survive. As in most disaster movies, the focus is on ordinary characters and their relationships in the impossibly tense story. Even in the face of disaster, people have to go about their daily lives. Comforting routines sometimes provide even more comfort when everything is falling apart. Most important, the very fact of impending disaster provides people with the opportunity to be transformed in the present. Dwelling on future catastrophic change always affects the ethics and relationships of right now.

When Jesus talks about the coming kingdom of God, it is not possible to separate the future from the present. The urgency of the kingdom applies right now. The choices have to be made today. Whether you are to die or to be spared, reconciliation and sacrifice for others must not be delayed.

In the movie, a character deliberately gives up her guaranteed place of safety from the disaster to a woman and child. A young woman cares more about being reconciled with her father than surviving.

The deep impact of the kingdom of God is not to be avoided or kicked into touch; it is to be embraced in our choices now as though Christ has come in glory.

O God, the protector of all who trust in you,
without whom nothing is strong, nothing is holy:
increase and multiply upon us your mercy;
that with you as our ruler and guide
we may so pass through things temporal
that we lose not our hold on things eternal;
grant this, heavenly Father,
for our Lord Jesus Christ's sake,
who is alive and reigns with you,
in the unity of the Holy Spirit,
one God, now and for ever.

Luke 18.1-14

'Will he delay long in helping them?' (v.7)

Ruth Burrows is a Carmelite nun who has written a number of books about prayer. She once wrote about one of her sisters in the convent who revealed that she had had no spiritual consolations in more than 25 years of living the religious life. Most people would have given up, but she was convinced that prayer was still the only answer to life. She claimed the experience of God's absence was so palpable that she knew he was there and that she should persist in prayer.

The first parable in today's reading is not focused so much on the widow as the unjust judge. He could not be further from what God is like in responding to lively petition, but we are led to see what God is actually like in responding to prayer when we are serious in our beseeching, but also when we are not.

In the 2006 film, *The Devil Wears Prada*, the fashion editor played by Meryl Streep is not wrong for having exceptional standards for her magazine; it is her contempt for others that separates her from genuine love. Her gawky young assistant, played by Anne Hathaway, who in the end makes the choice for love and self-respect, is only wrong for first believing that she should be written off as she was. The Pharisee is not condemned for his appreciation of sin and his concern for God's majesty, but for his judgement of others. He is probably the thin, praying ascetic, and the tax collector is probably round. What they both need is the realization of the grace and glory of God, who is the only real agent of change.

Gracious Father,
by the obedience of Jesus
you brought salvation to our wayward world:
draw us into harmony with your will,
that we may find all things restored in him,
our Saviour Jesus Christ.

COLLECT

Wednesday 16 July

Psalm 119.105-128
Judges 15.1 – 16.3
Luke 18.15-30

Luke 18.15-30

'How hard it is for those who have wealth to enter the kingdom of God!' (v.24)

There is an apocryphal story that a priest brought the sacrament of the sick to a dowager countess, like the character played by Maggie Smith in the ITV drama series, *Downton Abbey*. The butler, a stiff figure like Mr Carson, threw open the door in front of the priest and said, 'My lady, the Blessed Sacrament'. There is one person whom old Lady Grantham cannot look down on.

Meeting royalty in the United Kingdom has both formality and freedom to it. You always know that you are meeting someone special when the Queen passes by; but she makes herself subject to the responses of children wherever she goes. She chooses to give them priority, and they respond naturally.

What she demonstrates is what the rich young man was reluctant to learn from Jesus, which is that the true privilege of wealth is always to be of service to others. Wealth can be measured by money, talent, geography, time and, most of all, openness to God.

The 'Forbes List' of the world's richest people includes those who understand that the purpose of wealth is to give it away in the service of the common good. Wealth can make us blind and selfish, even as poor members of rich societies. Many more of us are at that eye of the needle place than we would care to admit. The gospel tells us to give ourselves away in order to find out a new definition of being on a rich list.

COLLECT

O God, the protector of all who trust in you,
without whom nothing is strong, nothing is holy:
increase and multiply upon us your mercy;
that with you as our ruler and guide
we may so pass through things temporal
that we lose not our hold on things eternal;
grant this, heavenly Father,
for our Lord Jesus Christ's sake,
who is alive and reigns with you,
in the unity of the Holy Spirit,
one God, now and for ever.

Luke 18.31-end

'Lord, let me see again' (v.41)

In the Danny Boyle movie of 2008, *Slumdog Millionaire*, the hero only just avoids being blinded to make him a more effective beggar on the streets of India. We know that there are deliberately maimed children and adults begging for the poorest of livings on the streets of many cities worldwide. It is hard for us to imagine, but it is a phenomenon with a dreadful but ancient lineage.

We do not know how this blind beggar came to his regular spot around which Jesus passed. We do know that he decides to be noisy and demanding: you have to be noticed to survive. But he does not ask for money or food; he asks for pity. As an unnamed person in the Gospel encounter with Jesus, he stands for you and me and any disciple. He is blind, but he knows his need. People who lack one of the senses make the others work harder. He can hear and feel the effect that Jesus has on the crowd. Here is someone to trust at last. Here is someone with the power to forgive.

He is brought before the one who will not maim him but heal him. Jesus has no interest except to make him whole. The blind beggar asks for sight, which will not only change his life, but take away his living. Asking for sight is a risk. Everyone rejoices at the miracle. Yet the newly sighted beggar now lives to witness the suffering and death that Jesus has predicted.

Gracious Father,
by the obedience of Jesus
you brought salvation to our wayward world:
draw us into harmony with your will,
that we may find all things restored in him,
our Saviour Jesus Christ.

Friday 18 July

Luke 19.1-10

'a chief tax-collector ... rich ... short in stature' (vv.2-3)

Virtue ethics have lately found a new prominence in Christian thinking and suggest that we focus on character so that we might grow into the full stature of Christ. The language of growth suggests that if we adopt certain diets as children, or stand in a 'grow bag', we will in some way become bigger. However, stature and size have no necessary correlation. Many – if not most – of our leading male actors on stage and screen who hold large audiences are not tall. This also applies to many gifted athletes.

Zacchaeus does not have a problem being of less than average height; he has demonstrated his power over a large section of the community by milking them of their money through tax extortion. In Thomas Berger's 1964 novel and Arthur Penn's 1970 movie *Little Big Man*, Jack Crabb claims to be the sole survivor of Custer's last stand at the Battle of Little Bighorn. As the little big man of Judaea, Zacchaeus meets his own last stand in a sycamore tree. He discovers as he looks down on Jesus that he has found a new centre of gravity, the welcoming and forgiving love of God.

From now on he works with a different currency. He realizes that he needs to be a provider rather than a collector, and a dispenser of riches not his own. He will be generous with his money, as we read. More than that, he will live the hospitality of Jesus who has come under his roof. Jesus was both the guest and the host in lots of other peoples' houses. He comes to us to be both, too.

COLLECT

O God, the protector of all who trust in you,
without whom nothing is strong, nothing is holy:
increase and multiply upon us your mercy;
that with you as our ruler and guide
we may so pass through things temporal
that we lose not our hold on things eternal;
grant this, heavenly Father,
for our Lord Jesus Christ's sake,
who is alive and reigns with you,
in the unity of the Holy Spirit,
one God, now and for ever.

Luke 19.11-27

'Do business with these until I come back' (v.13)

In Dickens' shortest novel, *Hard Times* (1854), we are treated to a distilled parody of a utilitarian approach to education and value in society. Mr Gradgrind is the epitome of optimism for a form of education that is restricted to fact rather than fancy.

In the gospel parable, the least productive servant of the king exercises discretion according to the facts of the king's public character and buries the talent he is given. He may have expected to be judged favourably for his caution. Everything is turned on its head by the expectation of trust and risk. Even Mr Gradgrind comes to see the error of his ways in a costly fashion. His daughter suffers a complete breakdown, which she blames upon his stifling of her imagination and emotional freedom.

What God actually requires is that we seek to be mountain climbers rather than valley dwellers. Life grows not through utilitarian maintenance of the status quo that keeps the institution running. Life grows through a spirit of Christian entrepreneurialism. *We* can do because *Christ* has done.

Of course, it is unfair to transfer the resources of the meagre person to the one who already has a great profit to present. God's mission, however, is not based on the kind of fairness that shares resources so equally, regardless of partnership, that there is a grim gruel of a future. Flourishing breaks out unexpectedly and unevenly. What really counts is the urgency of God's coming in Christ. The parable accentuates the kind of behaviour that disciples should live in the belief that the Lord's coming could be imminent.

Gracious Father,
by the obedience of Jesus
you brought salvation to our wayward world:
draw us into harmony with your will,
that we may find all things restored in him,
our Saviour Jesus Christ.

COLLECT

Monday 21 July

1 Samuel 1.1-20

'And she said, "Let your servant find favour in your sight."' (v.18)

What happens when all the treatments and investigations fail and you do not feel called to adopt a child? It is terrible to want children and to know that you cannot have them. It is tougher still when you know that your husband is fertile with another woman. The poet Sylvia Plath wrote a number of poems about reproduction, one of which gives voice to *The Childless Woman* whose womb, akin to a dried-out plant, 'rattles its pod'.

Although the reasons for it are unclear, Sylvia Plath later committed suicide. Hannah, however, will not give up. 'Promise me you'll always remember: you're braver than you believe, and stronger than you seem, and smarter than you think,' says Christopher Robin to Winnie the Pooh.

Hannah faces the misunderstanding and calumny of Eli because of the fervency of her prayer, but it is rewarded. She not only bears a son, but her experience and praise to God are also a prophetic sign of the calling of the Blessed Virgin Mary. Despised and powerless women become the agents of God's transforming power and grace. Rather than the despair of Sylvia Plath that nothing can happen, God performs a miracle. Not only are women not defined by fertility, they sing the song of a world turned the right way up by a woman saying 'Yes' to God.

COLLECT

Almighty and everlasting God,
by whose Spirit the whole body of the Church
    is governed and sanctified:
hear our prayer which we offer for all your faithful people,
that in their vocation and ministry
they may serve you in holiness and truth
to the glory of your name;
through our Lord and Saviour Jesus Christ,
who is alive and reigns with you,
in the unity of the Holy Spirit,
one God, now and for ever.

Psalms 30, 32, 150
1 Samuel 16.14-end
Luke 8.1-3

Tuesday 22 July

Mary Magdalene

Luke 8.1-3

'Mary, called Magdalene, from whom seven demons had gone out'
(v.2)

Today we celebrate the Feast of St Mary Magdalene, the 'thirteenth apostle' or the 'apostle to the apostles'. Mary is the first witness of the resurrection of Jesus in an age when the testimony of women did not count for much in a court of law. The artist, Caravaggio, painted a significant painting of Mary Magdalene. He created a moral storm by using a model who was also a courtesan. The situation was further aggravated because the same model also sat for the Blessed Virgin Mary in his *Flight into Egypt.*

The telling decision by Caravaggio is not meant to offend: the point is that neither woman is meant to be labelled. Both are the closest disciples of Jesus. The traditions about Mary as a reformed whore are late and unreliable. The traditions that sprang up after the resurrection were about a woman who went to Gaul to be an evangelist, the most natural response to witnessing the resurrection at first hand.

Donatello's statue of her in Florence reveals an old woman whose face and fashion reveal suffering and asceticism, but also great energy and hope. She is on the front foot, ready for action. Her clear calling is that of an apostle whose recovered mental illness gives her the sensitivity of one less layer of skin. Listen to her.

Almighty God,
whose Son restored Mary Magdalene to health of mind and body
and called her to be a witness to his resurrection:
forgive our sins and heal us by your grace,
that we may serve you in the power of his risen life;
who is alive and reigns with you,
in the unity of the Holy Spirit,
one God, now and for ever.

COLLECT

Wednesday 23 July

1 Samuel 2.12-26

'... they treated the offerings of the Lord with contempt' (v.17)

'The ceremony of innocence is drowned;
The best lack all conviction, while the worst
Are full of passionate intensity.'

This is part of W. B. Yeats' poem, *The Second Coming*, which he composed in 1919, using Christian imagery to describe the mood in post-war Europe. It is one of the most anthologized poems of the twentieth century. It connects well with the picture painted here of the misrule of Eli's sons. We can bring to mind contemporary evidence around the world where the poor and needy bear the cost of misrule. We can think of instances in history where heredity has been no guarantee of continuing strength or integrity.

The Remains of the Day, a novel by Kazuo Ishiguro (1989), is a first-person narrative by Mr Stevens, the butler at Darlington Hall. Largely through flashback, the reader comes to see the butler's delayed disillusionment with his employer, Lord Darlington, who had been an appeaser of the Nazis believing that they would deliver the continuity of his elitist way of life. Stevens is a victim of his own sense of dignity and hierarchy and the defence of these against life and flourishing. He realizes too late that he gave up the possibility of love, family and a decent future with Miss Kenton the housekeeper.

God does not sustain unworthy structures of power or dignity: he builds his kingdom with and for his people. The contrast is between the sons of Eli and the growing family of Hannah, which began with the miracle of Samuel's birth.

COLLECT

Almighty and everlasting God,
by whose Spirit the whole body of the Church
    is governed and sanctified:
hear our prayer which we offer for all your faithful people,
that in their vocation and ministry
they may serve you in holiness and truth
to the glory of your name;
through our Lord and Saviour Jesus Christ,
who is alive and reigns with you,
in the unity of the Holy Spirit,
one God, now and for ever.

Thursday 24 July

1 Samuel 2.27-end

'... no one in your family shall ever live to old age' (v.32)

Robert Graves' novel *I, Claudius* (1934) and the sequel, *Claudius the God* (1935) tell the tale of the Roman imperial family from Augustus to Nero. The story was told in the BBC drama serial of 1976 starring Derek Jacobi. The narrator is Claudius, the overlooked and rather comical grandson of Augustus, who survives his murderous clan longer than most. We are given a very intimate acquaintance with evil and madness.

As in God's judgement upon the sons of Eli, not many members of the imperial family made it to old age. Indeed, the family devours itself. The narrative provides a parallel for the end of the dynasty in the death of Nero.

Human structures of power, whether sacred or secular, can easily be perverted from godliness and the defenders of any system cannot assume that by complacent reliance upon their spiritual lineage, with Abraham as their father (John 8), they can behave as they like.

This applies to human beings and our personalities, too. In Edgar Allen Poe's 1839 short story, *The Fall of the House of Usher*, a house and the family who live there both fracture and die together after addiction and twisted relationships. Roderick Usher deliberately buries alive his sister, Madeleine. She appears to draw him into death with her.

Our bible story does not end in melancholy and death, however. It is the preparation for God doing a new thing in the call of Samuel to be the greatest judge and prophet in Israel.

> Almighty God,
> send down upon your Church
> the riches of your Spirit,
> and kindle in all who minister the gospel
> your countless gifts of grace;
> through Jesus Christ our Lord.

COLLECT

Friday 25 July

James the Apostle

Psalms 7, 29, 117
2 Kings 1.9-15
Luke 9.46-56

Luke 9.46-56

'... he set his face to go to Jerusalem' (v.51)

Today is the feast day of St James the Great, brother of John and one of the inner circle of Jesus's disciples who witnessed the transfiguration and who were in the Garden of Gethsemane with Jesus. The emblem of St James is the scallop shell, worn as a badge by pilgrims who travel the Camino de Santiago, the pilgrim route to Santiago de Compostela in northern Spain, whose cathedral houses the shrine of the saint.

In the 2010 Emilio Estevez film, *The Way*, Thomas Avery, in a combination of grief and homage to his son, decides to walk this ancient spiritual route through the Pyrenees where his son died. While walking the Camino, Tom meets others from around the world, all looking for greater meaning in their lives. Thomas occasionally sees his son alive and smiling among other pilgrims and people he meets along the way. The film is a gentle elegy about grief and faith and friendship.

Luke 9.51 is the decisive hinge verse of the gospel. Jesus sets his face resolutely towards Jerusalem. It takes another nine chapters of healings and teaching before he gets there. Everything is informed, however, by the journey. This is the prism through which the ministry of Jesus must be seen: he is on his way to suffering and death and to the vindication of the Father through his obedience.

COLLECT

Merciful God,
whose holy apostle Saint James,
leaving his father and all that he had,
was obedient to the calling of your Son Jesus Christ
and followed him even to death:
help us, forsaking the false attractions of the world,
to be ready at all times to answer your call without delay;
through Jesus Christ your Son our Lord,
who is alive and reigns with you,
in the unity of the Holy Spirit,
one God, now and for ever.

1 Samuel 4.1b-end

'The glory has departed from Israel' (vv.21,22)

Sir Steven Runciman was one of the foremost medieval historians of the twentieth century. His *History of the Crusades* (1951–54) is still widely read. In his third volume, *The Kingdom of Acre* (1954), he details the catastrophe of the defeat at the Battle of the Horns of Hattin, when the flower of crusader chivalry was defeated ignominiously by Saladin. King Geoffrey de Lusignan and his barons were convinced that they could win, not least because their army carried the alleged 'true cross' before them. The cross was captured along with the bulk of the army. The failure of the Crusader kingdom to defend itself through folly and hubris led to the Third Crusade and confrontation with the forces of Islam on an even greater scale. Defeat and stalemate were persistent outcomes.

This defeat at the hands of the Philistines was important to remember. An era had come to an end and the symbol of Israel's covenant with God had been taken by the enemy. Runciman also wrote about the fall of Constantinople in 1453 and the end of the Byzantine Empire. He quoted Sultan Mehmet II as he looked on the city:

'The Spider has wove her web in the imperial palace,
The Owl has sung her watch song upon the towers of Efrasiyab.'

Eli and his sons had died. Only Ichabod was left to symbolize that glory and identity had departed. Yet the clue is in the fact that this is the beginning of the First Book of Samuel. Soon Samuel will come into his strength and call the Israelites back to the Lord. Out of death, the Father of Our Lord Jesus Christ brings life; but new life only comes out of real death.

Almighty and everlasting God,
by whose Spirit the whole body of the Church
is governed and sanctified:
hear our prayer which we offer for all your faithful people,
that in their vocation and ministry
they may serve you in holiness and truth
to the glory of your name;
through our Lord and Saviour Jesus Christ,
who is alive and reigns with you,
in the unity of the Holy Spirit,
one God, now and for ever.

COLLECT

Monday 28 July

1 Samuel 5

'Send away the ark of the God of Israel' (v.11)

The Philistines might have captured the ark, but they soon regretted it. They carted it around from Ashdod to Gath to Ekron, but everywhere it went plague broke out, presumably because of the rat fleas that the bearers of the ark carried with them. They quickly concluded they were playing with fire and needed to return the ark to its original ownership.

Sacred objects often seem to have an aura about them such that their implicit message is: don't mess with the things of God. Ours is a culture where sacred objects and even saintly people get short shrift. 'Is nothing sacred?' goes the headline, and the answer is 'probably not'. And yet this demystification and reductionism makes everyone the poorer. Reverence for special buildings, special times and special people encourages us all to tread gently through the dreams of cultures, nations and religions. We are all enriched by acknowledging things that carry several layers of meaning, whether that be a gravestone, a Remembrance Day celebration, a Good Friday procession, a Royal Jubilee, or a table with bread and wine.

Are we ready to recognize the significance of the sacred in the midst of the mundane – even today?

COLLECT

Merciful God,
you have prepared for those who love you
such good things as pass our understanding:
pour into our hearts such love toward you
that we, loving you in all things and above all things,
may obtain your promises,
which exceed all that we can desire;
through Jesus Christ your Son our Lord,
who is alive and reigns with you,
in the unity of the Holy Spirit,
one God, now and for ever.

Psalms **132**, 133
1 Samuel 6.1-16
Luke 21.5-19

1 Samuel 6.1-16

'The cows went straight in the direction of Beth-shemesh' (v.12)

The Philistines have had enough. They need to send the ark back, along with a moderate fortune by way of apology. The priestly advice was to send it back on an unmanned cart pulled by two cows, hoping they would head back into Israelite territory. Providentially, the cows did as hoped, much to everyone's relief. The Israelites, busy bringing in their wheat harvest, were overjoyed to see the ark returning and promptly offered the cows as a burnt offering (which has to be a bit rough on faithful animals just doing an honest day's work ...).

If only it was that easy to sort out our disasters! If only we could send back our mistakes on a cart! A couple of wise cows wouldn't come amiss to most of us. But the same God who drew those cows towards the right border is the God who inspires our own all-too-feeble attempts at reconciliation and reparation. If we make a move – any move – towards putting right our mistakes, God's grace multiplies our efforts and blesses our intent. Our mistakes are only permanently damaging if we hold on to them and refuse to try and repair them.

Can we be humble enough to load our mistakes on to a cart and send them back with a genuine apology?

Creator God,
you made us all in your image:
may we discern you in all that we see,
and serve you in all that we do;
through Jesus Christ our Lord.

COLLECT

Wednesday 30 July

1 Samuel 7

'If you are returning to the Lord ... then put away the foreign gods' (v.3)

The ark might have been returned, but the Israelites still live in fear of the Philistines. Samuel has been off stage for some time, but now he returns and challenges the people to sort themselves out in terms of who they follow and worship. It works: 'So Israel put away the Baals and the Astartes and they served the Lord only' (v.4). When the Philistines get frisky again, they are roundly defeated. Israel gets its lost cities back and peace ensues with Samuel offering stable leadership as judge.

The key resistance had been hanging on to the old gods and mixing them with worship of Yahweh. How contemporary is that? We often want to mix the old gods with the true God. We don't want to lose touch with the idols that have had our heart – consumerism and the desire to possess; power and the desire to control; sex and the desire to stray. The uniqueness of the Judaeo-Christian way of telling God's story was that a mixed economy simply won't do. Nor will it. We're holed beneath the waterline if we hold on to alternative obsessions. God alone is our magnificent obsession.

But the only way we can prove this is by the way we live today (and every day).

COLLECT

Merciful God,
you have prepared for those who love you
such good things as pass our understanding:
pour into our hearts such love toward you
that we, loving you in all things and above all things,
may obtain your promises,
which exceed all that we can desire;
through Jesus Christ your Son our Lord,
who is alive and reigns with you,
in the unity of the Holy Spirit,
one God, now and for ever.

Psalms 143, 146
1 Samuel 8
Luke 21.29-end

1 Samuel 8

'Appoint for us ... a king to govern us, like other nations' (v.5)

This is a major change of gear in the story we've been following. Samuel has been both priest and judge, but his sons are simply not cut from the same cloth and the people seize the opportunity to demand a king, like other nations. The Lord assures Samuel that they're rejecting Yahweh, not him, and Samuel tries to warn them what this will mean in terms of royal oppression of all kinds. It's a sorry list, but the people are hell-bent on having their king, so the Lord says a king they shall have.

I once saw a notice in a shop in South Africa addressed to potential robbers. It stated simply: 'These premises are protected by God.' No arguing with that then! Israel had been protected by God, but the people somehow thought they would be better off being protected by a king. Mistake. If only we would understand that no human institution can offer us safety from harm, but God can offer us security in whatever life throws at us. It was going to be a hard lesson for the Israelites to learn. And we're not doing much better in our own day. A bit more protection, we think; more missiles, more police, more gated communities. But that's not it.

Safety lies in faith, not in certainty; in God, not in kings.

Creator God,
you made us all in your image:
may we discern you in all that we see,
and serve you in all that we do;
through Jesus Christ our Lord.

COLLECT

Friday 1 August

Psalms 142, **144**
1 Samuel 9.1-14
Luke 22.1-13

1 Samuel 9.1-14

'Let us turn back' (v.5)

The writer cleverly builds up the story of Saul being chosen to be king. He starts with an ordinary event of rural life – a search for lost donkeys – and leads us towards the momentous meeting with Samuel. And at one vital moment in the narrative, Saul gets tired of the whole search and suggests to his companion that they might as well turn back. The boy, fortunately, isn't so pessimistic and the search carries on.

There are often moments in life when we're tempted to think that a course of action is getting nowhere and we might as well give up. And if we do, who knows what shining moment we might miss? If I had dropped out of a mission in Hull, as I was tempted to do, I might never have met my future wife. If she hadn't seen an advert for a job in the Church Times, I might have happily continued as a parish priest all my days. Life is made up of chance encounters and near misses, any one of which can turn out to be seminal. God seems to weave them together into a fabric of opportunity and eventfulness, a fabric that is our life.

If ordinary events can be charged with such potential, what might happen today that might change our lives in significant ways? Will we notice?

COLLECT

Merciful God,
you have prepared for those who love you
such good things as pass our understanding:
pour into our hearts such love toward you
that we, loving you in all things and above all things,
may obtain your promises,
which exceed all that we can desire;
through Jesus Christ your Son our Lord,
who is alive and reigns with you,
in the unity of the Holy Spirit,
one God, now and for ever.

Psalm 147
1 Samuel 9.15 – 10.1
Luke 22.14-23

1 Samuel 9.15 – 10.1

'I am only a Benjaminite ... Why then have you spoken to me in this way?' (9.21)

Saul finds Samuel at last, but God has already prepared the ground and Samuel knows what he has to do. He reassures Saul about the donkeys but then slips in that 'Israel's desire' is fixed on him – in other words, he was to be their king. The idea is outrageous to Saul and he protests, but Samuel sees it through, sets him as honoured guest at the feast and then anoints him king the next morning as he leaves. Job done.

Saul's protest is entirely appropriate. The trouble is that God is no respecter of age, education, background, regiment or London club. God gets the person he needs, whether that person be Moses, David, Jeremiah, the Virgin Mary or the other Saul, the persecutor. None felt worthy, but – sorry – the decision belonged to God. Many of us are inclined to write ourselves off as belonging to the lower divisions, the hewers of wood and drawers of water. But wouldn't it be better to let God be the judge? God delights in talent-spotting, whether the talent be an Archbishop of Canterbury who used to be an oil executive or a newly redundant office worker who has a gift for befriending the elderly at a lunch club.

With God nothing is ruled out, except us ruling ourselves out.

Creator God,
you made us all in your image:
may we discern you in all that we see,
and serve you in all that we do;
through Jesus Christ our Lord.

COLLECT

217

Psalms 1, 2, 3
1 Samuel 10.1-16
Luke 22.24-30

1 Samuel 10.1-16

'Is Saul also among the prophets?' (v.11)

You have to admit Samuel is a bit of a tease. He tells Saul that three things will happen to him to prove that he really has been chosen by God to be king. He would meet two men who knew what his father was thinking, three men bringing lunch, and a band of prophets who would lead him into a prophetic frenzy. I guess if all of that happened to us, most of us would be impressed. And yet Saul still didn't feel able to share the big news with his father, but rather fobbed him off with the rather less significant story of the donkeys.

Most of us would like to be given the spectacular confirmation or guidance that Saul received that day, in the spirit of Woody Allen's comment: 'If only God would give me some clear sign. Like making a large deposit in my name at a Swiss bank.' But such clarity isn't common. For most of us, guidance comes from prayer and reflection, talking with close friends, facts on the ground, and a growing conviction that a course of action is right. In other words, God's guidance isn't an alternative to hard thinking but an aid to it, just as for many of us putting on our glasses is an aid to seeing clearly.

But if God sends you a band of prophets who lead you into a frenzy, don't ignore the experience. God will do what God will do.

Lord of all power and might,
the author and giver of all good things:
graft in our hearts the love of your name,
increase in us true religion,
nourish us with all goodness,
and of your great mercy keep us in the same;
through Jesus Christ your Son our Lord,
who is alive and reigns with you,
in the unity of the Holy Spirit,
one God, now and for ever.

Psalms **5**, 6 (8)
1 Samuel 10.17-end
Luke 22.31-38

1 Samuel 10.17-end

'See, he has hidden himself among the baggage' (v.22)

Samuel has another method of disclosing publicly who God has chosen to be king – even though he can't help telling the people off again for their disobedience in demanding a king. The field of candidates is narrowed down to Saul, but the new king is comically found hiding among the baggage. Is this the behaviour expected of a king?

When Edward VIII abdicated in 1936, his brother George very reluctantly found himself pulled from among the baggage. He had no desire to be king, not least because he had great difficulty in public speaking. It's all there in the film *The King's Speech*. But George VI was an inspirationally calm presence in the wartime years and just what the country needed. God knows the character of the heart, and that matters more than a long CV and a golden tongue. He even chose a carpenter from the hill country of an obscure Roman province to be the Saviour of the world.

Might he not then even choose you and me to do something far outside our comfort zone? Is God nudging you to make a move into some new territory? If so, don't hide among the baggage.

Generous God,
you give us gifts and make them grow:
though our faith is small as mustard seed,
make it grow to your glory
and the flourishing of your kingdom;
through Jesus Christ our Lord.

COLLECT

Wednesday 6 August

The Transfiguration of Our Lord

Psalms 27, 150
Ecclesiasticus 48.1-10
or 1 Kings 19.1-16
1 John 3.1-3

1 Kings 19.1-16

'Go out and stand on the mountain before the Lord, for the Lord is about to pass by' (v.11)

Elijah's experience of God was breathtaking, not in its power but in its gentleness. He wasn't to be found in wind, earthquake or fire, but in a sound of sheer silence. We often expect to find God in spectacular events, when worship is electric and spines are tingling, but God very often sneaks up on us in silence, in quiet places, in the smile of a child or the shape of a leaf.

The world often can't cope with displays of power. At the transfiguration, which we celebrate today, Peter couldn't cope with the disclosure of Christ's divinity and wanted to box it in. After the first atomic explosion at Hiroshima, which we lament today, no nation has been able to cope with the enormity of such horrific power as was released that day.

Both Elijah's and Jesus' experience encourages us not to look for God so much in spectacular demonstrations of power but in quiet encounters on mountainsides, when the veil is drawn back and we glimpse the aching depth of the divine in our midst. God is fully present today in the warp and weft of our lives. We need not so much to summon fire as to recognize Presence.

COLLECT

Father in heaven,
whose Son Jesus Christ was wonderfully transfigured
before chosen witnesses upon the holy mountain,
and spoke of the exodus he would accomplish at Jerusalem:
give us strength so to hear his voice and bear our cross
that in the world to come we may see him as he is;
who is alive and reigns with you,
in the unity of the Holy Spirit,
one God, now and for ever.

Thursday 7 August

1 Samuel 12

'Only fear the Lord, and serve him faithfully with all your heart'
(v.24)

When we near the end of our life, we are likely to survey it with a grand sweep, and to focus on one or two crucial messages we want to take out of it. This is what Samuel did in reminding the people of where they had come from (the survey), and in chastizing them for wanting a king but nevertheless instructing them to serve the Lord faithfully, for then they might avoid the destruction their disobedience warranted (the crucial messages). He was still cross that they didn't trust God as their only king, but he sensed that God could still use kingship as a vehicle for his purposes.

It's a helpful lesson in the value of the second best. God never writes us off, even when we make ridiculous decisions. God's very nature is to redeem whatever lies before him. If we lose the plot, God doesn't. If we mess up, God helps us find another way forward. God's purpose is that we, and all creation, shall be presented, redeemed and faultless, at the Banquet at the End of the World. But there isn't only one way of getting there. If we go off-piste, God will find another way to draw us to himself.

That's a great reassurance before we make today's mistakes!

Lord of all power and might,
the author and giver of all good things:
graft in our hearts the love of your name,
increase in us true religion,
nourish us with all goodness,
and of your great mercy keep us in the same;
through Jesus Christ your Son our Lord,
who is alive and reigns with you,
in the unity of the Holy Spirit,
one God, now and for ever.

COLLECT

221

Friday 8 August

1 Samuel 13.5-18

'... now your kingdom will not continue; the Lord has sought out a man after his own heart' (v.14)

Israel and the Philistines are at war, and Israel's prospects don't look good. After early successes the Israelites are seriously outnumbered and frankly terrified. Saul has waited patiently for Samuel to arrive before making his next move, but after a week he feels entitled to take responsibility for offering a sacrifice to God, an action normally taken by a priest but which a king could also take. But Samuel says this excuse isn't good enough. The issue is obedience and because Saul has failed, his dynasty will be overtaken by another. It's our first sight of David's line.

The bar set by some of the ancient prophets was excruciatingly high. Which of us would get over? Sometimes the bar is almost invisible, as in today's reading. Samuel was a week late; the situation was dire; surely a responsible king could approach God himself? But obedience is a high command, as Jesus found on the cross. Significantly, however, Jesus added mercy to the mix. Indeed, the very heart of the gospel is the forgiveness of sins. Thank God that in the life and teaching of Jesus we see these two as twin peaks – obedience to God and mercy from God. We reach for the stars but are also raised from the dust when we fail to get there.

Both peaks are available to us today.

Lord of all power and might,
the author and giver of all good things:
graft in our hearts the love of your name,
increase in us true religion,
nourish us with all goodness,
and of your great mercy keep us in the same;
through Jesus Christ your Son our Lord,
who is alive and reigns with you,
in the unity of the Holy Spirit,
one God, now and for ever.

Psalms 20, 21, **23**
1 Samuel 13.19 – 14.15
Luke 23.1-12

1 Samuel 13.19 – 14.15

'... the Lord has given them into our hand' (14.10)

Jonathan goes to reconnoitre the enemy positions and finds himself in a narrow defile. He and his armour bearer decide to attract the Philistines' attention and if they are invited to come nearer, then the Philistines' fate is sealed. So it was. The two of them killed about 20 men and the sheer nerve of this slaughter caused panic among the enemy soldiers, not helped by a confirmatory earthquake.

Seen in retrospect, it's easy to attach divine causation to the various victories and defeats of Israel. Our own experience of warfare is more ambiguous. The contradictory prayers of the British and the Germans in the two World Wars have set many a discussion going about the ways of God and the purpose of prayer. God's ways are the ways of peace, so all war is failure. God's action will always be directed to making a garment of peace out of the ragged strands of violence. In the meantime, the only way to live with the sorrow of war is by burying it in the mercy of the cross. Every death is a splinter of that cross. And Christians believe in the great reversal on Easter morning.

In the meantime, we remember not so much that the Lord has given the enemy into our hand as that he has everyone in his hand.

Generous God,
you give us gifts and make them grow:
though our faith is small as mustard seed,
make it grow to your glory
and the flourishing of your kingdom;
through Jesus Christ our Lord.

COLLECT

Monday 11 August

1 Samuel 14.24-46

'Now Saul committed a very rash act on that day' (v.24)

Every act in our lives has consequences. Whatever we do, whether right or wrong, we must have the courage to deal with what ensues. Sometimes we act well, and sometimes we act badly, and our acts affect not just ourselves but those around us. Saul's 'very rash' oath could have led to the death of his son.

Often we cannot undo that which we have done. What we can do is have the courage to acknowledge our mistakes and prayerfully ask the Lord for guidance. Christ has already atoned for our wrongdoings, and the way is always open for us to work with the help of the Holy Spirit and the people around us, to keep the balance in our lives. We praise God for the good acts that we do, and we ask God for empowerment to repair the damage when we act badly. Our entire life is a mixture of good and bad actions. This is life.

As an example, consider Peter who, despite swearing to Jesus that he would never desert him even if it meant his death, denied Jesus three times before the cock crowed twice – and when he realised what he had done, he broke down and wept bitterly. Having faith in Christ means that life does not stop at this point – even after deserting Jesus after the cross, the risen Lord empowered Peter to become the great apostle and the father of the Church.

COLLECT

Almighty Lord and everlasting God,
we beseech you to direct, sanctify and govern
 both our hearts and bodies
in the ways of your laws
 and the works of your commandments;
that through your most mighty protection, both here and ever,
we may be preserved in body and soul;
through our Lord and Saviour Jesus Christ,
who is alive and reigns with you,
in the unity of the Holy Spirit,
one God, now and for ever.

Psalms 32, **36**
1 Samuel 15.1-23
Luke 23.26-43

1 Samuel 15.1-23

'...to obey is better than sacrifice' (v.22)

In this challenging text we see one verse standing out, when Samuel said to Saul, 'Surely, to obey is better than sacrifice, and to heed than the fat of rams' (v.22).

For us as Christians, we believe that Jesus Christ on the cross is the ultimate sacrifice and the ultimate example of obedience. In Christ, obedience and sacrifice met and were entirely fulfilled. The result of this fulfilment was the glorious resurrection of Christ. This means that, whatever we do now, we do in Christ!

How do we deal with sacrifice and obedience after the resurrection of Christ? Sacrifice for us today has two sides: the first is when we continuously share in the ultimate sacrifice of Christ through taking Holy Communion; the second is when we present our lives and our bodies as a living sacrifice. Our obedience is an obedience to the teachings of Christ, opening our hearts and lives to the Lord Jesus Christ, the Risen One, to lead them and rule them. We need to make space for Christ, inviting the Holy Spirit into our lives!

For Christians, obedience and sacrifice are one, because obedience means sacrifice as we share the ultimate sacrifice, Jesus Christ. Through the cross and resurrection of Christ, we are liberated from an obedience to the Law and we obey now a person rather than a book; we are also liberated from offering sacrifices, because we have become living sacrifices.

Lord God,
your Son left the riches of heaven
and became poor for our sake:
when we prosper save us from pride,
when we are needy save us from despair,
that we may trust in you alone;
through Jesus Christ our Lord.

COLLECT

225

Wednesday 13 August

1 Samuel 16

'... they look on the outward appearance, but the Lord looks on the heart' (v.7)

Today more than ever we find satisfaction in the appearance of things. We are often deceived by what we see because we have not scratched beyond the surface to discover the true essence within. A good example is Christmas, when many cover the true nature of the occasion – a celebration of God becoming human – with a glitzy layer of consumerism and a shiny secular façade; even the message is sanitized so that it becomes unrecognizable and the Nativity becomes a perfumed, tidy, fairy tale.

Another example is when we divert our attention from being a worshipping, serving Church and we worship and serve buildings and all the rituals and paraphernalia that go with them. The Church is the wall-less instrument that God uses to transform people and serve humanity, and many of us have lost this, distracted by the Church as an organization that swallows everything else.

As it says in this passage, 'for the Lord does not see as mortals see; they look on the outward appearance, but the Lord looks on the heart' (v.7). This is also what Jesus said when he criticized the religious leaders: 'Woe to you, scribes and Pharisees, hypocrites! For you are like whitewashed tombs, which on the outside look beautiful, but inside they are full of the bones of the dead and of all kinds of filth' (Matthew 23.27). God is calling us to look beyond the surface, to the heart of all things.

COLLECT

Almighty Lord and everlasting God,
we beseech you to direct, sanctify and govern
    both our hearts and bodies
in the ways of your laws
    and the works of your commandments;
that through your most mighty protection, both here and ever,
we may be preserved in body and soul;
through our Lord and Saviour Jesus Christ,
who is alive and reigns with you,
in the unity of the Holy Spirit,
one God, now and for ever.

Thursday 14 August

1 Samuel 17.1-30

'Goliath, of Gath, whose height was six cubits and a span' (v.4)

Most of us have experienced the feeling of being insignificant when we have compared ourselves to someone whom we judge to be wonderful or imposing or great, and we think, 'I can never be like that person' or, 'I can never achieve that greatness'. Our hearts are filled with fear or awe, mixed with a feeling of weakness, perhaps even helplessness.

The people who witnessed Goliath's daily challenge were filled with fear and helplessness. David, however, rose to that challenge and resolved to stand up for what he believed in. This could have easily led to his death and the enslavement of his people. When David went to meet Goliath in battle, all present would have seen a heavily armoured giant, a hero of many battles, facing 'just a boy' (v.33) with no military experience whatsoever; they saw only the appearance of the combatants and, based on their appearance alone, everyone would have felt sure that this could only result in David's death.

We do this too – we judge ourselves all too often in a shallow way, not appreciating the abilities that God has given us, including the power of our faith and the immense power of the Holy Spirit. When we face a big challenge in our lives, remember that we are not facing this challenge alone, and let's make sure that we know that God has equipped us for those times when we must carry our own cross.

Friday 15 August

The Blessed Virgin Mary

Psalms 98, 138, 147.1-12
Isaiah 7.10-15
Luke 11.27-28

Luke 11.27-28

'Blessed is the womb that bore you and the breasts that nursed you!' (v.27)

The voice in the crowd, blessing the womb that bore Jesus and the breasts that nursed him, reflects the tight family relationships in the Middle East. In the eyes of his earthly society, the great acts of Jesus Christ could easily be attributed to how well his mother had raised him. The mother in the Middle Eastern culture directs the family even though the father is officially the head of the family. The voice in the crowd recognizes the successful effort and hard work on the mother's part in bringing Jesus up. Although Jesus draws our attention back to God rather than anyone else, this does not in any sense undermine the praise directed at Mary for her role in Jesus' life.

Mary's dedication, love and care, and how she raised Jesus, were all part of the personality of Christ and this is clearly expressed by the person in the crowd who called out. Wherever we travel, however we change and grow, we will always reflect something of the nature of our family, and especially our mother. Mary is an icon of humility and self-giving; she followed Christ, sticking with her Son, until his cross and resurrection; her life demonstrates unconditional love and a deep obedience to God and to the mission and the ministry of her son. Today we should follow Mary's wonderful example, learning from her so that we too can live a life of selfless devotion.

COLLECT

Almighty God,
who looked upon the lowliness of the Blessed Virgin Mary
and chose her to be the mother of your only Son:
grant that we who are redeemed by his blood
may share with her in the glory of your eternal kingdom;
through Jesus Christ your Son our Lord,
who is alive and reigns with you,
in the unity of the Holy Spirit,
one God, now and for ever.

Psalms 41, **42**, 43
1 Samuel 17.55 – 18.16
Luke 24.36-end

1 Samuel 17.55 – 18.16

'So Saul eyed David from that day on' (18.9)

Saul and David are perfect examples of something that is crucial in our lives; the success of David, who was one of Saul's servants, filled Saul with jealousy, and he felt threatened by the young David's success. Many of us feel threatened when we see those around us thrive and apparently outshine us. The feeling of jealousy itself is a very human one; it is not wrong to feel some jealousy on occasions. The important thing is how we deal with these feelings. We have two choices: the first choice is to turn this jealousy into a motivational force so that we work to improve ourselves and to aspire and to celebrate the success of others. The other choice is to allow jealousy to fester in our hearts until it acquires a self-destructive power.

Turning jealousy into a force for good requires humility and a security in who we are – and that is much more achievable when we have faith. Why? Because we already believe that God loves us whatever we have achieved and that, out of this love, he has given us gifts – our responsibility is to make the most of these gifts and to make them fruitful. Our success in life should not be at the expense of others; rather, our success should *benefit* those around us, and the success of others should be a cause for celebration and gratitude.

Almighty Lord and everlasting God,
we beseech you to direct, sanctify and govern
both our hearts and bodies
in the ways of your laws
and the works of your commandments;
that through your most mighty protection, both here and ever,
we may be preserved in body and soul;
through our Lord and Saviour Jesus Christ,
who is alive and reigns with you,
in the unity of the Holy Spirit,
one God, now and for ever.

COLLECT

229

Monday 18 August

Acts 1.1-14

'But you will receive power when the Holy Spirit has come upon you' (v.8)

St Luke, the doctor and writer, starts recording in this book not the acts of the apostles but the act of the Holy Spirit. Luke is passionate and enthusiastic about the presence and the role of the Holy Spirit in the Church. He writes the account of the ascension, but his focus is on the work of the Holy Spirit, which is the continuity of the presence of Christ in the world. Jesus is not with us in the body, but he is always with us through the Holy Spirit. This is an account of hope and power. The ascension is not a sad occasion when the world 'lost Christ'. Even today, it is a time to celebrate the era of the work of the Holy Spirit in us.

Through our baptism and the Eucharist, we go out into the world as the disciples of Christ, the risen and the ascended Lord, empowered just like the first disciples with the Holy Spirit. Through that same power of that same Spirit, we continue Christ's mission to be the light, the salt and the leaven in the world. By living our faith well, people do not see us – they see *Christ in us*! This is how we shine and how we become true agents of the Holy Spirit.

COLLECT

Almighty God,
who sent your Holy Spirit
to be the life and light of your Church:
open our hearts to the riches of your grace,
that we may bring forth the fruit of the Spirit
in love and joy and peace;
through Jesus Christ your Son our Lord,
who is alive and reigns with you,
in the unity of the Holy Spirit,
one God, now and for ever.

Tuesday 19 August

Acts 1.15-end

'... a witness with us to his resurrection' (v.22)

After nearly 2,000 years of the resurrection, we look at those disciples who influenced humanity by their witness to the resurrection of Jesus Christ, and as Christians we aspire to be like them. Witnessing to the resurrection of Christ is at the very heart of our mission as Christians and as a Church in the world. Yes, the disciples cast lots to find out who God wanted to continue the journey of witness with them from among those who had experienced the Lord's ministry first hand. Today, thank God, we do not need to draw lots because God has chosen all of us for the tremendous honour and privilege of witnessing to his resurrection. In our case, the lot is already cast and we are chosen to go into the world and make disciples in every time, in every place, in every culture!

The disciples whom God chose were people like us, living with their shortcomings as well as their gifts, and God used both for his glory. Today, it is our choice to put ourselves with all our shortcomings and gifts in the hands of God, to use us to witness to his love and the resurrection of his Son.

What a joy and what an honour to be disciples who can bring the message of liberation and love to all humanity by being ourselves in our lives – living examples of this message.

Gracious Father,
revive your Church in our day,
and make her holy, strong and faithful,
for your glory's sake
in Jesus Christ our Lord.

COLLECT

Wednesday 20 August

Psalm 119.57-80
1 Samuel 20.18-end
Acts 2.1-21

Acts 2.1-21

'Amazed and astonished ...' (v.7)

When the world stops being amazed by what we offer to it, by what we do and by what we say as Christians, we should know that we need to reconsider our baptism of fire. When Luke wanted to describe the Holy Spirit descending on the disciples, the best way he found was to depict it as 'tongues, as of fire' (v.3) because he was conscious that fire represents both power and warmth. As Christians, we have continued to receive this gift of the Spirit of the Lord in order to carry on our mission to amaze the world by reflecting the love of God in Jesus Christ and living in it with the power of the resurrection.

Sometimes, we lose this ability to amaze the world when we get too busy with our little selves, shifting the focus away from the Risen Lord, exactly like Peter when he shifted his gaze from the Lord to the storm and he began to sink. If we want to continue as the force for love and for the transformation of the world and if we want to keep receiving the gift of the Spirit, then we must make sure that our focus is on the Lord himself. Only then can we continue to receive the very same gift of the same Holy Spirit that worked in the disciples to amaze the world at Pentecost.

COLLECT

Almighty God,
who sent your Holy Spirit
to be the life and light of your Church:
open our hearts to the riches of your grace,
that we may bring forth the fruit of the Spirit
in love and joy and peace;
through Jesus Christ your Son our Lord,
who is alive and reigns with you,
in the unity of the Holy Spirit,
one God, now and for ever.

Thursday 21 August

Acts 2.22-36

'...listen to what I have to say' (v.22)

Who would have thought the fisherman who wrestled with the sea and faced the storms, the passionate, impulsive and emotional Peter, would stand in front of the crowd and utter these powerful, eloquent and profound words? The disciple who jumped into the sea because he was naked when he recognized the Lord, the one who said to Jesus, 'Yet if you say so, I will let down the nets' (Luke 5.5), the fisherman who was commissioned to be the 'fisher of men', stands before people of all nations to witness to his faith in his risen Lord and Master. Such courage has been, and will always be, the aspiration of the Church.

As we sail through life, armed with our faith in the same Lord and Master, we do not necessarily stand in front of crowds from every nation to witness to this faith, but each and every one of us has the opportunity to make a similar stand and proclaim the very gospel, not only through words but most importantly through deeds, through living the gospel and living the faith. The world today needs disciples like Peter more than ever, to witness boldly that when we proclaim the gospel, we do so through the Holy Spirit working within us. As Peter witnessed to the Spirit of the Risen Lord, so do we, every time we live our faith.

Gracious Father,
revive your Church in our day,
and make her holy, strong and faithful,
for your glory's sake
in Jesus Christ our Lord.

COLLECT

Acts 2.37-end

'Repent, and be baptized ... and you will receive the gift of the Holy Spirit' (v.38)

The Holy Spirit, as Jesus said, is like the wind that blows where it will – and we need to be always open to the Holy Spirit; we cannot place conditions on the work of the Holy Spirit, nor can we erect barriers against it.

As Peter asked the people to repent and to be baptized, we should today pause and examine our hearts, which is the essence of repentance, and reflect upon whether we live up to our vows of baptism. Being the light, the salt and the leaven in the world, as Jesus asked us to be, requires continuous self-examination so that we can change our ways. Jesus is our compass.

People of all nations, all colours, all genders, all backgrounds, all cultures, all abilities have experienced the power of the Holy Spirit, who empowers people to celebrate their differences. The Holy Spirit is our hope to find our identity and the way to belong to the household of God and rejoice in all our gifts. The call of Peter included all, and this invitation is for us today to go out and show the world the power of the same Holy Spirit. After nearly 2,000 years, we keep breaking bread together and lifting the cup together, witnessing to the presence of the Risen Lord in us and amongst us. This is the way to be true disciples of Jesus Christ and true citizens of his kingdom.

COLLECT

Almighty God,
who sent your Holy Spirit
to be the life and light of your Church:
open our hearts to the riches of your grace,
that we may bring forth the fruit of the Spirit
in love and joy and peace;
through Jesus Christ your Son our Lord,
who is alive and reigns with you,
in the unity of the Holy Spirit,
one God, now and for ever.

Psalm **68**
1 Samuel 23
Acts 3.1-10

Acts 3.1-10

'I have no silver or gold, but what I have I give you' (v.6)

When we pray, we enter into a two-way communication with God, and this should become our state of being. This relationship, just like all our relationships, can only flourish if we are willing to open up and to be vulnerable. God is not there to fulfil our shopping list of requests, however, and our prayers should not merely be a list of people we want looking after and a few life goals we would like the Lord magically to meet for us. An essential part of the vulnerability in prayer is that the Lord will always answer us, although not in the way we expect. The truth is that, while winning the lottery or reaching the pinnacle in our career might seem like the answer to our prayers, life is far more complicated than that.

The man lame from birth always asked for money; he never dreamed to ask for what he really needed, which was a cure. Consider how he would have reacted if Peter and John had given him a few coins: he would have taken the money, and carried on begging. Instead, we read of him 'walking and leaping and praising God'! When we pray, we open up our hearts to God and we listen. We might be surprised by what God has to say to us and what his plans for us are!

Gracious Father,
revive your Church in our day,
and make her holy, strong and faithful,
for your glory's sake
in Jesus Christ our Lord.

COLLECT

Monday 25 August

Acts 3.11-end

'... you killed the Author of life, whom God raised from the dead.
To this we are witnesses' (v.15)

'We are witnesses,' says Peter. These three words sum up the whole of this book of the Bible. The Acts of the Apostles are the acts of those who witness to the death and resurrection of Christ and the continuing work of his Spirit in the life of the Church. Remember how in Chapter 1 of Acts the Eleven choose a replacement for Judas on the basis of that person being *a witness* with them to all that had happened from Jesus' baptism by John up to the present time (Acts 1.22). Through these witnesses, God's purposes will be made known and faith in Jesus Christ will spread from Jerusalem to Rome. The Acts of the Apostles tells the astonishing story of how this happens, the Christian faith changing from a small Jewish sect to a global faith – and all in a few years and by the witness of an unlikely group of people. But the Holy Spirit is bearing witness through them.

Hence, the man who has been healed clings to Peter and John, amazed and confused by what has happened to him. The people are also astonished. And Peter bears witness. He says it is Jesus, the one they rejected and crucified, who has done this thing. It is by faith in his name that the man has received health. This Jesus is alive and working through his Church

COLLECT

Let your merciful ears, O Lord,
be open to the prayers of your humble servants;
and that they may obtain their petitions
make them to ask such things as shall please you;
through Jesus Christ your Son our Lord,
who is alive and reigns with you,
in the unity of the Holy Spirit,
one God, now and for ever.

Tuesday 26 August

Acts 4.1-12

'By what power or by what name did you do this?' (v.7)

What's in a name? Doesn't a rose by any other name still smell sweet? But the name of Jesus is different. His name carries power and authority. It opens doors. It is by faith in the name of Jesus that the crippled beggar at the beautiful gate is healed. And when the Jewish rulers ask Peter what authority he has to heal this man and in whose name he has done it – for the name corresponds directly to the authority to do it – he replies that is in the 'name of Jesus Christ of Nazareth' that this man stands before them in good health. Indeed, he goes on: 'there is no other name under heaven ... by which we must be saved' (v.12).

And so the Christian faith is not about 'what you know' but 'who you know'. To know and be known by Jesus is free entry to the banquet of heaven. In fact, the name Jesus means 'God rescues'. God has come in Jesus to gather us into his kingdom. This ministry of gathering and welcoming, of healing and saving, is continued by the Church. No ticket is required, the queue can be jumped, the lunch is free and the drinks are on the house. All you need do is mention his name.

Lord of heaven and earth,
as Jesus taught his disciples to be persistent in prayer,
give us patience and courage never to lose hope,
but always to bring our prayers before you;
through Jesus Christ our Lord.

COLLECT

237

Wednesday 27 August

Psalm **77**
I Samuel 28.3-end
Acts 4.13-31

Acts 4.13-31

'... we cannot keep from speaking about what we have seen and heard' (v.20)

Peter and John are told to keep quiet about Jesus. Amazed at their boldness and challenged by their lack of learning, the religious leaders just need them to shut them up. They are desperately trying to put the lid back on the infant Church. But it is too late. The genie was out of the bottle when Jesus rose from the dead and gave his Spirit to his friends. Now his followers, led by that same Spirit of Jesus, act in his name. They speak his words. They minister his healing. They offer his forgiveness. They beckon people into his kingdom. And they can't be stopped. The chief priests even mutter frustratedly to themselves, 'What will we do with them? For it is obvious to all who live in Jerusalem that a notable sign has been done through them; we cannot deny it' (v.16). And so Peter speaks the words that are the authenticating hallmark of all witness: 'We cannot keep from speaking about what we have seen and heard' (v.20).

This was the best evangelism then, and it is still the best evangelism now. Just as Peter simply spoke about what he had experienced, this is what the Church must do today. It doesn't matter whether we have had the right theological training; what matters is our experience of Jesus and speaking about it gently and boldly, and therefore carrying on his ministry.

COLLECT

Let your merciful ears, O Lord,
be open to the prayers of your humble servants;
and that they may obtain their petitions
make them to ask such things as shall please you;
through Jesus Christ your Son our Lord,
who is alive and reigns with you,
in the unity of the Holy Spirit,
one God, now and for ever.

Psalm **78.1-39***
I Samuel 31
Acts 4.32 – 5.11

Acts 4.32 – 5.11

'… everything they owned was held in common' (4.32)

Actions have consequences. That is the terrible truth of this terrible story. The selfless faithfulness of the infant Church, whose care for each other demands that all is held in common, is placed by Luke, the great storyteller of the New Testament, in stark contrast alongside the story of Ananias and Sapphira holding things for themselves. They keep a portion of the sale they have made; when their deceit is revealed, they fall down dead.

What does this story mean for us today? Will we fall down dead when we keep back resources for ourselves? Or fiddle a tax return? Or simply fail to be generous? Well, yes. That is the hard reality of this story: every time we act in own interests, we exclude others, we rob the common good, and something inside us dies. That vision of a Church which was one in heart and soul, that claimed no private ownership of possessions, that held things in common is compromised, and with it the earned right to declare the resurrection, to speak of a different reality, is also compromised. The result? The gospel itself is compromised. The witness of the Church is blunted. The poor are left more needy than before. Death, which is always the wage of sin, casts its shadow upon us.

Lord of heaven and earth,
as Jesus taught his disciples to be persistent in prayer,
give us patience and courage never to lose hope,
but always to bring our prayers before you;
through Jesus Christ our Lord.

COLLECT

Friday 29 August

Acts 5.12-26

'… in order that Peter's shadow might fall on some of them' (v.15)

I've written and preached about this passage more times than I care to remember. It is a piece of Scripture I keep coming back to.

Luke paints a vivid and compelling picture of the early Church growing and changing. People are added to its number. Signs and wonders are performed. And Peter is held in such esteem that, as he walks down the street, people carry out the sick and lay them on the pavement 'in order that Peter's shadow might fall on some of them as he came by'. How do we make sense of this verse? Can this be the same Peter that we read about in the Gospels, who always promised so much and delivered so little? Now people sense that even his passing shadow brings healing and blessing.

Peter has been changed. He has encountered the Risen Christ. He has been forgiven. He is learning what it means to love Jesus. He walks in that light. He isn't walking down the street in order to heal these people. He goes about his daily business, and from his presence blessings and healings flow. He casts a long shadow. And by his presence Christ is known. Peter is a true witness. He no longer acts in his own strength, but in the strength of the Risen Lord.

And if such a change can happen in Peter, there is not just hope for all of us, there is promise.

COLLECT

Let your merciful ears, O Lord,
be open to the prayers of your humble servants;
and that they may obtain their petitions
make them to ask such things as shall please you;
through Jesus Christ your Son our Lord,
who is alive and reigns with you,
in the unity of the Holy Spirit,
one God, now and for ever.

Psalms **76**, 79
2 Samuel 2.1-11
Acts 5.27-end

Acts 5.27-end

*'And we are witnesses to these things, and so is the Holy Spirit
whom God has given to those who obey him' (v.32)*

Sometimes the Acts of the Apostles is referred to as 'The Gospel of the Holy Spirit', for this book tells the story of a Spirit-filled and Spirit-guided Church expanding and growing. Its message is the good news of what God has done in Jesus Christ. In this reading, Peter again repeats the basic proclamation of the gospel: Jesus was killed, God raised him to life, forgiveness is found in him. Its method is witness through word and deed. And it is carried out by history's most unlikely collection of ambassadors – the twelve apostles and those who travelled with them. Few of them are learned or articulate by the world's standards, but it is this company of men and women who, spurred on by Jesus and sustained by the Spirit, succeed in taking the gospel across the known world and establishing Christian communities in many far-flung places. As Peter says here, it is both their witness and the witness of the Holy Spirit. All this enrages the religious leaders. But the first Christians consider it an honour to suffer for the sake of the gospel, and they carry on teaching and proclaiming Jesus as Messiah.

If, like Peter, we remain faithful, if we walk in the light of this gospel, then the same Spirit will be at work, witnessing through us. That is the astonishing Christian claim.

> Lord of heaven and earth,
> as Jesus taught his disciples to be persistent in prayer,
> give us patience and courage never to lose hope,
> but always to bring our prayers before you;
> through Jesus Christ our Lord.

COLLECT

Acts 6

*'... select from among yourselves seven men of good standing,
full of the Spirit and of wisdom' (v.3)*

As the Church grows, so its ministry grows. The apostles appoint
seven deacons with careful instructions that their job is to look after
widows. (By the way, the very fact that the widows are recognised
as an identifiable group tells us something about the nature of the
first Church and the persecution it faced.) But it seems that the Holy
Spirit has other ideas. No sooner have these deacons been
appointed than the Holy Spirit is leading them into new ministry.
Full of grace and power, Stephen does great wonders and signs
among the people. Others speak against him, and he is brought
before the council. One could be forgiven for wondering, who is
looking after the widows? Stephen's ministry of service – that is
what the word 'deacon' means – is leading him into witness.

How do we make sense of this? First of all, it tells us again that the
Church belongs to God, not us. Second, it shows us that ministry
cannot be tied down by our definitions and categories. Third, it
challenges us to see that all ministry, be it service or proclamation,
is an act of witness showing the world the new commandment of
love that is given by Christ. Hence, as Stephen is obedient to the
call of the Spirit, his face appears as that of an angel.

O God, you declare your almighty power
most chiefly in showing mercy and pity:
mercifully grant to us such a measure of your grace,
that we, running the way of your commandments,
may receive your gracious promises,
and be made partakers of your heavenly treasure;
through Jesus Christ your Son our Lord,
who is alive and reigns with you,
in the unity of the Holy Spirit,
one God, now and for ever.

Tuesday 2 September

Acts 7.1-16

'"Are these things so?" And Stephen replied…' (v.1)

The man who was chosen to wait at tables because the apostles needed more time for prayer and sermon preparation, preaches as his one and only recorded sermon the longest and most complex the Church has preached so far. Paul hasn't been converted yet, and up till now Peter's sermons have centred on the death and resurrection of Jesus and its significance for Israel.

Stephen takes us into new territory. The charge against him is that he spoke against the temple saying 'Jesus of Nazareth will destroy this place and will change the customs that Moses handed on to us' (Acts 6.14). 'Are these things so?' asks the High Priest (Acts 7.1).

Over the next three days we will read Stephen's reply. But this is where it is heading: Jesus himself is the temple. He won't be destroying what the prophets foretold, but fulfilling it in ways the leaders of Israel cannot yet see or comprehend. In my view, Stephen never quite gets to finish his speech. He is dragged out and stoned just as he is reaching his climax. By then, however, his thesis is clear, and the Council is furious. But his method is to tell again the great story of God's involvement with his people, a story that begins with Abraham, a story of how God is always reaching out to the people he loves.

God of glory,
the end of our searching,
help us to lay aside
all that prevents us from seeking your kingdom,
and to give all that we have
to gain the pearl beyond all price,
through our Saviour Jesus Christ.

COLLECT

Wednesday 3 September

Acts 7.17-43

*'God will raise up a prophet for you from your own people
as he raised me up' (v.37)*

Stephen presents Jesus in two ways. First, he shows how Jesus stands in the great prophetic tradition of Israel. The prophets, too, recalled Israel to its true vocation to be God's people and to worship and serve him faithfully and him alone. But Stephen also shows that Jesus is the one to whom all the prophets point. He is the prophet that God will raise up and through whom God will act to make an everlasting covenant. And so Stephen tells the story of salvation history. He explains how the prophets were rejected, how people did not listen to them, preferring other gods and other ways. He is preparing the ground for what he sees as the final and ultimate rejection of God, which is the rejection and crucifixion of Jesus.

If one of the themes of this book is witness – the Spirit-led witness of Christ through his Church – then there is much to learn here about how we tell the Christian story. Stephen addresses specific questions and concerns. He sets the story of Christ within the context of his listeners. He challenges them to look at their experience differently. Hopefully, we won't be stoned as a result. But we should expect misunderstanding and opposition. The story of Christ asks us to think about what we worship. For most of us today it isn't God.

COLLECT

O God, you declare your almighty power
most chiefly in showing mercy and pity:
mercifully grant to us such a measure of your grace,
that we, running the way of your commandments,
may receive your gracious promises,
and be made partakers of your heavenly treasure;
through Jesus Christ your Son our Lord,
who is alive and reigns with you,
in the unity of the Holy Spirit,
one God, now and for ever.

Thursday 4 September

Acts 7.44-53

*'... the Most High does not dwell in houses made
by human hands' (v.48)*

Stephen's conclusion is excoriating: 'the Most High does not live in houses made by human hands' (v.48). This is a direct attack on the temple. How could they be so stupid as to think that the God who made everything needed them to build him a house. Not only this, but those who received the law ordained by angels have failed to keep it. Like their forebears, they have opposed the Holy Spirit. They have ended up killing the Righteous One, who by his death and resurrection has become what the temple foreshadowed: the place where we worship – for in Christ, God tabernacles with us, and we with God. As Paul goes on to say in his letter to the Corinthians: 'Do you not know that you are God's temple and that God's Spirit dwells in you?' (1 Corinthians 3.16).

The council need no further evidence. Stephen is guilty as charged.

There is a challenge for us: what temples have we built? Where are our places of worship? Even in the Church, have we tried to confine God, constraining him in our rituals and customs? When do the things we love most in Church stop being channels of grace, and instead become barriers to God? And would we notice? Would we listen to Stephen if he came to our church? Or throw him into the street?

God of glory,
the end of our searching,
help us to lay aside
all that prevents us from seeking your kingdom,
and to give all that we have
to gain the pearl beyond all price,
through our Saviour Jesus Christ.

COLLECT

Friday 5 September

Acts 7.54 – 8.3

*'While they were stoning Stephen, he prayed,
"Lord Jesus, receive my spirit."' (7.59)*

The martyrdom of Stephen is one of the defining moments in the history of the early Church. It is a great act of apostolic witness. Stephen doesn't choose death. But he does not flinch from witnessing to the life-changing truth of Jesus Christ that leads to his death. His witness so enrages the religious council that, filled with fury, they drag him into the street and stone him.

Luke carefully tells this story to show how the witness, Stephen, is united with the Saviour, Jesus. He dies uplifted by a vision of Jesus in glory. Right to the end he continues to bear witness to the lordship of Christ. Like Jesus, he pleads forgiveness of those whose blindness compels them towards this hideous violence. 'Lord, do not hold this sin against them,' are his final words (7.60).

All this shows that the witness of the Church is the witness of Christ, and that, even in the smallest acts of witness or service, Christ is present with us through the Holy Spirit.

Stephen's clothes are laid at the feet of a young man called Saul. He approved of the killing. There is great lamentation for Stephen, but his witness has not ended. Saul's witnessing of this shocking and horrible death is part of what changes him; for it is to this persecutor of the Church that the baton of its witness is about to be passed.

COLLECT

O God, you declare your almighty power
most chiefly in showing mercy and pity:
mercifully grant to us such a measure of your grace,
that we, running the way of your commandments,
may receive your gracious promises,
and be made partakers of your heavenly treasure;
through Jesus Christ your Son our Lord,
who is alive and reigns with you,
in the unity of the Holy Spirit,
one God, now and for ever.

Saturday 6 September

Acts 8.4-25

*'Now those who were scattered went from place to place,
proclaiming the word' (v.4)*

The martyrdom of Stephen is significant for two other reasons. First, it marks the beginning of the first terrible persecution of the Church. Chapter 8 began with these words: 'That day a severe persecution began against the Church in Jerusalem' (v.1). But it also marks the beginning of a much broader evangelization. The Church is scattered. Those who persecuted the Church might have hoped that this would hasten its demise. On the contrary, far from inhibiting the spread of the gospel, this dispersal encourages it. Philip gets as far as Samaria. People respond to his proclamation. Some are healed. There is great joy in the city. News of this reaches Jerusalem, and Peter and John come to Samaria and through their ministry people receive the Holy Spirit.

Faith in Jesus Christ has not yet spread to the gentile world, but in this dispersal and witness that day comes closer.

It is hard to be a witness to Jesus Christ today. We may not face stoning or expulsion, but we do face ridicule and incomprehension. We are not witnessing in a culture that believes in God. Our task is in many ways much harder. But this book encourages us to see that God can be at work even in the setbacks to our ministry and that it is Christ's witness at work in us.

God of glory,
the end of our searching,
help us to lay aside
all that prevents us from seeking your kingdom,
and to give all that we have
to gain the pearl beyond all price,
through our Saviour Jesus Christ.

COLLECT

247

Monday 8 September

Acts 8.26-end

'What is to prevent me ...?' (v.36)

Power and responsibility had not distracted this Ethiopian from his religious duties or from searching the Scriptures for insight into the ways of God. What an answer to the longing in his heart as the Spirit brings Philip to unfold the Scripture's prophecy of the person and ministry of Jesus and help him take a crucial step in his discipleship!

This nameless man shows us a pathway for coming to deeper faith: he is, as many of us find ourselves, travelling a 'wilderness' road; he acknowledges something is missing from his spiritual life; he recognizes his need of grace; he sees an opportunity for a new level of commitment to God; and he is willing to ask for a sacramental action that will give both outward expression to his sense of bubbling hope and inner confirmation of his refreshed relationship with God.

We can be confident that God knows our spiritual hunger and will feed us in ways that suit our context and particular needs. These gifts of grace may be stunningly unexpected, but mostly they will pop up in the sacred simplicity of the ordinary day when we glimpse our heart-longing for God being answered – not through a mysterious coming or going, but in creation, in the smile of a child, a special Scripture verse, a timely message, events falling quietly into place, and that sense of deep peace that transcends the most difficult of circumstances.

How might God address your spiritual hunger today?

COLLECT

Almighty and everlasting God,
you are always more ready to hear than we to pray
and to give more than either we desire or deserve:
pour down upon us the abundance of your mercy,
forgiving us those things of which our conscience is afraid
and giving us those good things which we are not worthy to ask
but through the merits and mediation
of Jesus Christ your Son our Lord,
who is alive and reigns with you,
in the unity of the Holy Spirit,
one God, now and for ever.

Tuesday 9 September

Acts 9.1-19a

'I am Jesus, whom you are persecuting' (v.5)

Jesus doesn't minimize Saul's behaviour but names it for what it is: persecution. Jesus meets Saul head on, in the midst of his malice and, despite Saul's history and brutal intentions towards the followers of the Way, Jesus draws him into a radical revisiting of Jesus' own journey through darkness into the light of resurrection. For Saul, there is the day of crucifixion: the uncompromising deconstruction of Saul's sense of identity, authority, vision and life-purpose as he is faced with himself and the impact of his behaviour on Jesus. There is a period of darkness and waiting as his guilt and shame, dependence and powerlessness press in on him. And, finally, the hope of resurrection begins to emerge as Ananias bravely follows the Spirit's instructions and comes to Saul, to touch him, to call him 'Brother', to bring healing and baptism.

For some of us, this passage reawakens a longing for an unequivocal encounter with Jesus that would brush aside all our doubts. Far less appealing is the thought that we too might be like Saul, persecuting Jesus in some way. Saul's persecution of Jesus was public, zealous and vitriolic, creating fear among Christians everywhere. But us? Persecute Jesus? Surely not?

Perhaps it's time to ask the Holy Spirit of Jesus to show us how our actions or thoughts may be working against the kingdom of God, and how, in subtle ways, we too may be causing Jesus sadness and pain.

God of constant mercy,
who sent your Son to save us:
remind us of your goodness,
increase your grace within us,
that our thankfulness may grow,
through Jesus Christ our Lord.

COLLECT

Wednesday 10 September

Acts 9.19b-31

'… and immediately he began to proclaim Jesus in the synagogues' (v.20)

As Saul begins to live out his resurrection life by unashamedly proclaiming Christ, others understandably react with suspicion, reluctant to believe that something fundamental has shifted, that what they now see *is* a reformed character, with a perspective informed by love, not hate.

Saul knows he has been re-made in his encounter with Christ. He is 'a new creation' (2 Corinthians 5.17) and he has to trust that his redeemed behaviour and attitudes towards the followers of the Way will soon prove to others the genuineness of his transformation. For only someone who has experienced Jesus' loving acceptance and forgiveness and who is being led by his Spirit, can confidently say of Jesus, 'He is the Son of God', and can love God with his whole being, even if that means placing himself in the firing line for Christ.

Jesus saw Saul's potential and passion, and practised his own teaching, 'Love your enemies and pray for those who persecute you' (Matthew 5.44), offering Saul relationship. Jesus offers relationship to you and to me today, no matter what we have done or not done to help or hinder kingdom-growth, no matter if we have misused the name of Jesus in casual conversation, or taunted those around us who proclaim their faith in God.

God's power transformed Saul's attitude towards Jesus from persecution to proclamation. God's power can transform us too – from death to life, from fear to peace, from … to …

COLLECT

Almighty and everlasting God,
you are always more ready to hear than we to pray
and to give more than either we desire or deserve:
pour down upon us the abundance of your mercy,
forgiving us those things of which our conscience is afraid
and giving us those good things which we are not worthy to ask
but through the merits and mediation
of Jesus Christ your Son our Lord,
who is alive and reigns with you,
in the unity of the Holy Spirit,
one God, now and for ever.

Thursday 11 September

Acts 9.32-end

'... and then he knelt down and prayed' (v.40)

Undoubtedly, from the resurrection story before us, Peter's inspired ministry drew many people towards God's healing and powerful love. The Spirit's guidance sustained Peter as he went here and there among believers, for Peter knew that any ministry he undertook had to be preceded by acknowledging God's authority, and by spending substantial time in prayer in the name of Jesus Christ.

In far less trying circumstances than Peter faced, many of us still struggle to pray.

Prayer is mysteriously woven into the relationship between God and humanity. We pray because the Spirit first prays in us, moving us to call upon God using more familiar vocal prayer, and silent prayer as we wait upon God and listen with as receptive a heart as we can offer. It takes time for our minds to quieten, for our egos to move aside, but if our heart's intention is towards God in petition or intercession, we may notice a helpful thought, a pertinent Scripture, a word or picture, a memory, or clarity of feeling. Ultimately the next step in prayer or action emerges, as it did for Peter.

Maybe you have wondered what God was doing, when, like Dorcas's friends, you've watched someone you love face suffering and death. If, as you read this passage today, old feelings of pain, sadness or even anger have arisen to trouble your soul, bring them to God and then spend some time quietly listening for God's loving answer. It will come.

God of constant mercy,
who sent your Son to save us:
remind us of your goodness,
increase your grace within us,
that our thankfulness may grow,
through Jesus Christ our Lord.

COLLECT

Acts 10.1-16

'Your prayers and your alms have ascended as a memorial to God' (v.4)

At a pivotal point in the mission of God, two men of prayer from very different backgrounds are given divine guidance – an angelic instruction and reassurance for one, and a vision of great clarity with a thrice-repeated message for the other. Cornelius and Peter are being called to engage in something of immense significance, and we can feel the excitement mounting as each man experiences God's personal communication and makes his response.

These communications come in forms that some readers today may find hard to believe. However, there will be others of you for whom Cornelius' and Peter's spiritual experiences are a welcome reminder of something 'more real than real' which you've kept like a treasure in your heart, perhaps for years.

God plants within us a desire for more of God. As prayer and trust deepen, we open ourselves to God's personal communication to us, because God *still* connects with people – in ways that defy logic or scientific explanation. Whether through dreams, an angelic visitation, a providential unfolding of events, answered prayer, an awareness of the sacred in a special place, a sense of connection with creation, or even a timely call from a friend, God's ways of reaching out to us are perfectly suited to our needs and nature, and geared to the particular ministry to which God calls us.

How has God reached out to touch you, guide you, strengthen you at pivotal moments in your life?

COLLECT

Almighty and everlasting God,
you are always more ready to hear than we to pray
and to give more than either we desire or deserve:
pour down upon us the abundance of your mercy,
forgiving us those things of which our conscience is afraid
and giving us those good things which we are not worthy to ask
but through the merits and mediation
of Jesus Christ your Son our Lord,
who is alive and reigns with you,
in the unity of the Holy Spirit,
one God, now and for ever.

Saturday 13 September

Acts 10.17-33

'... here in the presence of God to listen to all that the Lord has commanded you to say' (v.33)

Few of us would make a 30-mile journey with people we didn't know to meet someone whom law and convention had put outside our experience – and comfort zones. But Peter, still pondering the vision that challenged his attitude to the exclusive Jewish food laws, and encouraged by a clear instruction from the Spirit, listens to the strangers' request, offers overnight hospitality, and then sets out with them willingly.

Cornelius welcomes Peter with such enthusiasm that he has to do what many spiritual leaders must do today, remind those present that God alone is worthy of worship. Each man hears the other's story. We can imagine their growing awe and excitement at the way God is working, their deepening joy in being agents of God's desire to break down the walls that divide (e.g. Ephesians 2.14), so that the Way of Jesus might ripple out beyond its natural origins in Judaism into the whole of the gentile world.

Whenever we prayerfully acknowledge God's presence, and are willing to work against un-freedom wherever we see it, the Spirit can move within and among us in ways that will exceed our best hopes and help fulfil the dream of God to gather all people into that great Love that creates, redeems and sanctifies.

What stereotypes prevent you from engaging with the 'strangers' you encounter each day? How far outside your comfort zones would *you* go for the sake of the Gospel?

God of constant mercy,
who sent your Son to save us:
remind us of your goodness,
increase your grace within us,
that our thankfulness may grow,
through Jesus Christ our Lord.

COLLECT

253

Monday 15 September

Psalms 123, 124, 125, **126**
2 Samuel 18.1-18
Acts 10.34-end

Acts 10.34-end

'Can anyone withhold the water for baptising these people ...?' (v.47)

Totally absorbed, the assembly listens to Peter's retelling of the good news of Jesus Christ. Speaking with the integrity of one who has been with Jesus from the start, has endured the harrowing day of crucifixion and experienced the truth of the resurrection appearances, Peter's presence brings Jesus closer to the gathered hearts.

Have you ever felt the presence of God at a Christian gathering – that loving intelligent energy pulsing around and within you? Then you will have an idea of what it was like that day – the air charged with the wonder and power of God, the Holy Spirit warming the group so each person's spirit bubbles over in praise and in speech uncluttered by intellectual sophistication. Following this unmistakable sign of God's delight, baptism is offered, affirming the sovereign movement of the Spirit, giving the new Gentile disciples an opportunity to make a public declaration of their faith and binding them into the widening fellowship of the name of Jesus.

What a lovely example of the Spirit of God moving 'where it chooses' (cf John 3.8). Those listening to Peter didn't have to complete a lengthy course of preparation before God blesses them; there is a simple sacred coming of the Spirit to those whose hearts are longing for God.

Those of us who are sticklers for correct ecclesiastical protocols can lighten up: in this story no one worries that baptism comes *after* the gift of the Holy Spirit!

COLLECT

Almighty God,
who called your Church to bear witness
that you were in Christ reconciling the world to yourself:
help us to proclaim the good news of your love,
that all who hear it may be drawn to you;
through him who was lifted up on the cross,
and reigns with you in the unity of the Holy Spirit,
one God, now and for ever.

Tuesday 16 September

Acts 11.1-18

'... who was I that I could hinder God?' (v.17)

Peter travels back to Jerusalem full of amazement and joy, but rumours have preceded him and he is met by questions and criticism. In the local believers we see the unfortunate human tendency to gossip and argue about who is 'in' and who is 'out' – whether it be in matters of faith, theology, praxis, class or ethnicity.

What lies behind this tendency in all of us is a complex mix of self-interest, the need to control, and fear – fear that somehow we will be diminished if we let 'them' become part of 'us'. Fear is not of God, and thankfully Peter is not a man of fear but a man of courage and prayer. He chooses not to engage in an argument to try to justify his action. Instead, he trusts the Holy Spirit to give him the words he needs. Peter's evocative truth-telling dissolves any hidden fear and those listening begin to see the hand of God in this extraordinary development. Their complaints evaporate, silenced by the beauty of God's dream of welcome, acceptance and love for *all* people.

Churches today are not immune to fear-based attitudes and behaviours that divide people and hinder God's longing for peace and justice. And so it will continue until we bring ourselves in penitence before our God and allow God to take control, cauterize our fear and release our compassion.

How quick are we to spread rumours or snub those who are 'different' – even at church?

Almighty God,
you search us and know us:
may we rely on you in strength
and rest on you in weakness,
now and in all our days;
through Jesus Christ our Lord.

COLLECT

Wednesday 17 September

Acts 11.19-end

'When he came and saw the grace of God, he rejoiced...'(v.23)

The Holy Spirit is at work in Antioch through two unnamed refugees who had settled in this fertile valley following Stephen's martyrdom. The men begin to reach out to the Greek population with the good news of Jesus, and soon reports of their efforts and the growing numbers of believers filter back to Jerusalem.

Sent to determine what is going on, Barnabas approaches the emerging Church in Antioch hopefully. Instead of exercising his authority by prematurely wading in to 'correct' divergent practice or theology, he takes the time to find out for himself what has been happening. And, having seen, he *rejoices*. He recognizes the Spirit of God at work and shares with those present in giving thanks for the continuing growth of the gospel among the Gentiles.

Barnabas lays down an important principle here: although 'church' may be done differently in different places, although things we hold dear may seem secondary to another group of Christians – even in our own parish – fundamentally, if we take the time to look, if 'the hand of God' is with them, the fruit of the Spirit *will* be apparent. Then we can do what Barnabas did: affirm their Godly work, foster genuine relationships and provide wise mentors to encourage in-depth spiritual formation.

By listening to people's longings, and the invitation of the Spirit, together we can build up the people of God in that place and reach out to serve the local community.

COLLECT

Almighty God,
who called your Church to bear witness
that you were in Christ reconciling the world to yourself:
help us to proclaim the good news of your love,
that all who hear it may be drawn to you;
through him who was lifted up on the cross,
and reigns with you in the unity of the Holy Spirit,
one God, now and for ever.

Thursday 18 September

Acts 12.1-17

'... the church prayed fervently to God for him' (v.5)

A kind angel, mindful of Peter's sleepy state, gently prods him into action as a mother might a drowsy child. Slightly stunned, Peter thankfully acknowledges that the Lord has rescued him from Herod Agrippa I's widening persecution of Church leaders in Jerusalem. But when he reaches a house church, he is refused entry! Ironically, those who had been praying for Peter's release are slow to believe Rhoda's good news, perhaps assuming that his guardian angel had taken on the guise of Peter – a not uncommon view at the time.

Do you ever assure your children or grandchildren that *their* guardian angels shield their spirit from all harm? How do you understand the many biblical references to angels? (e.g. Daniel 3 and 6, Luke 1, John 20)? What is your view – your story – of angels today?

Peter specifically wants his angel-assisted escape story shared with Jesus' brother James. In spite of James' earlier uncertainty about his brother's divinity and vocation, James was, by this time, an active leader among Jerusalem Christians, some of whom were still critical of Peter's unconventional ministry to the gentiles. It was important that James could tell this wider faith community of God's intervention on Peter's behalf, as an encouraging sign both of answered prayer and of God's confirmation of Peter's call to those beyond Judaism.

May we never underestimate the power of Spirit-led believers' prayer, or the possibility of angels' mysterious comings and goings – doing the Lord's bidding – even now.

Almighty God,
you search us and know us:
may we rely on you in strength
and rest on you in weakness,
now and in all our days;
through Jesus Christ our Lord.

COLLECT

257

Friday 19 September

Acts 12.18-end

'But the word of God continued to advance ...' (v.24)

For those panicking soldiers who had failed to keep Peter imprisoned, there is the sad, inevitable, death sentence imposed by a vengeful Agrippa, whose plans to appease a particular faction of the Jews by having Peter publicly tried and executed, have been thwarted.

Grandson of the first Herod, Agrippa's Roman upbringing and shrewd political sense meant that by AD 41, Emperor Claudius trusted him with the governorship of Galilee, Samaria, Judea and Peraea. But in AD 44, Agrippa's plans to emphasize his power over those dependent on him for their very food, take an unexpected turn.

Described in detail by contemporary Roman historian Josephus, the death of Agrippa comes after he is taken gravely ill, having failed to turn aside the shouts of feigned adulation from those attending his public address. Declared a god by those desperate to please him, Agrippa's end is painful and humiliating: for a tyrant opposed to the Way of Jesus, it is both a timely fall from power and understandably ascribed to the action of 'an angel of the Lord'.

The last few lines of this action-packed passage are encouragingly clear: God continues to build the Church as 'the word of God' advances. What a beautiful reality, the word of God, 'living and active' (Hebrews 4.12) rippling out to foster the kingdom through men and women of faith, fulfilling Isaiah 55.11: 'my word ... shall not return to me empty, but it shall accomplish that which I purpose.' And so it shall.

COLLECT

Almighty God,
who called your Church to bear witness
that you were in Christ reconciling the world to yourself:
help us to proclaim the good news of your love,
that all who hear it may be drawn to you;
through him who was lifted up on the cross,
and reigns with you in the unity of the Holy Spirit,
one God, now and for ever.

Psalm 147
2 Samuel 24
Acts 13.1-12

Acts 13.1-12

'... the Holy Spirit said ... being sent out by the Holy Spirit ... filled with the Holy Spirit ...' (vv.2,4,9)

Central to this passage is the apostles' continuing dependence on the guidance of the Holy Spirit. Nothing significant is decided or begun without waiting upon God in worship with fasting: worship to affirm their creaturely relationship with their Creator; fasting because abstinence helps focus their spiritual need of God. Nothing is achieved without the Spirit's enabling.

Frequently in Acts we see the Spirit actively setting direction and giving comfort, reminders, clarifications, detailed instructions and warnings to those whom God is sending out into the world with the radical news of Jesus. But what about today? What about us and the mission God gives to each one of us, to be as Christ in our communities? Is the Spirit of the living God as active today in you, in me?

Some reading this will say a resounding 'Yes', having personally experienced that timely, personal, wise and warm counsel that only God's Spirit can provide. Others may hesitate to be so emphatic, having little awareness of being led by the Spirit, or with a religious upbringing or current practice that has emphasised other aspects of the Christian faith.

If you are intrigued by the key role of the Holy Spirit in the supportive guidance of the apostles in Acts, if you want to experience more divine direction yourself, tell God of your longing and, if you can, pray with some others whom you trust that God's Spirit – already a glowing ember within you – may be rekindled.

Almighty God,
you search us and know us:
may we rely on you in strength
and rest on you in weakness,
now and in all our days;
through Jesus Christ our Lord.

COLLECT

Monday 22 September

1 Kings 1.5-31

'Now Adonijah … exalted himself, saying, "I will be king"' (v.5)

As King David's life draws to its end, an undignified scramble for the succession develops between the sons of two of David's wives. Adonijah the son of Haggith decides to anticipate David's death and has himself declared king without David's knowledge. But the prophet Nathan remains loyal, and moves swiftly to warn David's first wife Bathsheba of the threat to her son Solomon's promised succession. Both Bathsheba and Nathan petition the dying king, and David reaffirms to them that his intention is indeed that Solomon should succeed him as king.

Periods of dynastic change caused by death, deposition or retirement can be times of great instability and tension. Ancient quarrels may be resurrected and long-simmering feuds renewed as the contenders for the succession jostle for position. And it doesn't have to be a royal succession. As I write, the race for the Republican candidacy to run for president in the next United States election is underway, with all the mud-slinging and inflated promises that tend to accompany such a contest, whether abroad or in this country. And at a more local level, the reading of a will can expose hitherto unsuspected rivalries and tensions in families.

Adonijah exalted himself (v.5), and did not have the humility to seek the advice of his elders (v.6). How do we deal with our own inner power-drive, and how do we prevent it developing along destructive pathways?

COLLECT

Almighty God,
whose only Son has opened for us
a new and living way into your presence:
give us pure hearts and steadfast wills
to worship you in spirit and in truth;
through Jesus Christ your Son our Lord,
who is alive and reigns with you,
in the unity of the Holy Spirit,
one God, now and for ever.

Psalms **5**, 6 (8)
1 Kings 1.32 – 2.4; 2.10-12
Acts 13.44 – 14.7

1 Kings 1.32 – 2.4; 2.10-12

'I am about to go the way of all the earth' (2.2)

In this crisis, it may be that David has made a rod for his own back. The Bible indicates repeatedly that David, in addition to being a fine king and inspirational leader, was also a deeply flawed human being. In reference to Adonijah, there was a suggestion in yesterday's reading that David was over-indulgent with his son, and maybe even a little afraid of him (Chapter 1.6). At least when the crisis breaks he now acts decisively, reaffirming his promise to Nathan and Bathsheba concerning Solomon, and giving orders for the anointing of Solomon as king.

As his death approaches, David encourages his son to be of good courage, and to walk faithfully according to the law and commandments of God. If he does so, then his life and reign will prosper (2.2-3). It is regrettable that the lectionary compilers have omitted the remaining verses of the king's charge to Solomon (2.5-9). David here demands Solomon's continued retaliation on his father's enemies, urging him to pursue and take vengeance on those who had opposed him.

Another version of David's final words – minus the vengeance and bloodlust – can be found in 2 Samuel 23:1-7. But it is arguably the unsanitized version that more accurately reflects not only the highs and lows of the character of David himself, but also the complex mix of light and darkness that makes up our common humanity.

Merciful God,
your Son came to save us
and bore our sins on the cross:
may we trust in your mercy
and know your love,
rejoicing in the righteousness
that is ours through Jesus Christ our Lord.

COLLECT

1 Kings 3

*'Solomon loved the Lord ... only,
he sacrificed and offered incense at the high places.' (v.3)*

When God invites Solomon to ask him for what he wanted (v.5), he is setting the young man quite a challenge. The temptation for him must surely have been to take full advantage of the offer, in order to assure for himself riches and popularity. But Solomon's response indicates a depth of wisdom beyond his years, and God's response (vv.13-14) demonstrates the truth of some of the later teaching of Jesus about seeking God's kingdom first of all (Matthew 6.33).

Soon, Solomon's powers of discernment face an even sterner test as he is approached by two prostitutes, both claiming to be the mother of the same baby (vv.16-28). It may be an anachronism in this period to talk about acute psychological insight, but that is clearly what Solomon demonstrates as he distinguishes the attitude and response of the true mother from that of the fraud.

But even at this early stage, one or two disquieting hints indicate that all is not quite as it should have been. Solomon's marriage to the daughter of Pharoah king of Egypt must, given the history of the two nations, have put the integrity of the kingdom at risk. And this was coupled with delays in the completion of the temple, forcing Solomon and his people to sacrifice 'at the high places' (vv.2-3), with all their negative associations of pagan worship (cf. Leviticus 26.30; Numbers 33.52). This lack of single-heartedness was ultimately to cost Solomon dear.

COLLECT

Almighty God,
whose only Son has opened for us
a new and living way into your presence:
give us pure hearts and steadfast wills
to worship you in spirit and in truth;
through Jesus Christ your Son our Lord,
who is alive and reigns with you,
in the unity of the Holy Spirit,
one God, now and for ever.

Thursday 25 September

1 Kings 4.29 – 5.12

'But now ... there is neither adversary nor misfortune. So I intend to build a house for... the Lord my God' (5.4-5)

For the moment, any niggling doubts appear to have been forgotten as the knowledge of Solomon's wisdom and depth of understanding spread far beyond Israel's boundaries. Pictured here is an archetypal sage of the Near East, with a reputation for artistic as well as political interests. Earlier (1 Kings 3.10-14), we saw how God blessed Solomon with wealth and all the trappings of the good life; to these are now added fame, power and wisdom 'as vast as the sand on the seashore' (4.29).

And yet, hidden within the eulogistic tone, the tremors of uneasiness remain. The Hebrew idiom used for 'breadth of understanding' (4.29) is ambiguous: it is used elsewhere in the Hebrew Scriptures to denote arrogance (Psalm 101.5; Isaiah 9.9, 10.12). And Solomon's request to King Hiram for practical assistance in the building of the temple hints that this crucial work was not at the top of his list of priorities (5.5-6).

We should not assume that God's blessings on Solomon automatically imply that Solomon has a good character. If we read between the lines, a somewhat different picture begins to emerge: one of a leader who is insecure in his leadership, who surrounds himself with cronies and who is primarily concerned with ensuring his own comfort. As the Old Testament scholar Choon-Leong Seow has commented in the *New Interpreters' Bible (NIB)*: 'One may well envy Solomon, but this is not someone whom most of us would like.'

Merciful God,
your Son came to save us
and bore our sins on the cross:
may we trust in your mercy
and know your love,
rejoicing in the righteousness
that is ours through Jesus Christ our Lord.

COLLECT

Friday 26 September

Psalms 17, **19**
1 Kings 6.1, 11-28
Acts 15.22-35

1 Kings 6.1, 11-28

'…in the fourth year of Solomon's reign over Israel…he began to build the house of the Lord' (v.1)

With the willing assistance of Hiram, the building of the temple finally gets under way, and the process is described in exhaustive detail (vv.2-10). The omission of these verses from today's text highlights an often-puzzling question: what is the significance of all these intricate architectural details, and how do they reveal the word of God? Something of an answer to that question is suggested in verse 12: 'Concerning this house that you are building, if you will walk in my statutes … then I will establish my promise with you' (v.12). The significance of the building is inextricably linked to the people's obedience to God. This 'if … then …' motif first appeared in 1 Kings 3.14, and it seems to resonate with both promise and warning.

Things appear to be going according to plan – and yet a thread of anxiety continues to tremble beneath the surface of the narrative. There is no suggestion here that King Hiram's relationship with Solomon was anything but beneficial to both parties (as was Hiram's earlier relationship with David). But some have questioned why Israel, a nation supposedly at the peak of its power, needed to align itself with another nation at all. Were they not exposing themselves to unnecessary risk of domination by a foreign power by doing so? Choon-Leong Seow suggests that, ironically, Solomon's effort to bring about and ensure the divine presence actually put the freedom of his people in jeopardy.

COLLECT

Almighty God,
whose only Son has opened for us
a new and living way into your presence:
give us pure hearts and steadfast wills
to worship you in spirit and in truth;
through Jesus Christ your Son our Lord,
who is alive and reigns with you,
in the unity of the Holy Spirit,
one God, now and for ever.

Psalms 20, 21, **23**
1 Kings 8.1-30
Acts 15.36 – 16.5

1 Kings 8.1-30

'But will God indeed dwell on the earth?' (v.27)

The work on the temple is finally complete, and Solomon assembles all the elders and leaders of the tribes of Israel to witness the triumphant dedication. Central to the ceremony is the bringing up of the Ark of the Covenant, symbol of both God's presence with his people and a reminder of his covenant with them, to its final resting place in the inner sanctuary of the temple (vv.1-6). But we step aside from the narrative of Solomon's life and reign for a moment in order to reflect on a significant crossroads in the faith and belief of the Israelites.

The text at this point is laden with images resonant of Israel's religious past. Once the Ark had been installed and the priests re-emerged from the holy place, 'a cloud filled the house of the Lord … for the glory of the Lord filled the house of the Lord' (vv.10-11). The image conflates two symbols redolent of the exodus, where the glory of the Lord appeared in the cloud that accompanied the Israelites on their daytime wanderings through the desert (Exodus 16.10). But alongside these images of the immediate presence of God, a more mysterious reality is emerging: one that sees God as dwelling in deep darkness (8.12). The temple has indeed been built as a fitting dwelling place for the Lord, but its dedication is accompanied by a growing awareness that 'even heaven and the highest heaven' (v.27) cannot contain him.

Merciful God,
your Son came to save us
and bore our sins on the cross:
may we trust in your mercy
and know your love,
rejoicing in the righteousness
that is ours through Jesus Christ our Lord.

COLLECT

265

Monday 29 September

Michael and All Angels

Psalms 34, 150
Tobit 12.6-end *or* Daniel 12.1-4
Acts 12.1-11

Daniel 12.1-4

'Michael, the great prince, the protector of your people' (v.1)

The Bible teems with angelic presences. Abraham recognizes as 'the Lord' the angels who visit him in the guise of three men (Genesis 18.2-3). For the kingdom of Israel, God's angels were a heavenly army (1 Kings 22.19). After the Babylonian exile in 586 BC, angels became a more personalised presence: Daniel names both Michael, as in today's passage, and Gabriel (Daniel 8.16; 9.21). For Daniel, Gabriel is an interpreter of visions and a conveyor of wisdom; in Luke's Gospel, he is universally known as the angel of the annunciations to both Zechariah (Luke 1.19) and Mary (Luke 1.26). Matthew's Gospel tells of an angel who warned Joseph in a dream to flee with Mary and Jesus to escape Herod's murderous intentions, and again when it was safe for them to return home (Mathew 2.13-23). In Revelation, it is Michael and his angels who fight the final battle, defeating the enemies of God (Revelation 12.7).

Many people today – by no means all of them Christians – own a belief in the existence of angels; a number claim to have directly received angelic help. But whether in Scripture or in contemporary experience, the idea of angels tends to 'shape-shift' according to context and circumstance. Whether angels have been a part of our Christian experience or not, today's festival invites us to thank God for all the channels of his wisdom and goodness to us, and the means he continually offers for our guidance and protection.

COLLECT

Everlasting God,
you have ordained and constituted
    the ministries of angels and mortals in a wonderful order:
grant that as your holy angels always serve you in heaven,
so, at your command,
they may help and defend us on earth;
through Jesus Christ your Son our Lord,
who is alive and reigns with you,
in the unity of the Holy Spirit,
one God, now and for ever.

Tuesday 30 September

1 Kings 8.63 – 9.9

'I will cut Israel off from the land that I have given them' (9.7)

The magnificent celebrations accompanying the dedication of the new temple conclude with a seven-day festival, at the end of which the people 'blessed the king, and went to their tents, joyful and in good spirits' (8.66) on account of the Lord's goodness to them.

And then – another encounter between Solomon and the Lord; and an uneasy recurrence of the 'if ... then ...' motif (9.4-5) as God again hints at a promise and a warning. The danger here is that this can be read as justifying a crude cause-and-effect approach to God's response to the vagaries of human behaviour. Later biblical narrative reveals that, as Israel's relationship with her creator develops and deepens, so the biblical picture becomes much more complex and mysterious. The book of Job, which describes the plight of a righteous, God-fearing man almost overwhelmed by tragedy and suffering, sees this earlier simplistic correlation between obedience and blessing, disobedience and suffering being radically challenged. And Job learns that there are no easy answers.

What is clear, however, is that Solomon's actions and our own will bring consequences in their wake, whether or not we understand those consequences or feel them to be justified. When God calls a person into a relationship with him, in such a calling demands and responsibilities will be inextricably interwoven with peace, joy and spiritual enrichment. It is this interweaving that gives the relationship its depth and richness, and only so can it survive and thrive.

God, who in generous mercy sent the Holy Spirit
upon your Church in the burning fire of your love:
grant that your people may be fervent
in the fellowship of the gospel
that, always abiding in you,
they may be found steadfast in faith and active in service;
through Jesus Christ your Son our Lord,
who is alive and reigns with you,
in the unity of the Holy Spirit,
one God, now and for ever.

Wednesday 1 October

Psalm **34**
1 Kings 10.1-25
Acts 17.1-15

1 Kings 10.1-25

'Because the Lord loved Israel for ever, he has made you king...'
(v.9)

Solomon's prestige has spread worldwide, and this historic visit of the Queen of Sheba is representative of his now universal renown. In the Old Testament, only 1 Kings mentions this mysterious queen; Matthew 12:42 refers to her as 'the queen of the South' who 'came from the ends of the earth' to listen to Solomon's wisdom. Whatever other reasons there might have been for such an impressive state visit, it is clear that her coming is a considerable coup for Solomon.

It is here that the narrative takes on a wading-through-treacle quality, and we feel as if we are drowning in excess. To Solomon's existing riches the queen brings more (vv.2,10), but for all her own wealth, the opulence and magnificence of Solomon's house overwhelms her, and 'there was no more spirit in her' (v.5).

The imparting of wisdom is not all one-sided: the queen, indirectly, offers some of her own. Her praise of Solomon acknowledges the divine character of his kingship, and sees Solomon's qualities of justice and righteousness as a (super)natural consequence of his holy calling (v.9). The queen's words of praise carry a veiled warning, however. Solomon should take care not to get above himself, because none of the wealth, wisdom and renown that he enjoys are his by right, but only because God has chosen him for the fulfilment of his own sovereign purposes.

God, who in generous mercy sent the Holy Spirit
    upon your Church in the burning fire of your love:
grant that your people may be fervent
in the fellowship of the gospel
that, always abiding in you,
they may be found steadfast in faith and active in service;
through Jesus Christ your Son our Lord,
who is alive and reigns with you,
in the unity of the Holy Spirit,
one God, now and for ever.

Psalm 37*
1 Kings 11.1-13
Acts 17.16-end

1 Kings 11.1-13

'Then the Lord was angry with Solomon' (v.9)

It is at this point that the unease simmering just below the surface of the narrative erupts, and things begin to unravel. What was previously implicit is now expressed unambiguously, and the extent to which Solomon has deviated from God's will becomes transparently clear. We have known of Solomon's marriage to the daughter of the Egyptian Pharoah; now the narrative tells of the many other relationships with foreign women Solomon has contracted (v.1). The threat to Solomon's kingship was severe because these were not just any foreign women but women from nations with whom the Lord had strictly forbidden the Israelites to intermarry (v.2).

This may feel uncomfortably like xenophobia to the modern reader, but the original writer had no such concept in mind. The writer is concerned solely with Solomon's faithfulness to God, and it is on this point that the king's disobedience strikes at the heart of the matter in challenging the first two commandments: 'I am the Lord your God ... you shall have no other gods before me ... You shall not bow down to them or worship them' (Exodus 20.2,3,5). Solomon disobeyed and therefore 'did what was evil in the sight of the Lord' (v.6) and did not follow the Lord wholeheartedly as his father David had done. The Lord is angry with Solomon – an anger that was to have dire consequences for Israel and its future (vv.11-13).

Lord God,
defend your Church from all false teaching
and give to your people knowledge of your truth,
that we may enjoy eternal life
in Jesus Christ our Lord.

COLLECT

Friday 3 October

Psalm **31**
1 Kings 11.26-end
Acts 18.1-21

1 Kings 11.26-end

'[I] will build you an enduring house, as I built for David' (v.38)

The writing is on the wall for Solomon and his son and heir Rehoboam, as the prophet Ahijah tells Jeroboam (the son of Nebat, one of Solomon's servants) that *he* is God's choice to be the next king. Ahijah's prophecy has a ring of *déjà vu* about it, rehearsing again the solemn promise and warning that the Lord repeatedly gave to Solomon throughout his reign (v.38).

We are given some information about Jeroboam: that he was able and industrious, and that Solomon 'gave him charge over all the forced labour of the house of Joseph' (v.28). For reasons that are not totally clear, Jeroboam rebelled against the king (vv.26,27), although they may have included a reaction against the over-harsh demands imposed by Solomon on the tribe of Joseph (1 Kings 12.4). As with Solomon, the blessings that will be showered upon Jeroboam have nothing whatever to do with the prospective king's personal qualities or uprightness of character, but everything to do with the purposes of God.

Ahijah's prophecy is grim, and presages the breaking up of the kingdom (vv.29-36). In a vividly acted parable, Ahijah tears his new garment into twelve pieces. Ten pieces represent the number of tribes to be given to Jeroboam; one is to be left with Solomon's line, 'for the sake of my servant David' and for Jerusalem (v.32). The maths may be questionable – but the parable's grim meaning is crystal clear.

COLLECT

God, who in generous mercy sent the Holy Spirit
    upon your Church in the burning fire of your love:
grant that your people may be fervent
in the fellowship of the gospel
that, always abiding in you,
    they may be found steadfast in faith and active in service;
through Jesus Christ your Son our Lord,
who is alive and reigns with you,
in the unity of the Holy Spirit,
one God, now and for ever.

1 Kings 12.1-24

'... he disregarded the advice that the older men gave him' (v.8)

Solomon is dead, and all Israel goes to Shechem in order to see his son Rehoboam made king (v.1). Jeroboam takes advantage of the new regime, and asks the king for a more lenient treatment of his men than that which was meted out by Solomon (vv.3-4). Rehoboam's initial response bodes well, as he bids Jeroboam to return in three days, after the king has consulted with his counsellors.

However, it quickly becomes clear that the wisdom God bestowed in such abundance on Solomon has been withheld from his son. Ignoring the advice of those counsellors who had attended Solomon, Rehoboam instead turns to the young men with whom he had grown up. In a tragically mistaken attempt to impress his authority, Rehoboam squanders an unrepeatable opportunity to win everyone's good will and take the entire nation with him. His vow to subject the tribe of Joseph to even harsher treatment than his father had done irrevocably lost him the allegiance and loyalty of the vast majority of Israelites (vv.16-17).

Rehoboam's arrogance and inability to relent led to the breakup of the Israelite kingdom, and the fall-out from that event reverberated down the generations. Our own arrogance and youthful insecurities may not have resulted in such a catastrophic outcome, but time will have taught us that true wisdom lies in a willingness to listen to, and to learn from, the experience of those who have gone before us.

Lord God,
defend your Church from all false teaching
and give to your people knowledge of your truth,
that we may enjoy eternal life
in Jesus Christ our Lord.

COLLECT

Monday 6 October

1 Kings 12.25 – 13.10

'So he went another way … ' (13.10)

King Jeroboam initiated a number of building projects intended to promote a state religion that ensured his political power. It is too easy to use religion for selfish purposes, and when it is manipulated, the results are usually very damaging. Although this story is ancient, its themes are fresh. The fashioned gods of the day boost our egos, but they are shiny reflections of ourselves. Left to our own devices, we cannot save ourselves, and it takes a 'man of God' to approach the king and tell him his altars are worthless because they are simply the places where people come to worship themselves.

The man, we are told, is of God. This God is frightening not because he lives in high places but because he is real and exposes our masks. The man cuts through the sham of the compromised religion that, in effect, acts as a chaplaincy to the empire and foresees its end. He won't receive any gift from the king and won't commune in any way with what his kingdom represents. It is a resonant topic for today. How does a person of faith live and act in societies, institutions and cultures that are enmeshed in values and beliefs that are contrary to the way of love, reckless generosity and integrity that are central to their belief? The lives of Dietrich Bonhoeffer, Desmond Tutu and the many people of faith sitting in prisons around the world today confirm that the gospel can never be compromised and the world must be challenged – starting with ourselves.

COLLECT

O Lord, we beseech you mercifully to hear the prayers
    of your people who call upon you;
and grant that they may both perceive and know
    what things they ought to do,
and also may have grace and power faithfully to fulfil them;
through Jesus Christ your Son our Lord,
who is alive and reigns with you,
in the unity of the Holy Spirit,
one God, now and for ever.

Tuesday 7 October

1 Kings 13.11-end

'Alas, my brother!' (v.30)

This story outlines a comparison between a true prophet and a false one. The man of God we heard of yesterday allows himself to be deceived by an old prophet in Bethel. Whereas the man of God had, as prophets must, spoken truth to power, this other man seems to want to trip him up and says he's been told by an angel that the man of God can now eat and drink.

The consequent death of the man of God, however, convinces the Bethel prophet of his authenticity and holiness. He laments the man's death and asks to be buried with him. If he cannot share the man's integrity in life, it seems, he hopes to draw something of it for himself afterwards. Whereas the man of God seemed to be the shamed one, it is, we discover, the shame of the trickster that is unbearably heavy.

It is very easy to be convinced by those who say they speak the thoughts and words of God, especially when they sound plausible. This story advises caution. We must beware of quick clarity and the religious sound-bite. Sometimes people are using the name of God to bolster their own agendas and power games. Words always need to be weighed in the balance. How do they measure up to the values of truth, peace and, most of all, love? How are they playing with me and enticing me into conclusions that I am not worthy of as one called to service in the name of Jesus Christ?

Lord of creation,
whose glory is around and within us:
open our eyes to your wonders,
that we may serve you with reverence
and know your peace at our lives' end,
through Jesus Christ our Lord.

COLLECT

273

Wednesday 8 October

1 Kings 17

'The Lord listened to the voice of Elijah' (v.22)

Ahab hedges his bets and hopes for political harmony by trying to combine the worship of Yahweh and Baal. Then along comes Elijah whose name means 'My God is Yahweh!', challenging Ahab to follow the true God and declaring war on Baal, the god of rain and growth, by proclaiming that Yahweh controls the weather. It seems that his God is on his side. Even ravens, known for their selfish greed, bring him his food.

Elijah ends up being cared for, as many good people in the Bible are, by a woman – and a poor one at that. Elijah comforts her with words that are found throughout the Gospels: 'Do not be afraid' (v.13). So often Scripture suggests that to be fearful is one of the biggest threats to that relationship with God that we call faith.

The last part of today's reading also shows that death, which was also revered as a god in many parts of Elijah's world, is submissive to Yahweh. There is nothing that Yahweh cannot transform, nothing that cannot be brought to life. God hears Elijah's prayer and, like the story of St Kevin, where the saint prays with open hands so long that a blackbird nests and rears its young in one of them, there is something about his prayer that hatches newness and a future.

COLLECT

O Lord, we beseech you mercifully to hear the prayers
    of your people who call upon you;
and grant that they may both perceive and know
    what things they ought to do,
and also may have grace and power faithfully to fulfil them;
through Jesus Christ your Son our Lord,
who is alive and reigns with you,
in the unity of the Holy Spirit,
one God, now and for ever.

Thursday 9 October

1 Kings 18.1-20

'Is it you, you troubler of Israel?' (v.17)

Israel is a thirsty land in the middle of a great drought. God calls Elijah to do something very brave. He asks him to present himself to the godless King Ahab. Ahab has been searching for Elijah with evil intentions, and now God says it is time to show him who is in charge of heaven and earth.

This story introduces us to Obadiah whose name means 'servant of Yahweh'. He is a good man, a lover of God and someone who appears to respect Elijah. He is afraid to tell the king where Elijah is on two accounts: if Elijah has moved on, Ahab will be displeased and take it out on Obadiah; and if Elijah is still there, Ahab will do the prophet harm. Elijah makes it easier for him and simply tells him to go and get the King because he needs to see him because that's what God is asking of him.

The king addresses Elijah as the 'troubler of Israel'. What might it feel like for the Church to be called the 'troubler of our nation'? It feels the right time for Christians to recall the prophetic vocation of the gospel. We are used to a Church that is loyal to the past, but what would the Church that is loyal to the future look like? How would a Church that looks ahead, and sees what injustices must end, be shaped, behave, speak? Is it troubling that Christians are not thought to be troublers very often?

Lord of creation,
whose glory is around and within us:
open our eyes to your wonders,
that we may serve you with reverence
and know your peace at our lives' end,
through Jesus Christ our Lord.

COLLECT

275

Friday 10 October

1 Kings 18.21-end

'How long will you go limping with two different opinions?' (v.21)

The radical monotheism that we associate with Judaism seems not to have been established in Elijah's time. He asks the people why they follow both God and Baal and don't make their mind up? They are silent. Perhaps they don't understand the question? Has their religious dual citizenship, as it were, become comfortable and not at all a matter of concern? We can often be blind to the contradictions we live with as believers in God while at the same time courting the fashionable gods of the day.

Elijah puts Baal to the test. The prophets of Baal wind themselves up into a frenzy of self-mortification and movement, but with no result. Elijah just prays to his God, asking that it be made clear that he is the all-powerful and that Elijah is his servant. As throughout our tradition, from Moses to Pentecost, God is caught up in fire. He burns away dross and error. Those who come near are scorched forever.

There is an unsettling end to this story. Elijah, once he has proved his point, orders the prophets of Baal to be put to death in what must have been a carnage of blood and guts. It reminds us of the intensity and dangers of the religious competitions of the day and how God-fearers thought they were serving God best by murdering those who disagreed with them. Such curdled and hateful belief can still rear its head in our times.

COLLECT

O Lord, we beseech you mercifully to hear the prayers
    of your people who call upon you;
and grant that they may both perceive and know
    what things they ought to do,
and also may have grace and power faithfully to fulfil them;
through Jesus Christ your Son our Lord,
who is alive and reigns with you,
in the unity of the Holy Spirit,
one God, now and for ever.

Psalm **68**
1 Kings 19
Acts 21.17-36

1 Kings 19

'It is enough; now, O Lord, take away my life ... ' (19.4)

Elijah's had enough. He's run away scared because Jezebel is after his life and, while on the run, he seems to give up and basically tells God to finish him off. It's a nice human portrait of Elijah that we get here, someone we can identify with perhaps. God is having none of it and provides food via an angel to keep him on the journey. He still has work for Elijah to do, and to call him back to his first love of God, to inspirit his energy, Elijah is taken to mount Horeb.

The other gods of the day were thought to show their strength through natural phenomena and violent demonstrations. Here, however, Yahweh reveals himself to be different. There is a power but a gentleness to this revelation, a beauty and a terror. The 'sheer silence' in which God's presence dwells has an X-ray quality to it, penetrating and searching the world with a holiness that can't be voiced.

God is often spoken of in frightening terms as if he is a traffic warden of souls, out to get us and condemn us. The Bible so often shows that God is be feared not because he is frightening but rather because he is real. His reality exposes our masks and superficiality, and this, like silence itself, is both horrific and liberating, as at last we are shown what we have become and who we really are. Such knowledge is needed if our vocations are to be lived fully.

Lord of creation,
whose glory is around and within us:
open our eyes to your wonders,
that we may serve you with reverence
and know your peace at our lives' end,
through Jesus Christ our Lord.

COLLECT

Monday 13 October

Psalm 71
1 Kings 21
Acts 21.37 – 22.21

1 Kings 21

'... you have sold yourself to do what is evil' (v.20)

Humanity is not best represented by the characters in today's story! Ahab is greedy and wants someone else's land and has a dramatic strop when he doesn't get his way. His wife plots the murder of Naboth and the theft of the land. Two 'scoundrels' are employed to do the dark deed. The story is frighteningly open about the motives that can drive the abuses of power. It is a story that highlights the tension between the demands of the state and the rights of the people.

Elijah is an angry man when confronted with the abuses of the king against the hard-working farmer. He berates the king's religious failings, and the king listens and acknowledges that he has indeed done wrong and needs to repent.

As we read the bible it can be tempting to translate the word 'justice' as being punitive, but so much of the word's use refers more to a restorative justice, a putting right of wrongs and making life fairer, harmonious, peaceful. The prophets are those who speak out to challenge injustice. But to wave the angry finger is never enough. Those with influence need to be transformed, and shared visions for society need to be retuned. One archbishop in South America noted that when he feeds the poor he is regarded as being a saint, but when he asks why the poor have no food he is thought to be a communist. True justice is the social form of that love that God commands.

COLLECT

Almighty God,
you have made us for yourself,
and our hearts are restless till they find their rest in you:
pour your love into our hearts and draw us to yourself,
and so bring us at last to your heavenly city
where we shall see you face to face;
through Jesus Christ your Son our Lord,
who is alive and reigns with you,
in the unity of the Holy Spirit,
one God, now and for ever.

Psalm **73**
1 Kings 22.1-28
Acts 22.22 – 23.11

1 Kings 22.1-28

'... whatever the Lord says to me, that I will speak' (v.14)

This story nicely shows the difference between Israel's court prophets and individual prophets. The court prophets tell the king what he wants to hear and get rewarded for it. Micaiah, however, says what he believes God is saying and pays a cost for it. The Judean king is braver and is willing to hear critical prophecy, but this is a hard thing to do for all of us; until there is self-scrutiny and the fearless knowledge that must go with it, there can be no full movement of God's spirit to use us for his purposes. Our own agendas push him out.

Micaiah's warnings have the effect of hardening the people's views rather than changing them. The words of a true prophet are often not recognized and received until they have aged or died; the cost of speaking truth to power is the pain of being persecuted or ignored – until the pain of truth breaks through and becomes generally accepted. When Martin Luther King Jr said that segregation of black and white was dead, he added that they now had to wait to see how long some prolonged the funeral. Truth has its moments, and those who speak early and begin its transformative effects are those who make the sacrifices. Micaiah sits with reduced rations in prison – like so many have since.

Gracious God,
you call us to fullness of life:
deliver us from unbelief
and banish our anxieties
with the liberating love of Jesus Christ our Lord.

COLLECT

Wednesday 15 October

Psalm **77**
1 Kings 22.29-45
Acts 23.12-end

1 Kings 22.29-45

'I will disguise myself and go into battle' (v.30)

Ahab is portrayed here as a hero but as a villain too. He causes war, ensures Judah's support but then doesn't hold back in sacrificing his ally to save his own skin. An arrow hits him, however, and while showing courage on the battlefield, he eventually succumbs to his wounds and dies. The author relates this to Elijah's prophecy (1 Kings 21.19).

Part of Ahab's cunning was to disguise himself, while encouraging Jehoshaphat to keep in his own robes. Many myths and stories, of course, see heroes killed while in disguise, and the danger of masks has been explored through the centuries, from Greek drama to Jungian psychology. Masks quickly eat into our faces and it can be difficult to know where the mask ends and we begin. The spiritual journey is a painful stripping away of disguise and pretension, projection and mixed messaging towards an authentic way of being human and transparent. Wherever masks are worn, in the ancient stories, battles are fought and death follows. As Jung said: 'Whatever we ignore or hide in ourselves for the sake of ambition will always come back, knife in hand, to take its revenge'.

Almighty God,
you have made us for yourself,
and our hearts are restless till they find their rest in you:
pour your love into our hearts and draw us to yourself,
and so bring us at last to your heavenly city
where we shall see you face to face;
through Jesus Christ your Son our Lord,
who is alive and reigns with you,
in the unity of the Holy Spirit,
one God, now and for ever.

Psalm **78.1-39***
2 Kings 1.2-17
Acts 24.1-23

Thursday 16 October

2 Kings 1.2-17

'... but now let my life be precious in your sight' (v.14)

The king has fallen through either a window or a roof grid and, severely injured, sends for an oracle to discern whether he will survive or not. His mistake is to send for an oracle from Baal rather than Yahweh, and it is this fact that Elijah exposes and condemns. Not even three 50-men divisions can stop Elijah speaking. His words are fiery. Elijah often appears when unexpected or unwanted – and with some impressive results!

Mention of him being hairy with a leather belt (v.8) reminds us of that other prophet, John the Baptist, who came as a speaker of truth, calling people back to the ways of God through repentance and a ritual river washing. He too in his different times was challenging people to return to God and not to be lured away by all the oracles of the respected, opinionated or loud.

So much of life can be spent living down to the messages that the culture or our environment tell us about ourselves, whereas prophets ask us to start living up to the message that comes from heaven – of God's grace, creativity and love for his people. When John, the Elijah figure, pushed Jesus down into the water to drown all the damaging voices, it was only one voice that Jesus could hear when he came up out of the water telling him he was a son and was beloved. Prophets ensure we are listening in the right places.

Gracious God,
you call us to fullness of life:
deliver us from unbelief
and banish our anxieties
with the liberating love of Jesus Christ our Lord.

COLLECT

2 Kings 2.1-18

'Tell me what I may do for you, before I am taken from you?' (v.9)

In the Jewish Scriptures, people tend to view death as the natural conclusion to a life rather than as some feared enemy. This story, from which a faith in resurrection later develops, gives the sense that Yahweh is a God of life and that there is existence with him beyond the confines of our earthly living. For those who looked for the Messiah in the time of Jesus, it was to be Elijah returned from heaven who would announce his arrival – hence John the Baptist's Elijah overtones.

Elisha is appointed as Elijah's successor, inheriting his spirit and powerful mantle. We get another important theme here – that faith in God is something that is inherited and handed down. We have a duty to pass on the truths that have inspired us and helped us through life to another generation. We cannot expect them to discover the riches of the soul for themselves. This is a day to recall all those who nurtured and encouraged your own Christian discipleship – and then to ask whom you must now help.

As faithful vocation is handed on in this passage, so the whole impression is of life, glory and expectancy. To the jaundiced of the world, everything will look rather yellow, but to the faithful, life will be constantly opened up as we are carried by grace and enabled to do good things in the time given to us.

COLLECT

Almighty God,
you have made us for yourself,
and our hearts are restless till they find their rest in you:
pour your love into our hearts and draw us to yourself,
and so bring us at last to your heavenly city
where we shall see you face to face;
through Jesus Christ your Son our Lord,
who is alive and reigns with you,
in the unity of the Holy Spirit,
one God, now and for ever.

Psalms 145, 146
Isaiah 55
Luke 1.1-4

Saturday 18 October

Luke the Evangelist

Isaiah 55

'... listen, so that you may live' (v.3)

We remember St Luke today and might easily forget that he is the author of over a quarter of the New Testament. His Gospel and Acts of the Apostles are both beautifully written, and it is shocking to think of a Christian faith without some of the stories that only Luke recounts – the Good Samaritan, the Prodigal Son, the Pharisee and the Publican, and the Road to Emmaus among them. Writing some time between 75 and 130 AD, his contribution to the nurturing and understanding of what it means to follow Jesus Christ is incomparable.

There is a tradition that Luke was a doctor. Whereas the body is quite skilled at healing itself, the soul isn't quite so adaptable. Human souls can only be healed from the outside, by love. From the beginning of Luke's Gospel, with his portrait of the nativity and of love breaking into a ruined world, to the end when Jesus speaks love to the good thief and later to his failed disciples, Luke knows that our healing comes from outside ourselves and that God always takes the first steps.

The passage from Isaiah is very appropriate for Luke. As the rain and snow water the parched earth and bring things to growth, so the good news from God brings joy and completion to the human heart (vv.10-11). As the theologian Karl Barth said, we cannot speak of God by just talking about man in a loud voice. Our thoughts are not God's thoughts (v.8). The gospel comes to challenge our lazy, limited and comfortable thinking. It comes to open our eyes to see the world as God's sees it.

Almighty God,
you called Luke the physician,
whose praise is in the gospel,
to be an evangelist and physician of the soul:
by the grace of the Spirit
and through the wholesome medicine of the gospel,
give your Church the same love and power to heal;
through Jesus Christ your Son our Lord,
who is alive and reigns with you,
in the unity of the Holy Spirit,
one God, now and for ever.

COLLECT

Monday 20 October

2 Kings 5

'He said to him, "Go in peace"' (v.19)

Go in Peace. Elisha's simple blessing for Naaman acts as the quiet centre of this great story of pride and humility, greed and generosity, fear and possibility from the book of 2 Kings. Everything spins around this point. Naaman's desire for healing, the servant girl's imagination, the king of Aram's power, the king of Israel's fear, Gehazi's pursuit of wealth, and Elisha's faith and intuition. Pretty much all of life is involved. And perhaps for the characters in the story, and for those of us hearing or reading it, the key to all our yearnings can be found in the spirit of Elisha's blessing.

The moment in the story when the blessing is given is interesting. Naaman's request to be given permission for a convenient offering to his master's god Rimmon might have caused Elisha to despair after Naaman had been healed and claimed that there is only a God in Israel. But Elisha accepts this complexity and makes the blessing. No doubt today will bring its complexities. Perhaps the very best thing that we can do today is to offer some blessing of peace, in word or gesture, to the people whose complexities we will encounter. In so doing we will surely also be stepping into the spirit of Jesus whose resurrection greeting was 'Peace be with you' (John 20.19-21).

COLLECT

Almighty and everlasting God,
increase in us your gift of faith
that, forsaking what lies behind
and reaching out to that which is before,
we may run the way of your commandments
and win the crown of everlasting joy;
through Jesus Christ your Son our Lord,
who is alive and reigns with you,
in the unity of the Holy Spirit,
one God, now and for ever.

Psalms 87, **89.1-18**
2 Kings 6.1-23
Acts 26.24-end

2 Kings 6.1-23

*'... he cut off a stick, and threw it in there,
and made the iron float' (v.6)*

This passage from 2 Kings is full of miracles. The miracle of the axe head (the iron that was made to float by Elisha), unexplainable knowledge of the King of Aram's plans (even 'the words that you speak in your bedchamber' (v.12)) and Elisha's unseen protectors ('the mountain was full of horses and chariots of fire' (v.16)). Miracles are at the heart of the story of the prophet Elisha and his relationship with the God of Israel. There are strong similarities here with the stories of saints like Columba of Iona. So what are we to do with these miracle stories – or more importantly what might they be doing to us?

However we receive these stories – as actual events that happened as described in time and place, or as mythic tales representative of greater truth (like the possibilities revealed by faith, or the overarching goodness of God through all circumstances) – they have a capacity for good and a vibrancy of faith that will not leave us unchanged. And either way, as we approach the close of the season of Trinity, we are reminded of the lived experience of the Christ-community over two millennia, the mystery and miracle that is God the Holy Trinity. So may we approach the next phase of this day with a sense of the day's miraculous possibility. And let the iron float!

God, our judge and saviour,
teach us to be open to your truth
and to trust in your love,
that we may live each day
with confidence in the salvation which is given
through Jesus Christ our Lord.

COLLECT

Wednesday 22 October

2 Kings 9.1-16

'... open the door and flee; do not linger' (v.3)

Get out, while you can! Today's passage from 2 Kings takes us into an unsavoury world of Iron Age political manoeuvring and violence. The anointing of Jehu as king while another king still lives is just the start. The destruction of the (admittedly almost uniformly wicked) house of Ahab is being organized. No one will be spared. The story is beginning to resemble a ruthless mafia war. It feels as if the only sane moment in the story comes when Elisha tells the trainee prophet whom he has instructed to go and anoint Jehu to 'open the door and flee; do not linger'.

We rightly place a lot of store on loyalty, remaining at our post and hanging on in there. The Desert Fathers and Mothers discovered the importance of remaining in their place of calling. And, wherever possible, we try in the spirit of Jesus the Christ to bring peaceful, non-violent change from within, committing ourselves to stay and be part of the solution. But just occasionally the situation in which we find ourselves and those we care about needs to be exited, as soon as possible. Violence, abuse, deceit and manipulation are corrosive and destructive to the human spirit. May we find the wisdom and courage to know if and when the right moment has come to leave a situation behind.

COLLECT

Almighty and everlasting God,
increase in us your gift of faith
that, forsaking what lies behind
and reaching out to that which is before,
we may run the way of your commandments
and win the crown of everlasting joy;
through Jesus Christ your Son our Lord,
who is alive and reigns with you,
in the unity of the Holy Spirit,
one God, now and for ever.

Thursday 23 October

2 Kings 9.17-end

'What have you to do with peace?' (vv.18,19)

Sometimes it seems as if the Old Testament offers stories that are more about how we should *not* behave, rather than how we *should* or *could*. Today's passage continues in the vein of yesterday's reading, taking us yet further down a stomach-churning route of deceit, vengeance and unrestrained violence. In a passage that famously contains the reference to Jehu driving like a maniac, almost *everyone* behaves in a deranged manner. Driving is the least of it. Of course, someone might say, we are reading this through twenty-first century eyes, the Iron Age was different, and it's a mistake to impose our values on an ancient story. But it's precisely through engaging with stories like these that our values will be formed and refined. In this case, we either accede to their underlying assumptions – such as 'they had it coming' – or we seek a better way.

We can perhaps take one phrase from the story and allow it to help us find that better way. 'What have you to do with peace?' asks Jehu of one of the messengers of King Joram (v.18). Let's allow this phrase, in the name and spirit of the Christ, to be at work in us today. So both in the small, local, seemingly mundane situations of the day, and in the bigger, global issues of the day, let's ask ourselves: 'What have you to do with peace?'

God, our judge and saviour,
teach us to be open to your truth
and to trust in your love,
that we may live each day
with confidence in the salvation which is given
through Jesus Christ our Lord.

COLLECT

287

Friday 24 October

Psalms **88** (95)
2 Kings 12.1-19
Acts 28.1-16

2 Kings 12.1-19

'... for they dealt honestly' (v.15)

The story of how *not to live* as told in 2 Kings continues. We've left behind the violence and retribution, but today it's the turn of financial impropriety. Embezzlement. Theft. And lack of accountability. For an astonishing 23 years, no running repairs are made to the House of the Lord as the priests keep back the element of the donations that is meant to be used for that purpose. Twenty-three years! The House must have been in a dreadful state. Amazingly, the king finally seems to realize that something is amiss (we can imagine perhaps rain falling on him at prayer one day through a hole where a roof used to be) and he asks the obvious question. Reforms are made, and in the end an honest system is put in place.

This story of course acts as a reminder of how corruption of any sort can easily take over an institution, and the longer it is in place, the harder it becomes to sort it out. So perhaps this is an encouragement to us to be part of the solution in this earthy area – to make sure that we are honest in our own affairs and alert to corruption where we see it. This, of course, may be a demanding experience, but there's something completely life-enhancing about being honest, something 'blessed' in being 'pure in heart' (Matthew 5.8) and in pure in action ...

COLLECT

Almighty and everlasting God,
increase in us your gift of faith
that, forsaking what lies behind
and reaching out to that which is before,
we may run the way of your commandments
and win the crown of everlasting joy;
through Jesus Christ your Son our Lord,
who is alive and reigns with you,
in the unity of the Holy Spirit,
one God, now and for ever.

Saturday 25 October

2 Kings 17.1-23

'They did wicked things, provoking the Lord to anger' (v.11)

In today's passage, the writers of the book of 2 Kings are looking back at their people's story and wondering how things had ended up going so wrong, with Israel following Samaria into defeat and exile at the hands of the mighty Assyrians. Their conclusion is straightforward. The people had committed a whole catalogue of 'wicked things, provoking the Lord to anger' (v.11). They had rejected God's commandments, made false idols, entered into prohibited religious practices and 'sold themselves to do evil'. The downfall of Israel (and later the kingdom of Judah too) is down to their own disobedience.

Israel at the time of 2 Kings was, of course, a very different place and time to our own. With the benefit of the New Testament, we may want to add to the idea of God's anger at our wrongdoing the possibility of the sadness of God at our missing the mark. However, the principles of learning to be truly human in the way of God remain the same. Righteousness and holiness matter. So what might it mean for us to reject the 'wicked things', and do the good things? There will be a personal aspect to this, shaping our own behaviour today, but also a corporate aspect. What might we do today to help our own society to reject the wicked things?

God, our judge and saviour,
teach us to be open to your truth
and to trust in your love,
that we may live each day
with confidence in the salvation which is given
through Jesus Christ our Lord.

COLLECT

Monday 27 October

Psalms **98**, 99, 101
2 Kings 17.24-end
Philippians 1.1-11

2 Kings 17.24-end

'But every nation still made gods of its own' (v.29)

Something close to ethnic cleansing rears its ugly head in this passage from 2 Kings. The king of Assyria removes the people of Israel to Assyrian territory and settles migrants in Samaria from all over the Assyrian empire. Naturally, they bring their own religious traditions and worship their own gods. Even while these new arrivals are attempting to stop the threat of rogue wild animals by adding worship of the local god, the God of Israel, to their practice, they continue to worship their own gods. This, to the writers of 2 Kings, is anathema: 'You shall not worship other gods; but you shall worship the Lord your God' (vv.35–36).

We live in a complex and dynamic world, where people of many origins and faiths live side by side. How can this passage help us, if at all, here and now? The story of the Christ opens up new possibilities. Of course every people has its own religious roots. Is it possible to see Jesus as a gift to each of those traditions, and perhaps in some way their as yet unknown fulfilment? Paul in Athens hints at this possibility, applauding the religious practice of the people, and speaking about their devotion to 'an unknown god' (Acts 17.23). May we, with integrity, humility and quiet confidence, live and share the story of the Christ and St Paul's 'unknown god' wherever we are today ...

COLLECT

Blessed Lord,
who caused all holy Scriptures to be written for our learning:
help us so to hear them,
to read, mark, learn and inwardly digest them
that, through patience, and the comfort of your holy word,
we may embrace and for ever hold fast
　　the hope of everlasting life,
which you have given us in our Saviour Jesus Christ,
who is alive and reigns with you,
in the unity of the Holy Spirit,
one God, now and for ever.

Psalms 116, 117
Wisdom 5.1-16
or Isaiah 45.18-end
Luke 6.12-16

Tuesday 28 October

Simon and Jude, Apostles

Luke 6.12-16

'And when day came, he called his disciples and chose ...' (v.13)

Today we celebrate two lesser-known disciples of Jesus, Simon and Jude. In his description of the calling of the disciples, Luke gives them brief descriptions. Simon is Simon who was called the Zealot. Jude is Judas son of James. And that's about it. Jude may be the author of the epistle of that name. Matthew and Mark in their Gospels appear to rename Jude as Thaddaeus, perhaps to avoid confusing him with Judas Iscariot. Elsewhere in the Gospel narratives, Simon and Jude are elusive. So amongst the twelve disciples, some of whose names are highly familiar, we find two who are barely known. They are perhaps the patron saints of 'anyone and everyone'.

This is encouraging. Discipleship of Jesus is not about being successful, lauded, applauded or even known. We are still called by him, and he calls us by name. Our calling is to follow and serve. The remembering by others of our name or our deeds is irrelevant. This runs contrary to today's culture of fame seeking and celebrity. But it is the way of the Christ. So, how might we pursue being unknown disciples today? Can we be content to remain unseen, our work hidden from view? And, whether seen or unseen now, in the very end, which is of course a whole new beginning, we *will* be remembered (Luke 23.42-43).

COLLECT

Almighty God,
who built your Church upon the foundation
of the apostles and prophets,
with Jesus Christ himself as the chief cornerstone:
so join us together in unity of spirit by their doctrine,
that we may be made a holy temple acceptable to you;
through Jesus Christ your Son our Lord,
who is alive and reigns with you,
in the unity of the Holy Spirit,
one God, now and for ever.

Wednesday 29 October

Psalms 110, 111, 112
2 Kings 18.13-end
Philippians 2.1-13

2 Kings 18.13-end

'On what do you base this confidence of yours?' (v.19)

At last, some clear air to breathe. In 2 Kings 18, we meet Hezekiah, the king of Judah who 'did what was right in the sight of the Lord just as his ancestor David had done' (2 Kings 18.3). Where every other king before has got it wrong, Hezekiah seems to get it right. He ends all the idol worship and trusts God – who is with him, and in whose company he prospers. But then, perhaps inevitably, a great threat begins to emerge. Six years into Hezekiah's reign, King Shalmaneser of Assyria conquers Samaria and Israel. A few years later King Sennacherib of Assyria brings his armies into Judah. A large army is sent to besiege Jerusalem. The testing of Hezekiah is coming.

Rabshakeh, one of the Assyrian generals, taunts the people of Judah at the walls of Jerusalem and has a particular message for King Hezekiah: 'On what do you base this confidence of yours?' (v.19). This is a tough but important question for Hezekiah to hear. So far things have gone pretty well. But what is it all based upon? Is God truly with him? And can he survive the awesome threat of the Assyrians? Sometimes questions are best left hanging in the air. So may we receive this question ourselves today, let it have room, and not insert our responses too quickly. On what do you base this confidence of yours?

COLLECT

Blessed Lord,
who caused all holy Scriptures to be written for our learning:
help us so to hear them,
to read, mark, learn and inwardly digest them
that, through patience, and the comfort of your holy word,
we may embrace and for ever hold fast
   the hope of everlasting life,
which you have given us in our Saviour Jesus Christ,
who is alive and reigns with you,
in the unity of the Holy Spirit,
one God, now and for ever.

Thursday 30 October

2 Kings 19.1-19

'... he tore his clothes, covered himself with sackcloth' (v.1)

What are your losses at this time? What, or who, are you grieving? In today's passage from 2 Kings, Hezekiah is told of the taunting message from the general of the Assyrian army encamped outside the walls of Jerusalem. His response is one of grief. He tears his clothes and covers himself with sackcloth. 'This day' he says in a message to Isaiah 'is a day of distress, of rebuke, and of disgrace' (v.3). Hezekiah doesn't try to minimize the threat, ignore it or run away from it. The danger is massive and real. It needs acknowledging. Later in the passage we find him in prayer. But his first action is to express his grief at what is unfolding.

When we face great challenge, loss or failure, it's vital to give space to the feelings that arise in us. The act of tearing clothes and covering with sackcloth – early forerunners perhaps of the Jewish mourning practice of 'sitting shivah' – acknowledge the depth of loss, creating space for grief to be expressed and, in time, for it to give way to new life. Today's passage is a reminder to us of the need for us to acknowledge our own losses, griefs and anxieties. Don't rush from this space. Find a way to express what you feeling.

Merciful God,
teach us to be faithful in change and uncertainty,
that trusting in your word
and obeying your will
we may enter the unfailing joy of Jesus Christ our Lord.

COLLECT

293

Friday 31 October

2 Kings 19.20-36

'I will turn you back on the way by which you came' (v.28)

King Hezekiah's message to the prophet Isaiah, and his prayers to God, are finding a positive answer. Isaiah's reply is full of confidence and hope for Hezekiah, and ominous for the warlike Sennacherib, king of Assyria. He will be turned back 'on the way by which he came' (v.28). At one level this may mean simply that Sennacherib's armies will be forced to retreat down the same road along which they advanced. At another level, this warning is suggesting that Sennacherib will receive the same (violent) treatment that he has meted out to others. And this is what comes about. The army besieging Jerusalem is destroyed – 185,000 dead – and upon his return to Nineveh, Sennacherib is murdered by his own sons.

Human society has always been keen on people getting their just deserts. I don't expect that to change, and in many ways that can be appropriate. A problem comes whenever we seem to advocate just deserts (usually meaning retribution) to others while ignoring our own faults. Perhaps today's passage is a reminder that in the end, and in God's righteous care, there will be a settling process in which people's actions – our own included – will find their deserving home. As Jesus suggested, our weeds will be burned, and our wheat will be gathered in (Matthew 13.24-30). May today be a good day for growing wheat ...

COLLECT

Blessed Lord,
who caused all holy Scriptures to be written for our learning:
help us so to hear them,
to read, mark, learn and inwardly digest them
that, through patience, and the comfort of your holy word,
we may embrace and for ever hold fast
    the hope of everlasting life,
which you have given us in our Saviour Jesus Christ,
who is alive and reigns with you,
in the unity of the Holy Spirit,
one God, now and for ever.

Psalms 15, 84, 149
Isaiah 35.1-9
Luke 9.18-27

Saturday 1 November

All Saints' Day

Isaiah 35.1-9

'A highway shall be there, and it shall be called the Holy Way'
(v.8)

Today we celebrate All Saints' Day, one of the greatest days of the Church year, in which we remember and honour all those who have tried to walk 'the Holy Way' of the Christ before us. We are just some of the very latest in a long and wonderful line of those who have been captivated by Jesus – by his life, wisdom and presence. And how good that our reading today is one of the most inspiring texts from the Jewish Scriptures, a passage that would have helped form Jesus and shape his own understanding of his people, himself and his own calling.

Life can feel like a wilderness, like desert, like dry land, but on the Holy Way through this arid landscape, we are not alone. Christ and the saints are with us! And, there will come a time when it will be as if a new springtime has come to the desert. 'The wilderness and the dry land shall be glad' (v.1) and 'waters shall break forth in the wilderness, and streams in the desert' (v.6). Today is a gift. So let's allow its joy to permeate all that we do. Let's nurture our thankfulness for the saints who have gone before, and let's allow a song of joy to form within us. What that song sounds or looks like is up to you. Whatever it is – let it 'break forth'!

Almighty God,
you have knit together your elect
in one communion and fellowship
in the mystical body of your Son Christ our Lord:
grant us grace so to follow your blessed saints
in all virtuous and godly living
that we may come to those inexpressible joys
that you have prepared for those who truly love you;
through Jesus Christ your Son our Lord,
who is alive and reigns with you,
in the unity of the Holy Spirit,
one God, now and for ever.

COLLECT

Monday 3 November

Revelation 1

'I am alive for ever and ever' (v.18)

The last book of the Bible is a window onto God's ultimate purposes. The author of Revelation is John, a Christian visionary whom tradition associates with John the Evangelist, though his literary style and theological concerns are so different from that of the author of the fourth Gospel as to make this historically unlikely. In spite of that, these prophecies have the stamp of authenticity. They come from the heart of a suffering and expectant Church. John is inspired by the Spirit to record a series of visions and send them by letter to the seven churches of Asia with the authority of the living Christ.

The opening vision is of Christ himself 'one like the Son of Man' (v.13), a figure who appears in the book of Daniel, but is here revealed as the risen Lord. Christ speaks with the authority of his victory over death; he holds the keys to the afterlife and sees into the future. The vision is to assure those who are facing suffering that they are not alone; the Lord knows what is in store for them and gives them the courage to face it.

We do not know what lies ahead for us today or in the future, but the living Christ is always near us and tells us not to be afraid.

COLLECT

Almighty and eternal God,
you have kindled the flame of love in the hearts of the saints:
grant to us the same faith and power of love,
that, as we rejoice in their triumphs,
we may be sustained by their example and fellowship;
through Jesus Christ your Son our Lord,
who is alive and reigns with you,
in the unity of the Holy Spirit,
one God, now and for ever.

Tuesday 4 November

Revelation 2.1-11

'Be faithful until death, and I will give you the crown of life' (v.10)

The Christian community of Ephesus belonged to one of the most vibrant cosmopolitan cities of the ancient world. They had plenty of opportunity to grow and also plenty of temptation to embrace teachings, practices and philosophies that were alien to the gospel. The Church has had to struggle with false teaching. The risen Christ commends them for their readiness to test the claims of interlopers, but chides them for having lost their first love. The Church of Smyrna, on the other hand, is still rich in faith, but needs to prepare for suffering in the future.

As we contemplate the judgement of the risen Christ on these two ancient churches, we can ask ourselves what might be written to us and to the Christian communities we belong to. Have we lost that first love, so that our worship and witness have become routine and uninspiring? Are we prepared to suffer for the sake of Christ? We cannot avoid testing in the Christian life, and testing is ultimately helpful to us. It reveals the true intentions of our hearts and strengthens us to live more generously towards God and one another. Much is forgiven to those who love much, and growing faithfulness to Christ is the mature response to the love that will not let us go. From a Christian perspective, love conquers all, even death.

God of glory,
touch our lips with the fire of your Spirit,
that we with all creation
may rejoice to sing your praise;
through Jesus Christ our Lord.

COLLECT

297

Wednesday 5 November

Psalms **9**, 147.13-end
or **119.153-end**
Daniel 2.25-end
Revelation 2.12-end

Revelation 2.12-end

'... hold fast to what you have until I come' (v.25)

The letter to Pergamum recognizes the extreme hostility surrounding the Christian community in that city. Pergamum is 'where Satan's throne is' (v.13), which may refer to the fact that this city was renowned for religious worship of the Roman emperor. Once again the Church is struggling with false teaching, but it is 'holding fast to my name' (v.13).

The Church in Thyatira is commended for its good works and yet criticized for compromise with 'Jezebel'. It is not clear who this figure was, but it seems likely that members of the Church were in danger of compromising their faith by having business dealings with groups who practiced immorality. Such dealings had a social component and some members of the Church had been drawn in deeper perhaps than they had intended.

Sexual immorality and idolatry were often seen by the early Christians as two halves of the same coin. How might this speak to us in our tolerant and relaxed age? We can all be influenced by networks where Christian values are compromised; where the virtues of honesty, faithfulness and moderation are seen as wimpish, even contemptible. We should reflect on our habits of mind and body – on what we read, watch and relax with. The temptation to worship material things, sensations, or just novelty, is very real. Christian faithfulness is a tough but sane alternative to seduction by the world.

COLLECT

Almighty and eternal God,
you have kindled the flame of love in the hearts of the saints:
grant to us the same faith and power of love,
that, as we rejoice in their triumphs,
we may be sustained by their example and fellowship;
through Jesus Christ your Son our Lord,
who is alive and reigns with you,
in the unity of the Holy Spirit,
one God, now and for ever.

Psalms 11, **15**, 148 *or* **143**, 146
Daniel 3.1-18
Revelation 3.1-13

Thursday 6 November

Revelation 3.1-13

'I know your works' (vv.1,8)

There is no escape from God's all-seeing, all-perceiving presence. Yet appearances sometimes deceive. Behind the reputation for being a 'lively' Church, the Christian community in Sardis is spiritually dying. The Church has lost touch with authentic Christian life. The Church of Philadelphia receives a very different judgement. This community has little power, and yet it has remained faithful. It is the only one of the seven churches that does not have some deadly flaw and is therefore not urged to repent, but is reassured that it will be spared in the hour of trial and persecution. From the point of view of the risen Christ, the Philadelphian Church is a model of holiness – a pillar in God's temple, bearing the name of God.

There have been many attempts in our time to distil the marks of a healthy Church. We tend to think that growth in numbers of worshippers, a lively presence in the community and the ministry of gifted individuals are signs of God's approval and blessing. Yet behind such a veneer can lie unchecked ambition, careerism, manipulation. The small, struggling apparently powerless Church, on the other hand, may be the place of real Christian life – neither glamorous, nor successful, but simply faithful.

What is the Spirit of God saying to our own churches today? Do we belong to a community that is self-satisfied or one that seeks to satisfy the Lord?

God of glory,
touch our lips with the fire of your Spirit,
that we with all creation
may rejoice to sing your praise;
through Jesus Christ our Lord.

COLLECT

299

Friday 7 November

Revelation 3.14-end

'I reprove and discipline those whom I love' (v.19)

The last of the churches receives its letter of judgement from the 'Amen', the faithful and true witness. The news is not good. The letter to the seventh of the Asian churches has always inspired more comment than the previous six because its spiritual condition is so easily recognized. The Church of Laodicea is neither dead nor alive. It is neither one thing nor another – neither spectacularly sinful nor truly holy. Perhaps we see ourselves here!

Although the Lord's rebuke is harsh – he threatens to spit the Church out of his mouth (v.16) – a burning love shines through the fierceness of his judgement. There is a remedy for the Church's indifference. The grace of the gospel is inexhaustible, and earnest repentance will be rewarded. A realistic spiritual audit will reveal the community's pathetic state, but the result of such painful honesty will be salvation, medicine for the soul. The Christ of the seer's vision urges the Church to turn back from the brink with the great invitation portrayed in Holman Hunt's famous painting 'The Light of the World'. Christ does not force an entrance into his Church, nor into the human heart, but remains, knocking at the door, waiting for our response. His judgement is the consequence of his never-defeated love, inviting our response of love in return.

COLLECT

Almighty and eternal God,
you have kindled the flame of love in the hearts of the saints:
grant to us the same faith and power of love,
that, as we rejoice in their triumphs,
we may be sustained by their example and fellowship;
through Jesus Christ your Son our Lord,
who is alive and reigns with you,
in the unity of the Holy Spirit,
one God, now and for ever.

Psalms **18.31-end**, 150 *or* 147
Daniel 4.1-18
Revelation 4

Revelation 4

'… there in heaven a door stood open!' (v.1)

After the opening letters to the Asian churches and their angelic guardians, John the seer is presented with an open door into heaven and is lifted in the Spirit into the heavenly court. He finds himself in the presence of God the Creator who has made all things by his own will (v.11). There is no picture of God here; he is simply compared to a range of bright and luminous precious stones, hidden by the vivid rainbow. The sea of crystal represents chaos overcome in the creation of the world. The living creatures first appeared in Ezekiel and are angelic energies, representing the omnipresence of God. The impression is of light and movement, energy and ceaseless praise. Heaven is not a static place; there is plenty going on!

Much of the imagery here comes from various parts of the Old Testament and from other Jewish apocryphal writings that influenced the early Christians. The imagery also shows the influence on the seer's mind of the layout, decoration and furnishings of the Jerusalem temple, which was regarded as the earthly counterpart of the heavenly throne room. The praise of God in heaven is ecstatic and continuous. All creation is destined to find its meaning and its fulfilment in the worship of God.

God of glory,
touch our lips with the fire of your Spirit,
that we with all creation
may rejoice to sing your praise;
through Jesus Christ our Lord.

COLLECT

Monday 10 November

Revelation 5

'I saw … a Lamb standing as if it had been slaughtered' (v.6)

The Greek word for Revelation, *apocalypse*, implies the uncovering of secrets. The secrets of God are contained in the scroll – that is, in human history as told through Scripture. The only one worthy to reveal the secrets of the Scriptures is the one who is their subject, Jesus Christ. In spite of the multitude of angels around the throne, God bestows his secrets and his promises only to a human figure. Christ stands here for the whole human race. Christ is both the Son of David (which is why he is named as the conquering Lion of Judah) and the sacrificed Lamb of God who still bears the wounds of his passion. The fruit of his sacrifice is shown by the presence of the saints who have been ransomed by his death from every tribe and nation. It is because the Lamb/Lion is uniquely qualified to open the scroll and reveal the depth of God's judgement and love that the angels and the elders fall down and worship.

Today's reading invites us to remember that our personal faith is a small part of a big canvas: all human history is there – all hope, all suffering, all destiny. All this is potentially judged and redeemed by Christ. Nothing that is human is alien to him.

COLLECT

Almighty Father,
whose will is to restore all things
in your beloved Son, the King of all:
govern the hearts and minds of those in authority,
and bring the families of the nations,
divided and torn apart by the ravages of sin,
to be subject to his just and gentle rule;
who is alive and reigns with you,
in the unity of the Holy Spirit,
one God, now and for ever.

Tuesday 11 November

Revelation 6

'Sovereign Lord, holy and true, how long...?' (v.10)

The breaking of the first four seals unleashes the four terrible horsemen of the apocalypse, each more ferocious than the last, and each with a mandate to kill and destroy. The opening of the fifth seal reveals the cause of the bloodshed, the sufferings of the martyrs, whose precious souls are gathered under the altar. They must wait for their liberation a little longer until all those destined to be martyred have joined them. This detail of the martyrs' souls is intended to strengthen those who are facing persecution. They are to see themselves as part of the final sacrifice that leads to redemption.

The opening of the sixth seal extends the destruction brought by the four horsemen to the whole cosmos: sun, moon, stars and sky are horribly transformed. There is nowhere to hide in this suddenly unpredictable world, as all are confronted with 'the wrath of the Lamb' (v.16). This is a paradoxical image: the figure who represents sacrificial obedience is transformed into the agent of divine vengeance.

Whatever we make of the fierce imagery of judgement, we can appreciate the insight that those who perpetrate violence against the innocent always do so at cost to themselves. Any image they might have of God becomes distorted by their guilt. The only safe place in the cosmos is with the martyrs, under the altar, where Christ's sacrifice avails until the end of time.

God, our refuge and strength,
bring near the day when wars shall cease
and poverty and pain shall end,
that earth may know the peace of heaven
through Jesus Christ our Lord.

COLLECT

Wednesday 12 November

Revelation 7.1-4, 9-end

'… a great multitude that no one could count' (v.9)

There is a pause in the opening of seals as John's vision looks first back and then forward to introduce the theme of final redemption. First, he refers back to the salvation of the saints. The servants of God are marked on the foreheads to show that they belong to God. This is the meaning of their baptism. They have been bought by God, transferred to God's ownership. At first glance the redeemed servants of God – the 144,000 – look like a representative group modelled on the tribes that make up Israel. But looking forward ('after this I looked…', v.9) John also sees the redeemed saints as a worldwide community so large that they cannot be counted. This indicates that, though in some sense believers are representatives of the whole of humanity, the final scope of salvation is unlimited. The multitude is seen in heaven, joining the worship of heaven alongside the angels, the elders and the living energies of God.

The dialogue with 'one of the elders' (v.13) reinforces the point that earthly suffering is part of the vocation of those who follow the Lamb. We may feel we do not suffer much compared to those who are persecuted. We should nevertheless consider how our baptismal faith is strengthening and sustaining us to cope with the sufferings that inevitably come our way in the course of life.

COLLECT

Almighty Father,
whose will is to restore all things
in your beloved Son, the King of all:
govern the hearts and minds of those in authority,
and bring the families of the nations,
divided and torn apart by the ravages of sin,
to be subject to his just and gentle rule;
who is alive and reigns with you,
in the unity of the Holy Spirit,
one God, now and for ever.

Thursday 13 November

Revelation 8

'... the smoke of the incense, with the prayers of the saints, rose before God' (v.4)

We return now to the opening of the last of the seals. Instead of unleashing immediate divine action, the breaking of this seventh seal ushers in a time of silence. This may be a deliberate recall of the silence that accompanied parts of the Jewish temple service, or it may be a profound recollection of the silence before creation, a moment of waiting before the destruction of the old world and the start of the new. The prayers of the suffering saints continue to rise to God, and now at last they are answered as the seven angels herald the break-up of the world.

What are we to make of this awesome vision of the end? Troubling though the imagery must seem to us, it is not an act of divine abandonment. It is rather the way in which human cruelty and malice are played out to their final consequences. The earth itself implodes under the impact of human sin. We can take this both as a warning and as a hope. The warning is that greed and selfishness could overwhelm all the good that God has made, turning his creation into a hell on earth. But God's passion for salvation is also revealed here. There can be no healing until evil is purged; this destruction serves the ultimate good.

God, our refuge and strength,
bring near the day when wars shall cease
and poverty and pain shall end,
that earth may know the peace of heaven
through Jesus Christ our Lord.

COLLECT

Friday 14 November

Psalms 28, **32** *or* 17, **19**
Daniel 7.1-14
Revelation 9.1-12

Revelation 9.1-12

'... they will long to die, but death will flee from them' (v.6)

A star now falls out of the sky opening up a bottomless pit, the fathomless abyss of evil from which all human evils arise. God's judgement now focuses on the demonic source behind the rebellious human spirit. The choking darkness and the locusts that emerge from it recall the plagues of Egypt. Those who do not bear God's seal of salvation are subject to torture. They long to die, but there is no release.

We are naturally repelled by this image. We cannot imagine how torture could lead to genuine repentance. However, in a harsher world with no concept of human rights, it is not hard to see how John might have believed that any means are justified to turn sinners to salvation. Underneath the harshness is the passion of God, who did not spare his own Son but delivered him up for the redemption of the world. The opening of the pit reveals that abyss of evil is ruled by a supernatural enemy, Abaddon, or Apollyon. For the Christians John was writing to, the Roman emperor was the embodiment of tyranny and pride. Here, it is revealed that he has a fearsome spiritual counterpart who rules from the abyss. But his rule, like that of the emperor's, is destined to come to an end.

COLLECT

Almighty Father,
whose will is to restore all things
in your beloved Son, the King of all:
govern the hearts and minds of those in authority,
and bring the families of the nations,
divided and torn apart by the ravages of sin,
to be subject to his just and gentle rule;
who is alive and reigns with you,
in the unity of the Holy Spirit,
one God, now and for ever.

Saturday 15 November

Revelation 9.13-end

'The rest of humankind … did not repent' (v.20)

Two further woes follow, representing the next phase of divine judgement. Once again, it is the prayers of the saints from under the altar that trigger them. The bound angels at the mouth of the Euphrates suggest that a surge of destructive power has been held in waiting for the precise moment when it is to be released. Now that moment comes and a vast horde of cavalry overruns a third of humankind. This supernatural force is extravagantly equipped to destroy, not only by emitting the plagues of fire, smoke and sulphur, but also by the lion heads and serpent tails of the horses. Terrible though the destruction is, its aim is to warn and heal. It is meant to reveal the ultimate sterility of evil. But the warning does not succeed. Those spared the cavalry's destruction continue in their destructive behaviour.

What does this say to us? It reminds us that human beings are natural worshippers, and if God is not enthroned in the heart, he is usurped by something less than himself. If we are worshipping something less than God, then we are enslaved. Only God, as the source of our being, can liberate us to be the selves he desires us to be, the selves that we long to be. Repentance is no more and no less than the spiritual therapy that we all urgently need.

God, our refuge and strength,
bring near the day when wars shall cease
and poverty and pain shall end,
that earth may know the peace of heaven
through Jesus Christ our Lord.

COLLECT

Monday 17 November

Revelation 10

*'... it was sweet as honey in my mouth, but when I had eaten it,
my stomach was made bitter' (v.10)*

Between the sixth and the seventh trumpets there is an interlude: a mighty angel descends with a little scroll. He explains that, when the seventh trumpet is blown, 'the mystery of God will be fulfilled, as he announced to his servants the prophets' (v.7). This passage is about the commissioning of John the Seer, and here he identifies himself with those who have been privileged to know the divine mysteries through the ages. Indeed, his commissioning, as seen in the command to eat the scroll, mirrors that of Ezekiel (Ezekiel 3.3). John has delivered God's word to the churches in chapters 2–3. Now he must prophesy to the nations.

We are all, to a greater or lesser degree, called to be prophets of God's word. With that comes an honour – the sweetness of knowing that something precious has been entrusted to us to share with others. But it may also come with a bitterness – the word to be shared may be difficult and make us unpopular; it may call others to repentance or divulge an inconvenient truth; it may cause us suffering. God's promise to us, as to all his prophets throughout the ages, is that he is faithful to those whom he calls. What message has God entrusted to you?

COLLECT

Heavenly Father,
whose blessed Son was revealed to destroy the works of the devil
and to make us the children of God and heirs of eternal life:
grant that we, having this hope,
may purify ourselves even as he is pure;
that when he shall appear in power and great glory
we may be made like him in his eternal and glorious kingdom;
where he is alive and reigns with you,
in the unity of the Holy Spirit,
one God, now and for ever.

Tuesday 18 November

Revelation 11.1-14

'... after the three and a half days, the breath of life from God entered them' (v.11)

The two witnesses, variously identified as Moses and Elijah, Peter and Paul, or two representative figures, are empowered to prophesy to the nations. Whoever they are, their fate mirrors that of their prophetic prototype, Christ. Their prophecy is powerful, authoritative and unstoppable. Until their work is finished, they cannot be killed; just as it is not until Christ utters the words 'it is finished' that he breathes his last. As he lies in the tomb for three days, so their bodies lie degraded and unburied while others rejoice. As Christ himself is resurrected, they receive again the breath of life from God; and as Christ ascends to heaven, so they receive the call 'Come up here!' (v.12). It is, if you like, the story of the faithful Christian life in miniature.

It is not just the story of our lives, though, but a cycle we experience regularly as we grow in faith: the cycle of witness, suffering, death, resurrection and ascension, or closeness to God. We are charged to witness to God's purifying love. Suffering comes with the territory. Death is a necessary and authentic part of Christian life. But living that life after the pattern of its author and perfecter, we know, wherever we are now in that cycle, that death is not the end.

Heavenly Lord,
you long for the world's salvation:
stir us from apathy,
restrain us from excess
and revive in us new hope
that all creation will one day be healed
in Jesus Christ our Lord.

COLLECT

309

Wednesday 19 November

Revelation 11.15-end

'The kingdom of the world has become the kingdom of our Lord'
(v.15)

'Thy kingdom come' is a phrase we say quite regularly – every week or even every day, perhaps more than once. If we have in mind some injustice – local or global – when we say it, we may pray earnestly for God's kingdom to break into that situation. More likely, they are words that follow on swiftly from 'hallowed be thy name' and we do not reflect on what they mean in practice.

In this passage, the sounding of the seventh trumpet heralds that the kingdom has come. The elders who fall down before him worship the Lord Almighty who is and who was (v.17). There is no need for the usual third part of this acclamation – who is to come – as that time is now. The kingdom of the world has become the kingdom of God, where he now rules with power. It is a reign characterized by worship in heaven and by the judgement of the earth: reward or destruction for each according to his or her deeds. It reminds us that, implicit in the coming of God's kingdom, is the exercise of his just rule and the judgement of those who have rejected it. Dare we say 'thy kingdom come' in our lives today? Yes, but only if we also earnestly pray 'forgive us our trespasses'.

COLLECT

Heavenly Father,
whose blessed Son was revealed to destroy the works of the devil
and to make us the children of God and heirs of eternal life:
grant that we, having this hope,
may purify ourselves even as he is pure;
that when he shall appear in power and great glory
we may be made like him in his eternal and glorious kingdom;
where he is alive and reigns with you,
in the unity of the Holy Spirit,
one God, now and for ever.

Psalms 61, **62** *or* **37***
Daniel 9.20-end
Revelation 12

Thursday 20 November

Revelation 12

'The great dragon was thrown down' (v.9)

Chapter 12 sees the beginning of the second part of the Book of Revelation. We are introduced to a lurid cast of characters through which the cosmic battle of good versus evil will be played out. The description of these characters and their actions conjures up cartoon-like scenes: a red dragon who, with the flick of his tail, scatters stars from heaven to earth; a great battle between the Archangel and the Devil and their troops. These images have certainly captured the imagination of artists across the years. It is easy for them to remain exaggerated Technicolor images in our own minds, but they speak of something black and white: the desperate reality of the struggle between good and evil.

Through his vision, John is reminding his audience to remain faithful to Christ in a world of overt pressure and mortal danger, of subtle deception and damaging compromise. The battle of good verses evil is writ large in their circumstances. It is no less prominent in our own; we simply don't use the same language to discuss it. Sometimes, however, when we are struggling and feel our own lives are a battleground, envisaging the comprehensive defeat of that which seems to be defeating us in such graphic terms can be extraordinarily helpful.

Heavenly Lord,
you long for the world's salvation:
stir us from apathy,
restrain us from excess
and revive in us new hope
that all creation will one day be healed
in Jesus Christ our Lord.

COLLECT

Friday 21 November

Psalms **63**, 65 *or* **31**
Daniel 10.1 – 11.1
Revelation 13.1-10

Revelation 13.1-10

'It opened its mouth to utter blasphemies against God' (v.6)

In Revelation 13 we meet two beasts that, with the dragon, form a kind of 'evil trinity'. They are both derived from traditional Jewish mythical figures. Today's beast is Leviathan, the terrifying sea monster we also encounter in Job and the Psalms. Within this context the beast represents the Roman Empire and its heads bear blasphemous names because the emperors claimed divine titles for themselves, such as 'Lord', 'Divine' and 'Saviour'.

It is easy to play down the sin of blasphemy. It has become rather trivialized by its association with the utterance of casual profanities such as 'Oh God!' It was, however, the sin for which Christ himself was framed and condemned by the chief priests. It involves the misuse of the divine name and the assumption of divine identity: it is a subtle form of idolatry that replaces worship of God with the worship and exaltation of self. We are all prone to it and it manifests itself in various ways, one of which is an overreliance on our own strength and resources. There is the temptation to feel, particularly when things are going well, that we are powerful enough to achieve our goals by our own strength, making ourselves super-successful mini-gods rather than looking to the one true God. Let us, with Job, remember who caught Leviathan with a fish-hook (Job 41.1).

COLLECT

Heavenly Father,
whose blessed Son was revealed to destroy the works of the devil
and to make us the children of God and heirs of eternal life:
grant that we, having this hope,
may purify ourselves even as he is pure;
that when he shall appear in power and great glory
we may be made like him in his eternal and glorious kingdom;
where he is alive and reigns with you,
in the unity of the Holy Spirit,
one God, now and for ever.

Saturday 22 November

Revelation 13.11-end

'... it makes the earth and its inhabitants worship the first beast'
(v.12)

Today's mythical beast is Behemoth, the beast of the earth. It looks like a lamb but speaks like a dragon revealing its nature and function: deception. It leads the people astray with great signs, making them create and worship an image of the first beast.

If the atrocity of yesterday's beast was blasphemy, the focus of today's is idolatry. This is an all-consuming idolatry, which impacts on every area of human life. It defines identity and regulates involvement in business and society. Those who worship the beast are owned by him, branded on the hand and forehead with the mark of his name. Their every thought, their every deed reveals to whom they belong: the dragon and not the Lamb.

The branding on head and hand is evocative of the Great Commandment received by Moses and delivered to Israel. The people are to bind the words of this command on their forehead and hand. Those words are: 'Hear, O Israel: The Lord is our God, the Lord alone. You shall love the Lord your God with all your heart, and with all your soul, and with all your might' (Deuteronomy 6.4-5). In the days of Moses, in the days of John the Seer, in our own day, this is the only antidote to idolatry.

Heavenly Lord,
you long for the world's salvation:
stir us from apathy,
restrain us from excess
and revive in us new hope
that all creation will one day be healed
in Jesus Christ our Lord.

COLLECT

Monday 24 November

Psalms 92, **96** *or* **44**
Isaiah 40.1-11
Revelation 14.1-13

Revelation 14.1-13

'... they sing a new song before the throne' (v.3)

The Lamb and the redeemed are gathered together for worship. John hears a voice from heaven: a sound of beauty, power and harmony. We identify the sound of many waters with the vision of Jesus in chapter 1. With it is heard thunder, reminding us of the voice of the Father from the Gospels. Accompanying those two is the flowing melody of the harpists. Can we hear the voice of the Spirit here? This is the sound of Trinity in unity.

The occasion is the singing of a new worship song. The term 'new song' has specific connotations, celebrating victory in a holy war (Psalms 98.1-3; 144.9-10). We already know the words since we heard them in chapter 5. It is a song to the Lamb: 'You are worthy ... for you were slaughtered and by your blood you ransomed for God saints from every tribe and language ...' (Revelation 5.9). This is a song only the redeemed can learn and its words are the chant of every Christian life. It becomes the song of our heart when we first accept Christ's great love for us. But it is also the song we are called to sing each day. Sometimes our tune is joyful, hopeful; sometimes meditative or sorrowful; sometimes even flat or sharp. But the words are always the same: You are worthy, Jesus Christ, for by your sacrificial love you have redeemed us. Alleluia!

COLLECT

Eternal Father,
whose Son Jesus Christ ascended to the throne of heaven
    that he might rule over all things as Lord and King:
keep the Church in the unity of the Spirit
and in the bond of peace,
and bring the whole created order to worship at his feet;
who is alive and reigns with you,
in the unity of the Holy Spirit,
one God, now and for ever.

Tuesday 25 November

Revelation 14.14 – end of 15

'... the hour to reap has come, because the harvest of the earth is fully ripe' (v.15)

No one knew the day nor the hour of the coming of the Son of Man, but it has arrived. This is the moment of judgement anticipated in the Gospels: the harvest at the end of the age, which represents the culmination of all things. In this vision we witness two stages of judgement: the harvest of the grain, followed by the grape.

In the first, Christ raises his sharp sickle and reaps the righteous with one clean swing. This is an image of salvation. But then it is the turn of the vintage of the earth, ripe with unrighteousness. This is a sour vintage indeed. The grapes are gathered up and trodden in the winepress, from which flows more blood than can possibly be imagined. It is a deeply disturbing image: a tsunami of blood rushing from the winepress. Whose blood is this? The blood of the unrighteous who are being finally crushed, or the blood of the martyrs shed by violent means?

The image is multi-faceted and opinions vary, but what is clear is that it represents the immeasurable suffering caused by evil. We note too that the winepress is trodden outside the city, the very place where evil was defeated by the shedding of the blood of the Son of Man upon the cross, whose blood is sufficient to cleanse all humanity.

God the Father,
help us to hear the call of Christ the King
and to follow in his service,
whose kingdom has no end;
for he reigns with you and the Holy Spirit,
one God, one glory.

COLLECT

Wednesday 26 November

Revelation 16.1-11

*'Go and pour out on the earth the seven bowls
of the wrath of God' (v.1)*

The 'wrath of God' has rather fallen out of fashion as a topic for preaching in mainstream Western Christianity. Many would say that is a good thing and would feel uncomfortable about this reading in which bowls of God's wrath are poured upon the earth. It is imagery that would be at home in the medieval period, but is insufficiently subtle for our age.

However, while the wrath of God is downplayed, the wrath of man is still very much in evidence in today's world. Hatred and violence abound, fuelling injustice, poverty and war. Is it right that while we are busy pouring out our own wrath upon the earth, we deny God permission to do likewise?

Instead of disallowing God his wrath, why not ask for a share in it? God is enraged by disregard for the poor, by violation of the vulnerable and by the malicious prejudice that denies any of his children their full humanity. When we witness cruelty against the innocent, are not our hearts filled with rage? This rage is our sharing in the wrath of God. It is what gives us the zeal to seek justice for the wronged, relief for the suffering and heed the cries of the lowly crushed by the mighty. May our hearts burn with God's wrath and glow with his mercy.

Eternal Father,
whose Son Jesus Christ ascended to the throne of heaven
    that he might rule over all things as Lord and King:
keep the Church in the unity of the Spirit
and in the bond of peace,
and bring the whole created order to worship at his feet;
who is alive and reigns with you,
in the unity of the Holy Spirit,
one God, now and for ever.

Thursday 27 November

Revelation 16.12-end

'It is done!' (v.17)

The seventh and final bowl is emptied. Immediately, we hear the voice from the throne declaring, 'It is done!' We are reminded of the last words of Jesus from the cross in John's Gospel: 'It is finished' (John 19.30). If we remain on Calvary, we will make further connections with this passage from the Apocalypse as rocks split and the earth shakes.

What has been 'finished' on the cross is the saving work of Jesus entrusted to him by the Father: the sacrifice is complete and, by it, death has been defeated. What has been 'done' in this vision is the final judgement of evil, represented by the fall of Babylon. But this is not the only time the triumphant cry, 'It is done!' is uttered from the One seated on the throne. It will occur again in Revelation 21.6 on completion of the new creation and the descent of the new Jerusalem from heaven. It is not enough simply to defeat evil; that which was destroyed by evil must be restored. It is not enough to defeat death; new life must spring from the resurrection. It is not enough to destroy Babylon; the new Jerusalem must be created.

'Behold, I make all things new', promises Christ (Revelation 21.5, *AV*). This is the phrase to remember when sin and death have wreaked destruction in our own lives.

God the Father,
help us to hear the call of Christ the King
and to follow in his service,
whose kingdom has no end;
for he reigns with you and the Holy Spirit,
one God, one glory.

COLLECT

Friday 28 November

Psalms **139** *or* **51**, 54
Isaiah 41.21 – 42.9
Revelation 17

Revelation 17

'... it was and is not and is to come' (v.8)

We meet in this passage the 'great whore of Babylon' and the beast, whose identification has long been a source of scholarly speculation. Consensus would say Rome, in the sense that the Rome of John's time represented the latest incarnation of the idolatrous city Babylon. It is important for the Seer that his readers recognize the demonic nature of the imperial power, regardless of whether they are experiencing persecution at its hands. Otherwise they may be seduced away from the true God to a deceptive counterfeit and, as Paul writes to the Romans of his day, 'exchange the truth about God for a lie' (Romans 1.25).

The beast is described three times in this chapter as the one who 'was and is not and is to come'. The language parodies one of Revelation's key titles for God, as the one who 'was and is and is to come' (1.4,8; 4.8). The beast may masquerade as divine, but its destiny is non-being: it is not eternal and will perish. Rather, the one who declares seven times in Revelation 'I am coming' is the one who will reign forever, Jesus Christ. May our 'being' be defined by his, and our hearts look for his coming, wherever we are and whatever we do today.

COLLECT

Eternal Father,
whose Son Jesus Christ ascended to the throne of heaven
    that he might rule over all things as Lord and King:
keep the Church in the unity of the Spirit
and in the bond of peace,
and bring the whole created order to worship at his feet;
who is alive and reigns with you,
in the unity of the Holy Spirit,
one God, now and for ever.

Psalm 145 *or* **68**
Isaiah 42.10-17
Revelation 18

Saturday 29 November

Revelation 18

'Alas, alas the great city' (vv.10,16,19)

Chapter 18 comprises a lengthy lament over Babylon the fallen. It is stitched together using quotations and allusions from biblical dirges and taunt-songs over the destroyed cities of God's enemies. But what are the reasons for Babylon's judgement? Why has she fallen? The charges are heaped up throughout the chapter and summarized in verses 23–24: her commercial practices use wealth to exploit and oppress; by her hubris she seduces people into blasphemy and idolatry; she has blood on her hands: not just that of God's faithful, but of any who have stood in the way of her expansion in pursuit of power.

Although parts of Revelation can seem far removed from the world in which we live, we can recognize the sins of our age in the fall of Babylon. The last few years have seen protests in many of the world's major cities against similar practices in response to global crises, and social and economic inequalities caused by corporations and financial markets. In the face of the seductive power of wealth, flattery and material success, it is worth recalling the fate of Babylon, deprived of all beauty, light and life as she was cast into the sea. How might we better order our lives to reflect God's heavenly city, rather than colluding with those earthly powers that encourage us in selfishness and greed?

God the Father,
help us to hear the call of Christ the King
and to follow in his service,
whose kingdom has no end;
for he reigns with you and the Holy Spirit,
one God, one glory.

COLLECT

319

Seasonal Prayers of Thanksgiving

Blessed are you, Sovereign God of all,
to you be praise and glory for ever.
In your tender compassion
the dawn from on high is breaking upon us
to dispel the lingering shadows of night.
As we look for your coming among us this day,
open our eyes to behold your presence
and strengthen our hands to do your will,
that the world may rejoice and give you praise.
Blessed be God, Father, Son and Holy Spirit.
Blessed be God for ever.

Blessed are you, Sovereign God,
creator of heaven and earth,
to you be praise and glory for ever.
As your living Word, eternal in heaven,
assumed the frailty of our mortal flesh,
may the light of your love be born in us
to fill our hearts with joy as we sing:
Blessed be God, Father, Son and Holy Spirit.
Blessed be God for ever.

Blessed are you, Sovereign God,
king of the nations,
to you be praise and glory for ever.
From the rising of the sun to its setting
your name is proclaimed in all the world.
As the Sun of Righteousness dawns in our hearts
anoint our lips with the seal of your Spirit
that we may witness to your gospel
and sing your praise in all the earth.
Blessed be God, Father, Son and Holy Spirit.
Blessed be God for ever.

Blessed are you, Lord God of our salvation,
to you be glory and praise for ever.
In the darkness of our sin you have shone in our hearts
to give the light of the knowledge of the glory of God
in the face of Jesus Christ.
Open our eyes to acknowledge your presence,
that freed from the misery of sin and shame
we may grow into your likeness from glory to glory.
Blessed be God, Father, Son and Holy Spirit.
Blessed be God for ever.

Passiontide

Blessed are you, Lord God of our salvation,
to you be praise and glory for ever.
As a man of sorrows and acquainted with grief
your only Son was lifted up
that he might draw the whole world to himself.
May we walk this day in the way of the cross
and always be ready to share its weight,
declaring your love for all the world.
Blessed be God, Father, Son and Holy Spirit.
Blessed be God for ever.

Easter Season

Blessed are you, Sovereign Lord,
the God and Father of our Lord Jesus Christ,
to you be glory and praise for ever.
From the deep waters of death
you brought your people to new birth
by raising your Son to life in triumph.
Through him dark death has been destroyed
and radiant life is everywhere restored.
As you call us out of darkness into his marvellous light
may our lives reflect his glory
and our lips repeat the endless song.
Blessed be God, Father, Son and Holy Spirit.
Blessed be God for ever.

Blessed are you, Lord of heaven and earth,
to you be glory and praise for ever.
From the darkness of death you have raised your Christ
to the right hand of your majesty on high.
The pioneer of our faith, his passion accomplished,
has opened for us the way to heaven
and sends on us the promised Spirit.
May we be ready to follow the Way
and so be brought to the glory of his presence
where songs of triumph for ever sound:
Blessed be God, Father, Son and Holy Spirit.
Blessed be God for ever.

From the day after Ascension Day
until the Day of Pentecost

Blessed are you, creator God,
to you be praise and glory for ever.
As your Spirit moved over the face of the waters
bringing light and life to your creation,
pour out your Spirit on us today
that we may walk as children of light
and by your grace reveal your presence.
Blessed be God, Father, Son and Holy Spirit.
Blessed be God for ever.

From All Saints until the day before
the First Sunday of Advent

Blessed are you, Sovereign God,
ruler and judge of all,
to you be praise and glory for ever.
In the darkness of this age that is passing away
may the light of your presence which the saints enjoy
surround our steps as we journey on.
May we reflect your glory this day
and so be made ready to see your face
in the heavenly city where night shall be no more.
Blessed be God, Father, Son and Holy Spirit.
Blessed be God for ever.

The Lord's Prayer and The Grace

Our Father in heaven,
hallowed be your name,
your kingdom come,
your will be done,
on earth as in heaven.
Give us today our daily bread.
Forgive us our sins
as we forgive those who sin against us.
Lead us not into temptation
but deliver us from evil.
For the kingdom, the power,
and the glory are yours
now and for ever.
Amen.

(or)

Our Father, who art in heaven,
hallowed be thy name;
thy kingdom come;
thy will be done;
on earth as it is in heaven.
Give us this day our daily bread.
And forgive us our trespasses,
as we forgive those who trespass against us.
And lead us not into temptation;
but deliver us from evil.
For thine is the kingdom,
the power and the glory,
for ever and ever.
Amen.

The grace of our Lord Jesus Christ,
and the love of God,
and the fellowship of the Holy Spirit,
be with us all evermore.
Amen.

An Order for Night Prayer (Compline)

The Lord almighty grant us a quiet night and a perfect end.
Amen.

Our help is in the name of the Lord
who made heaven and earth.

A period of silence for reflection on the past day may follow.

The following or other suitable words of penitence may be used

**Most merciful God,
we confess to you,
before the whole company of heaven and one another,
that we have sinned in thought, word and deed
and in what we have failed to do.
Forgive us our sins,
heal us by your Spirit
and raise us to new life in Christ. Amen.**

O God, make speed to save us.
O Lord, make haste to help us.

**Glory to the Father and to the Son
and to the Holy Spirit;
as it was in the beginning is now
and shall be for ever. Amen.
Alleluia.**

The following or another suitable hymn may be sung

Before the ending of the day,
Creator of the world, we pray
That you, with steadfast love, would keep
Your watch around us while we sleep.

From evil dreams defend our sight,
From fears and terrors of the night;
Tread underfoot our deadly foe
That we no sinful thought may know.

O Father, that we ask be done
Through Jesus Christ, your only Son;
And Holy Spirit, by whose breath
Our souls are raised to life from death.

The Word of God

One or more of Psalms 4, 91 or 134 may be used.

Psalm 134

1   Come, bless the Lord, all you servants of the Lord, ◆
    you that by night stand in the house of the Lord.

2   Lift up your hands towards the sanctuary ◆
    and bless the Lord.

3   The Lord who made heaven and earth ◆
    give you blessing out of Zion.

**Glory to the Father and to the Son
and to the Holy Spirit;
as it was in the beginning is now
and shall be for ever. Amen.**

Scripture Reading

*One of the following short lessons or another suitable
passage is read*

You, O Lord, are in the midst of us and we are called by
your name; leave us not, O Lord our God.

Jeremiah 14.9

(or)

Be sober, be vigilant, because your adversary the devil is
prowling round like a roaring lion, seeking for someone
to devour. Resist him, strong in the faith.

1 Peter 5.8,9

(or)

The servants of the Lamb shall see the face of God, whose
name will be on their foreheads. There will be no more
night: they will not need the light of a lamp or the light of the
sun, for God will be their light, and they will reign for ever
and ever.

Revelation 22.4,5

The following responsory may be said

Into your hands, O Lord, I commend my spirit.
Into your hands, O Lord, I commend my spirit.
For you have redeemed me, Lord God of truth.
I commend my spirit.
Glory to the Father and to the Son
and to the Holy Spirit.
Into your hands, O Lord, I commend my spirit.

Or, in Easter

Into your hands, O Lord, I commend my spirit.
   Alleluia, alleluia.
Into your hands, O Lord, I commend my spirit.
   Alleluia, alleluia.
For you have redeemed me, Lord God of truth.
Alleluia, alleluia.
Glory to the Father and to the Son
and to the Holy Spirit.
Into your hands, O Lord, I commend my spirit.
   Alleluia, alleluia.

Keep me as the apple of your eye.
Hide me under the shadow of your wings.

Gospel Canticle

Nunc Dimittis (The Song of Simeon)

**Save us, O Lord, while waking,
and guard us while sleeping,
that awake we may watch with Christ
and asleep may rest in peace.**

1   Now, Lord, you let your servant go in peace:
    your word has been fulfilled.

2   My own eyes have seen the salvation
    which you have prepared in the sight of every people;

3   A light to reveal you to the nations
    and the glory of your people Israel.

Luke 2.29-32

Glory to the Father and to the Son
and to the Holy Spirit;
as it was in the beginning is now
and shall be for ever. Amen.

Save us, O Lord, while waking,
and guard us while sleeping,
that awake we may watch with Christ
and asleep may rest in peace.

Prayers

Intercessions and thanksgivings may be offered here.

The Collect

Visit this place, O Lord, we pray,
and drive far from it the snares of the enemy;
may your holy angels dwell with us and guard us in peace,
and may your blessing be always upon us;
through Jesus Christ our Lord.
Amen.

The Lord's Prayer (see p. 323) may be said.

The Conclusion

In peace we will lie down and sleep;
for you alone, Lord, make us dwell in safety.

Abide with us, Lord Jesus,
for the night is at hand and the day is now past.

As the night watch looks for the morning,
so do we look for you, O Christ.

[Come with the dawning of the day
and make yourself known in the breaking of the bread.]

The Lord bless us and watch over us;
the Lord make his face shine upon us and be gracious to us;
the Lord look kindly on us and give us peace.
Amen.

Reflections for Daily Prayer:
Advent 2014 to the eve of Advent 2015

Reflections for Daily Prayer returns
for the 2014–15 Church year with
another range of illustrious
contributors! Confirmed writers
so far include Gillian Cooper,
Peter Graystone, Malcolm Guite,
Mark Ireland, Martyn Percy,
John Pritchard, Ben Quash,
Angela Tilby, Frances Ward and
Jeremy Worthen

£16.99 • 336 pages
ISBN 978 0 7151 4366 7
Available May 2014

**Also
available
for the
Amazon
Kindle!**

Reflections for Daily Prayer:
Lent and Holy Week 2014

Do you enjoy reading *Reflections for Daily Prayer* and wish you
could share its benefits with others? This shortened edition of
Reflections is ideal for group or church use during Lent, or for
anyone seeking a daily devotional guide to the most holy
season of the Christian year. It is also an ideal taster for those
wanting to begin a regular pattern of prayer and reading.

Authors: Ian Adams,
Christopher Cocksworth,
John Pritchard, Angela Tilby

**Please note this book
reproduces the material for Lent
and Holy Week found in the
volume you are now holding.**

£3.99 • 48 pages
ISBN 978 0 7151 4367 4
Available November 2014

Reflections for Daily Prayer
App

Make Bible study and reflection a part of your routine wherever you go with the Reflections for Daily Prayer App for iPhone, iPad and iPod Touch.

Download the app for free from the Apple App Store and receive a week's worth of reflections free. Then purchase a monthly, three-monthly or annual subscription to receive up-to-date content.

Use your iPhone QR code reader to scan this symbol and visit the Reflections for Daily Prayer page at the App store.

Resources for Daily Prayer

Common Worship: Daily Prayer

The official daily office of the Church of England,
Common Worship: Daily Prayer is a rich collection of
devotional material that will enable those wanting to
enrich their quiet times to develop
a regular pattern of prayer. It includes:

- Prayer During the Day
- Forms of Penitence
- Morning and Evening Prayer
- Night Prayer (Compline)
- Collects and Refrains
- Canticles
- Complete Psalter

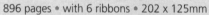

896 pages • with 6 ribbons • 202 x 125mm		
Hardback	978 0 7151 2199 3	**£22.50**
Soft cased	978 0 7151 2178 8	**£27.50**
Bonded leather	978 0 7151 2100 9	**£45.00**

Time to Pray

This compact, soft-case volume offers two simple,
shorter offices from *Common Worship: Daily Prayer*.
It is an ideal introduction to a more structured
personal devotional time, or can be used as a
lighter, portable daily office for those on the move.

Time to Pray includes:

- Prayer During the Day
  (for every day of the week)
- Night Prayer
- Selected Psalms

£12.99 • 112 pages • Soft case
ISBN 978 0 7151 2122 1

Order now at **www.chpublishing.co.uk**
or via **Norwich Books and Music**
Telephone **(01603) 785923**
E-mail **orders@norwichbooksandmusic.co.uk**